D1438147

Jamie McGuinness left university mid-way through studying engineering, to discover the world; after prospecting for gold in the western deserts of Australia, training huskies in Sweden and selling Trans-Siberian train tickets in Hong Kong, he even found his place in it – as a Himalayan trekker.

To satisfy a yesteryear sense of exploration, for much of the year Jamie can be found in Nepal leading treks and climbs or exploring the forgotten corners of the country. His latest project is publishing trekking guides for less frequented regions of Nepal on the Internet. When not filling information blanks he can be found surfing or skiing in New Zealand.

Trekking in Langtang, Helambu & Gosainkund
First edition: October 1997

Publisher
Trailblazer Publications
The Old Manse, Tower Rd, Hindhead, Surrey, GU26 6SU, UK
Fax (+44) 01428-607571
E-mail: trailblazer@compuserve.com

British Library Cataloguing in Publication Data
A catalogue record for this book is available from the British Library

ISBN 1-873756-13-5

© **Jamie McGuinness**
Photographs

© **Trailblazer Publications**
Text and maps

Editor: Anna Jacomb-Hood
Cartography and index: Jane Thomas

Every effort has been made by the author and publisher to ensure that the information contained herein is as accurate and up to date as possible. However, they are unable to accept responsibility for any inconvenience, loss or injury sustained by anyone as a result of the advice and information given in this guide.

Printed on chlorine-free paper from farmed forests by
Technographic Design & Print (☎ 01206-303323) Colchester, Essex, UK

TREKKING
IN
LANGTANG
HELAMBU & GOSAINKUND

JAMIE McGUINNESS

WITH ADDITIONAL MATERIAL BY
BRYN THOMAS

TRAILBLAZER PUBLICATIONS

Acknowledgements

Nepal has become a second home for me thanks to the delightful people and the monumental nature of the land.

As always Mr Puru, the staff and guests of Hotel Karma considerably enlivened my long stays in Kathmandu. So too have the many trekkers and travellers I met. From on the trail I would like to thank: Bernie (Australia), Matze (Germany) and the trekkers who accidentally took the Syabru Bensi to Sherpagaon route and who, together with Shane Capron, subsequently provided details for that section; Vicky Morrison (UK) for showing me the Helambu trek through a first-timer's eyes and Johan Melse (Netherlands) for double-checking the Gosainkund section.

Temba Tamang (Syabru Bensi) put me on to the story of the settling of the Langtang valley, Ayako Sadakane (Japan and Langtang village) and Kami Gyalbo Sherpa (Sing Gompa) provided information on the surrounding areas. Kalsang Lama (Tarkeghyang), Maria (HRA doctor, Manang), Wendy Brewer Lama (TMI) and Durga Poudel (Assistant National Park Warden of Langtang National Park) faithfully answered innumerable questions on their areas of expertise. Paldor was climbed and Christmas and New Year celebrated in the company of Sue Behrenfeld, Renate and Shane Capron.

In Kathmandu, the Department of Hydrology and Meteorology of the Ministry of Water Resources helpfully provided climatic information. The staff at the Ministry of Tourism and the Department of Immigration also deserve mention for allowing me to stay so long in Nepal.

Kerry Moran's eloquent and appreciative *Nepal Handbook* has continued to provide me with inspiration and helped untangle the complexities of this wonderful country. Robert R Desjarlais' exceptionally perceptive book *Body and Emotion* opened my eyes to the real Yolmo culture.

The whole project began with Bryn Thomas having faith enough for a second book. The first half of the Kathmandu chapter is adapted from his book *Trekking in the Annapurna Region* and various other sections received substantial input from him.

Sue Behrenfeld and Lynanne Stanaway pre-edited the text while Shane Capron field-checked some of the maps and added many useful comments.

Thanks also to the UK production team: Jane Thomas for redrawing my sketch maps, Anna Jacomb-Hood for editing the text and Bryn for assembling the book.

A request

Comments and suggestions are welcomed: please send any to 54a Darwin Rd, Gisborne, New Zealand or leave them at Hotel Karma, Thamel, Kathmandu. Alternatively e-mail me at treks@clear.net.nz or meet me in the hills.

Cover photo: Approaching Paldor (5928m) and Base Camp in the Ganesh Himal. Both Langtang and Ganesh Himals feature some excellent wilderness trekking, as well as teahouse trekking. (photo: Jamie McGuinness)

CONTENTS

INTRODUCTION

Why has trekking in Nepal rapidly become such an essential part of almost every budget traveller's Asian tour and a prime destination for adventure travellers in general? Apart from Mt Everest and the majestic Himalaya range, it is the endearing people of Nepal who have made holidaying and trekking here easier than in the surrounding countries. Organising almost anything in Kathmandu is a comparative breeze. The general trustworthiness of the Nepalis ensures that relatively little goes wrong. Trekking itself is also hassle-free travelling; there's no need to worry about reservations or waiting for buses and no squalid, polluted, noisy cities. Instead, once on the trail there is little to worry about. In the morning just pack up and go, during the day enjoy the peace, the nature and the exercise, and in the evening chat over a hearty meal.

Perhaps the most difficult decision for a trekker heading to (or already in) Nepal is where to go. If you've just gotta see Mt Everest, it's easy. However, many more people choose Annapurna for its variety of treks – anything from four days to four weeks – and for its range of peoples and landscapes. Langtang is the third most popular of the main trekking regions. Most trekkers I talked to were somewhat vague as to why they had chosen Langtang; for many it was to do with time restrictions and a desire to do something slightly different. The unanimous comment, however, was that Langtang had pleasantly surprised them. For new and veteran trekkers alike, it is a superb trekking region.

Because *Trekking in Langtang, Helambu and Gosainkund* is geographically accurate if a little unwieldy, when referring to all three in the text I have called them the Langtang or the Langtang region. The specific area is referred to as the Langtang Valley.

The treks in the Langtang Valley, Gosainkund and Helambu each have their own character. The walk up the Langtang Valley roughly follows the river through pleasant forests and occasional villages before reaching the open alpine country encircled by massive snowy peaks and glaciers. A 5000m/16,400ft viewpoint provides a stunning panorama, and this is all possible in 10 days. Because of its less developed nature the alpine regions of the Langtang Valley also offer the best easy camping in Nepal (independent camping rather than a camping tour). And for the really adventurous a challenging high pass, the Kangja La, beckons.

Helambu, on the other hand, is most definitely a cultural trek; although there are mountain views, it is the people and their villages that are most memorable. Rice paddies, water buffalo and fine-featured Hindus change to Buddhist gompas, forests, high grazing areas and the round, smiling faces of Tibetans.

The Gosainkund trek follows a pilgrimage route. It's a fine open ridge walk with the high point being a series of beautiful lakes set amid craggy mountains. The trek also usefully links Helambu with the Langtang Valley.

So how exactly does the Langtang compare to Everest and Annapurna? The Langtang Valley is a compressed version of the Everest trek. The walk-in is only a couple of days and with a single hill it is rather less testing than the eight-day Everest walk-in. Once up there, the mountains of Langtang are slightly smaller than their Khumbu cousins (only 7000m/23,000ft not 8000m/26,250ft!) but since you are at a lower altitude, they still rank as decidedly impressive. Both areas have exploration possibilities but in the Langtang they are less extreme.

The diversity in the Langtang region is, however, no match for Annapurna but the walking is generally easier and the whole experience less touristy. The mountains of the Langtang are closer; they seem almost touchable compared to the distant feel of Annapurna. Crossing the 5120m/16,800ft Kangja La is definitely more challenging than Annapurna's Thorung La (mountain pass), although, it has to be admitted, perhaps less worthwhile. In Helambu many lodges are still very much the traditional family home rather than the trekker-orientated hotels of Annapurna so the culture is more accessible and less adapted to mass tourism.

Treks in the Langtang are usually shorter but not necessarily softer. All have the advantage of ease of access from Kathmandu. Indeed for some options the trail begins on the edge of the Kathmandu Valley or is only half a day away by road. There is no need to fly. And all, while distinct treks in their own right, can be linked for more variety.

I hope your trek in the Langtang gives you as much pleasure as researching this guide gave me.

PART 1: PLANNING YOUR TREK

What is trekking?

I see fields of green and skies of blue and I think to myself, 'Oh, what a wonderful world'. **Louis Armstrong**

And there are few more wonderful experiences than trekking in Nepal.

For the first time trekker the prospect of trekking in the Himalaya can be daunting as well as thrilling. Trekking in Nepal is an altogether different experience from a week's backpacking in the Rockies or bushwalking in Tasmania. Rather than wilderness, this is a countryside free from roads, with villages caught in a time warp and terraced fields stacked up huge hillsides. The paths are timeless pilgrimage routes, trails between villages or tracks to high grazing pastures. It is by no means untouched but it is an incredibly beautiful natural world. Only higher up in the alpine valleys are the villages left behind, replaced by herders' huts. Higher stills are the ice castles of the Himalaya.

The practical aspects of trekking are surprisingly easy. In the villages and along the way are lodges and teahouses where meals are ordered from menus in English. Alternatively, on a trekking tour three-course meals are served by your crew. Without the need to carry food and camping equipment, backpacks are light, and if you have a porter you need carry only your daypack. So trekking is really little more than a pleasurable ramble through quaint villages, gazing in wonder at the terraced hillsides and wandering amid incredible mountain scenery.

The satisfaction of trekking is in the process; most trekking days are not particularly long so there is time to spot wildlife, take photographs, chat along the way and relax over lunch or a reviving cup of tea.

But there are challenges. The first is the physical effort required. Although you'll hopefully be lightly laden, hill-climbing still requires plenty of effort. Pleasure can be had from frequent rests to admire the scenery which, even after a mere 10 minutes, alters satisfyingly and often dramatically. Take comfort, too, in the frequent teahouses which are often strategically placed. The second challenge is the discomfort of sickness. This is Asia and no matter how careful you are, you should count on some bowel problems, though these are usually minor and seem trivial compared to the whole wonderful experience. To enjoy the Himalaya you don't have to be the tough outdoor type. Like rucksacks and cameras, trekkers come in all shapes and sizes and with widely differing aspirations. Trekking is physical but certainly not beyond the majority of people. Most important is knowing that you enjoy the concept. Bring along a traveller's curiosity and a sense of humour, and before you know it you'll relish the thought of another trek.

With a group or on your own?

Nepal, long suspicious of foreign influence and colonial powers, began opening its borders only in 1948. The first tourists (as opposed to mountaineers and researchers) arrived in 1955 but it was not until 1965, when Colonel Jimmy Roberts set up Mountain Travel, that the first commercial treks began. The concept was similar to the expedition approach used by mountaineers, with guides, porters and tents. These holidays proved a great success and essentially the same format is used today by most trekking companies.

An alternative to this self-sufficient approach is teahouse trekking. Along the main trade routes the hill peoples of Nepal traditionally had a code of hospitality towards traders and travellers. It was only a matter of time before small groups of adventurers started taking advantage of this by staying in the basic teahouses and lodges. Now around 40,000 people trek this way each year, staying in the much improved lodges and teahouses along the routes. Of the 8400 trekkers who visited the Langtang in 1995 (the latest figures) 5400 trekked independently, the rest were group trekkers.

The trekking infrastructure in the Langtang has now developed to a stage where many options are possible, ranging from expedition-style with tents and porters to an independent trek using the local lodges and carrying only a sleeping-bag and jacket. It is simply a case of choosing the option most appropriate for you.

TEAHOUSE TREKKING

Dotted along the main trails, family-owned lodges cater specifically for independent trekkers. They can provide anything from a cup of tea to a full meal and a bed so, for the entire trek, there's no need to carry food or shelter. Teahouse trekking, as it's usually called, is easy to organise; just a day or two of planning and bureaucracy-bashing in Kathmandu and away you go. It's also cheap – luxuries aside, US$10/£6.25 a day easily covers food and accommodation. The facilities and level of comfort in the Langtang lodges are improving rapidly. Once infamously smoky and rather too authentically medieval, they are now modest hotels. See p113.

As well as being economical, teahouse trekking gives you the freedom to set your own schedule. This is particularly handy if you get sick or feel like a rest; commercial group treks have to push on mercilessly. The freedom to explore is, however, limited by the location of lodges.

The main difference between the approaches is the style of interaction with the local people. Staying in lodges provides rewarding opportunities to mix with your Nepali hosts, many of whom speak reasonable English. How much you interact depends on you; some trekkers come away speaking Nepali, others seem happy to spend most of their time in the company of other trekkers. On an expedition-style trek you miss out on the enjoyable need to interact with villagers, though this is partially redeemed by the crew, an often substantial team who look after, entertain and add Nepali colour to a guided trek.

Trekking alone

Many people trek by themselves. Unless you are trekking during the monsoon or off standard routes you will constantly meet other trekkers in lodges and on the trail. While you can remain by yourself, most people end up walking in small groups and staying at the same lodges.

There are few risks in hiking alone except in one region – see the warning on p212. Villagers often ask how many people you are trekking with; if you want to be cautious you can always say your friend is just behind but violent crimes against foreigners are still rare. Women are slightly more vulnerable and locals do caution against women hiking alone. Dressing sensibly and behaving modestly is essential. When stopping for the night, check that there is another woman or other trekkers staying there.

If you would prefer to begin your trek with a partner, scan or advertise on the notice boards around Thamel, especially at the Himalayan Rescue Association (HRA) office, Pumpernickel Bakery and the board outside Kathmandu Guest House. You'll also meet other trekkers at the Department of Immigration as you get your permit. Other possibilities include hiring a porter-guide through a trekking company or trying to join an existing group.

Is a guide or porter necessary?

Assuming you will be taking this book with you, there's no need for a guide of the human kind on the established trekking routes. The lodges are impossible to miss, route finding presents few problems and basic English is widely understood. However, trekking with some local people can be an enlightening, entertaining and rewarding cultural exchange.

Hiring a porter-guide is an option that gives you the advantages of both the independent approach and the group trek. You retain control and you have the opportunity for greater insight and interaction that a guide can provide as well as having a much lighter load to carry. A porter-guide should speak reasonable English, know the region and carry 10-15kg plus their equipment. Usually they are young and aspiring to become a full guide or sirdar. They are happy to work for one person or a small group. See p98.

A cheaper option is to hire a porter at the trail head. He will probably speak little English but will know the route well. Once at a lodge they tend to look after themselves but on the trail they can be helpful, especially in route-finding and deciding where to stop for lunch.

People sometimes feel guilty about hiring someone simply to carry a load but you shouldn't. You will be giving them a considerably lighter load than the 30kg+ that trekking companies dish out (who still have plenty of takers for employment) and you directly benefit the local economy.

Commercial teahouse trekking

While becoming popular in the Annapurna and Everest regions, foreign companies have yet to offer similar teahouse-organised treks in Langtang. The reasons are that lodges still don't offer real double rooms and they cost a trekking company more than trekking expedition style. Nepalese trekking companies can offer teahouse packages; however they charge more than you would spend if you paid for a guide separately and paid the lodge bills yourself.

FREE CAMPING

The Langtang Valley is one of the best areas in Nepal for backpacking, as Americans call it, or free camping; carrying a tent, stove and some food and camping where you feel like. Elsewhere in the country there are lodges just about wherever you need them or the logistics of carrying supplies for 15 to 20 days means taking porters, and food and fuel for them, all the way.

EXPEDITION-STYLE TREKS

What more enjoyable way to be woken up than with a '*namaste didi* (good morning sister), bed tea?' A bowl of hot washing water encourages you to rise then, once packed, breakfast awaits your attention. On the trail the walking is made easier because 'members' (the trekkers) carry only a daypack – the porters hump the rest. The sherpas ensure you don't get lost, pitch the tents and serve the meals. The kitchen crew conjure up three course meals which are served on tables complete with table linen. This is trekking first class and, like any luxury, is all too easy to get accustomed to.

Trekking expedition style has a few minor advantages. There is more visual privacy and everyone's nocturnal goings-on are less likely to disturb others. On the down side, lodge dining rooms are definitely warmer and more comfortable than a dining tent.

Arranging a guided trek in Nepal

Armed with the addresses of trekking companies in Nepal, a number of people have tried to arrange a trek by mail or fax from their home country. Some have had success, others experience frustration. In fact, especially for the Langtang region, it's better simply to arrive in Nepal and start making arrangements there. You won't be met at the airport but that's about all that will be missing. Allow a day for comparing companies, then a couple more for the trekking company to get a crew and supplies together, and you'll be ready to go.

This approach is cheaper than a home-booked, package tour. You are not paying for office services in your home country, which may amount to more than the actual trek cost, or a set standard of luxury that you may not entirely desire. Other advantages are greater flexibility on the choice of itinerary and changes en route. The disadvantages are that quality is less assured and you have no comeback if there are problems.

If you intend to join a group trek on arrival, be prepared to wait a few days while you contact a number of trekking companies in Thamel; insist on meeting the other tour members otherwise you won't be the first person to find that they are mysteriously not coming after all! Alternatively, advertise on the various trekkers' notice boards in Kathmandu. There is little chance of joining an overseas-booked trek in Kathmandu; bookings are either made via overseas agents only or privately booked by people who prefer to go with their friends. There are a few companies that advertise set trekking dates, but these usually depart even if only two people book. Sometimes, although not always, this is just a different way of advertising trek-organising expertise.

Arranging a guided trek at home

The glossiness of brochures aside, what sets one company above another is the quality of their trek leaders. A good Western leader backed up by a local sirdar or guide is a powerful combination. However, many companies, particularly if the group is small, provide only a local guide who may have excellent organisational abilities but be less able to act as a cultural interface between the trekkers and Nepalis. You are equally likely to land a good one through a Kathmandu trekking agency as through the foreign trekking companies. Often, the best local leaders form their own trekking companies or work as climbing expedition sirdars.

Expedition-style trekking is a pleasant routine suited to those who enjoy being looked after and, with everything planned in advance, is perfect for people with limited time. Normally the package includes airport pick-up, a guided tour plus a day or two in Kathmandu, hotel accommodation, and everything while trekking.

A selling point for companies is the independence that trekking with tents allows. In reality, on the standard trails porters prefer to stay in or near villages so the group is just as reliant on these as is the teahouse trekker. However, off the main trails and in the true wilderness areas, the expedition approach is a pleasant, and indeed sometimes the only alternative for a group.

HOME COUNTRY TREKKING COMPANIES

While all trekking companies offer Everest and Annapurna treks, fewer offer Langtang trips. The larger companies should have a brochure at your local travel agency. Some travel agencies specialise in adventure travel. Smaller trekking companies advertise in magazines and shops which specialise in outdoor activities.

Most larger companies offer audio-visual presentations in main centres. Some will also send out a video on request. These can give you a better picture about the company and what to expect. In particular ask about the trek leader.

Nepal offers a range of other activities that combine well with a trek – see p36. Some can be booked via your travel agent but it is always cheaper and usually easy to book these in Kathmandu.

Trekking agencies in the UK
• **Classic Nepal** (☎ 01773-873497, fax 01773-590243) 33 Metro Ave, Newton, Derbyshire, DE55 5UF.
• **Encounter Overland** (☎ 0171-370 6845, fax 0171-244 9737) 267 Old Brompton Rd, London SW5 9JA.
• **Exodus Expeditions** (☎ 0181-675 5550, fax 0181-673 0779) 9 Weir Rd, London SW12 OLT.
• **ExplorAsia/Abercrombie & Kent Travel** (☎ 0171-973 0482, fax 0171-730 9376) Sloane Square House, Holbein Place, Sloane Square, London SW1W 8NS.
• **Explore Worldwide** (☎ 01252-319448. fax 01252-343170) 1 Frederick St, Aldershot, Hants GU11 1LQ.
• **Guerba Expeditions** (☎ 01373-858956, fax 01373-858351) Wessex House, 40 Station Road, Westbury, Wilts BA13 3JN.
• **Himalayan Kingdoms** (☎ 01179-237163, fax 01179-74493) 20 The Mall, Clifton, Bristol BS8 4DR. Their expeditions section (☎ 01142-763322) organises more ambitious adventure trekking and mountaineering holidays.
• **Himalayan Quest** (☎ 01926-450835) 12 Euston Place, Leamington Spa, Warks CV32 4LY.

- **KE Adventure Travel** (☎ 017687-73966, fax 017687-74693) 32 Lake Rd, Keswick, Cumbria CA12 5DQ).
- **Naturetrek** (☎ 01962-733051, fax 01962-733368) Chautara, Bighton, Nr Alresford, Hampshire SO24 9RB offer bird-watching tours in several regions of Nepal.
- **OTT Expeditions** (☎ 01142-588508, fax 01142-551603) 62 Nettleham Rd, Sheffield S8 8SX.
- **Roama Travel** (☎ 01258-860298, fax 01258-861382) Shroton, Blandford Forum, Dorset DT11 8QW.
- **Sherpa Expeditions** (☎ 0181-577 2717, fax 0181-572 9788) 131a Heston Rd, Hounslow, Middx TW5 ORD.
- **World Expeditions** (☎ 01628-74174, fax 01628-74312) 7 North Rd, Maidenhead SL6 1PL.

Trekking agencies in Continental Europe

- **Austria Okistra** (☎ 0222-347526) Turkenstrasse 4, A-1090 Wien. **Supertramp Reisen** (☎ 01222-5335136) Helferstorfer St 4, A-1010 Wien.
- **Belgium Connections** (☎ 02-512 50 60) Kolenmarkt 13, rue Marche au Charbon, Brussel 1000 Bruxelles, with branches in Antwerpen (☎ 03-225 31 61), Gent (☎ 091-23 90 20) and Liege (☎ 041-22 04 44).
- **Denmark Green Tours** (☎ 33-13 27 27) Kultorvet 7, DK-1175 Kobenhavn K. **Inter-Travel** (☎ 33-15 00 77) Frederiksholms Kanal 2, DK-1220 Kobenhavn K. **Marco Polo Tours** (☎ 33-13 03 07) Borgergade 16, 1300 Kobenhavn K. **Topas Globetrotters** (☎ 86-89 36 22) Skaersbrovej 11, 8680 Ry.
- **Germany Explorer** (☎ 0211-379 064) Huttenstrasse 17, 4000 Dusseldorf 1. **SHR Reisen** (☎ 0761-210 078) Kaiser Joseph Strasse 263, D-7800 Freiburg.
- **Iceland Icelandic Student Travel** (☎ 01-615656) V/Hringbraut, IS-101 Reykjavik.
- **Ireland Maxwells Travel** (☎ 01-779 479) D'Olier Chambers, 1 Hawkins St, Dublin 2. **Funtrek** (☎ 01-733 633) 32 Batchelors Walk, O'Connell Bridge, Dublin 1.
- **Italy CTS** (☎ 06-46791) V. Genova 15, 00184 Roma.
- **Netherlands NBBS** (☎ 071-22 1414) Schipholweg 101, PO Box 360, 2300 AJ Leiden. Branches in Groningen (☎ 050-126 333), Amsterdam (☎ 020-20 5071), Utrecht (☎ 030-314 520) and Rotterdam (☎ 010-414 9822). **De Wandelwaaier** (☎ 020-622 6990) Herngracht 329, 1016AW Amsterdam. **Terra Travel** (☎ 020-275129) Singel 190H, 1016AA Amsterdam.
- **Norway Terra Nova Travel** (☎ 47-2 42 14 10) Dronningens Gate 26, N-0154, Oslo 1. **Eventyrreiser A/S Adventure Travel** (☎ 22-11 31 81) Hegdehaugsvn 10, 0167 Oslo.

• **Spain Expo Mundo** (☎ 03-412 59 56) Diputacion, 238 Stco, 08007 Barcelona.
• **Sweden Aeventyrsresor** (☎ 08-654 1155) Hantverkargaten 38, PO Box 12168, S-102 24 Stockholm. **Himalayaresor** (08-605 5760) Box 17, S-123, 21 Farsta.
• **Switzerland S.S.R.** (☎ 01-242 30 00) Backerstr. 52, CH 8026, Zurich. **Suntrek Tours** (☎ 01-462 61 61) Birmensdorferstr. 187, CH-8003 Zurich. **Case Depart Voyages** (☎ 021-311 13 61) Avenue de Bethusy 4, Case Postale 107, CH-1000, Lausanne 4.

Trekking agencies in the USA
• **Above the Clouds Trekking** (☎ 508-799 4499, fax 797 4779) PO Box 398, Worcester, MA 01602.
• **Adventure Center** (☎ 415-654 1879, ☎ 800-227 8747, fax 654 4200) 1311 63rd St, Suite 200, Emeryville, CA 94608 – agents for Explore (UK).
• **Geeta Tours & Travels** (☎ 312-262 4959) 1245 West Jarvis Ave, Chicago IL 60626.
• **Himalayan Travel** (☎ 800-225 2380, fax 203-359 3669) 2nd Floor, 112 Prospect St, Stamford CT 06901 – agents for Sherpa Expeditions (UK).
• **InnerAsia** (☎ 415-922 0448, ☎ 800-777 8183) 2627 Lombard St, San Francisco, CA 94123.
• **Journeys** (☎ 313-665 4407, ☎ 800-255 8735, fax 665 2945) 4011 Jackson Rd, Ann Arbor, MI 48103. Also includes some treks specially for families.
• **Mountain Travel & Sobek Expeditions** (☎ 510-527 8100, ☎ 800-227 2384) 6420 Fairmount Ave, El Cerrito, CA 94530. Wide range of upmarket treks.
• **Narayan's Gateway to Nepal** (☎ 303-440 0331, fax 440 6958) 948 Pearl St, Boulder CO 80302 is run by a Nepalese family based in Colorado and Kathmandu. Study programmes are offered.
• **Overseas Adventure Travel** (☎ 800-221 0814) 349 Broadway, Cambridge MA 02139 offer a number of treks in this area.
• **Safaricentre** (☎ 310-546 4411, ☎ 800-223 6046, fax 546 3188) 3201 N Sepulveda Blvd, Manhattan Beach, CA 90266 – agents for Exodus (UK).
• **Wilderness Travel** (☎ 510-548 0420, ☎ 800-368 2794) 801 Allston Way, Berkeley, CA 94710.

Trekking agencies in Canada
•**Adventure Centre** (☎ 416-922 7584) 17 Hayden St, Toronto, Ontario M4Y 2P2.
• **Mountain Travel & Sobek Expeditions** (☎ 604-876 5511) 101 511 West 14th Ave, Vancouver BC V5Z 1P5, offers upmarket treks.
• **Market Square Tours** (☎ 800 661 3838) 54 Donald St, Winnipeg, Manitoba, R3C 1LC – agents for Exodus (UK).

• **Travel Cuts**, also agents for Exodus (UK), have offices in **Edmonton** (☎ 403-488 8487) 12304 Jasper Ave, Edmonton, Alberta, T5N 3K5, **Toronto** (☎ 416-979 8608) 187 College St, Toronto, Ontario M5T 1P7 and **Vancouver** (☎ 604-689 2887) 501 602 West Hastings St, Vancouver BC, V6B 1P2.

• **Trek Holidays**, agents for Explore (UK), have offices in **Calgary** (☎ 403-283 6115, 336 14th St NW, Calgary, Alberta T2N 1Z7), **Edmonton** (☎ 403-439 9118, 8412 109th St, Edmonton, Alberta T6G 1E2), **Toronto** (☎ 416-922 7584) 25 Bellair St, Toronto, Ontario M4Y 2P2 and **Vancouver** (☎ 604-734 1066, 1965 West 4th Ave, Vancouver BC V6J 1M8.

• **Worldwide Adventures Inc** (☎ 416-963 9163, from USA ☎ 1-800-387 1483) 920 Yonge St, Suite 747, Toronto, Ontario M4W 3C7 – agents for World Expeditions (Australia).

Trekking agencies in Australia

• **Adventure World** has branches in **Adelaide** (☎ 9231 6844, 7th floor, 45 King William St, Adelaide SA 5000), **Brisbane** (☎ 229 0599, 3rd floor, 333 Adelaide St, Brisbane Qld 4000), **Melbourne** (☎ 03-9670 0125, 3rd floor, 343 Little Collins St, Melbourne Vic 3000), **Perth** (☎ 221 2300, 2nd floor, 8 Victoria Ave, Perth WA 6000) and **Sydney** (☎ 9956 7766, toll free 008-221 931, 73 Walker St, North Sydney, NSW 2059).

• **Ausventure** (☎ 02-960 1677, fax 969 1463) Suite 1, 860 Military Rd, (PO Box 54) Mosman, NSW 2088. This long-established adventure travel company offers a comprehensive range of treks.

• **Back Track Adventures** (☎ 07-368 4987) 226 Given Terrace, Paddington, QLD 4064.

• **Exodus Expeditions** (☎ 02-552 6317) 81A Glebe Point Rd, Glebe, NSW 2037 – agents for Exodus (UK).

• **Outdoor Travel** (☎ 03-9670 7252, fax 9670 3310) 55 Hardware St, Melbourne, Vic 3000 – agents for Sherpa Expeditions (UK).

• **Peregrine Adventures** is a Nepal specialist with branches in **Melbourne** (☎ 03-9663 8611, fax 9663 8618, 2nd floor, 258 Lonsdale St, Melbourne, Vic 3000) and **Sydney** (☎ 02-9241 1128, 5th floor, 58 Pitt St, Sydney, NSW 2000) and offers a good range of treks.

• **Peregrine Travel** (08-9223 5905) 192 Rundle St, Adelaide, SA 5000.

• **Summit Travel** (☎ 09-321 1259) 1st floor, 862 Hay St, Perth WA 6000.

• **World Expeditions** (☎ 02-9264 3366, fax 9261 1974) 3rd floor, 441 Kent St, Sydney NSW 2000.

Trekking agencies in New Zealand

• **Adventure World** (☎ 09-524 5118, 0800-652 954, fax 520 6629) 101 Great South Rd, Remuera, PO Box 74008, Auckland – agents for Exodus and Explore (UK).

• **Suntravel** (☎ 09-525 3074, fax 525 3065) PO Box 12-424, Penrose,

Auckland – agents for Peregrine Adventures (Australia.)
• **Venture Treks** (☎ 09-379 9855, fax 770 320) PO Box 37610, 164 Parnell Rd, Auckland – agents for Sherpa Expeditions (UK).
• **Himalaya Trekking** (☎ 06-868 8595, 025-466 465), 54a Darwin Road, Gisborne.

Getting to Nepal

BY AIR

Booking early is recommended, especially for the peak season. Check travel agencies and the travel sections of newspapers and magazines. Shopping around or at least making a few phone calls can often save lots of money. Also check the restrictions associated with the ticket. Note that tour operators often hold large numbers of seats, releasing the ones that aren't needed only a few weeks before departure. If you have been wait-listed, there is a reasonable chance of picking up a seat then.

Singapore Airlines and Thai International are the only quality airlines that fly into Kathmandu. Other carriers include Pakistan International Airlines (PIA), Indian Airlines, Royal Nepal (RNAC), Bangladesh Biman and Aeroflot. Apart from Royal Nepal and Indian Airlines which operate daily flights into Kathmandu, most airlines have only two flights a week. British Airways and another European carrier are considering introducing services to replace Lufthansa which pulled out in April 1997.

From the West From the UK, the cheapest return tickets (around £450) are on Biman and Aeroflot. The quickest flight from London is on Royal Nepal which touches down only in Frankfurt and the Gulf. Biman flies from Rome and Aeroflot from many European cities.

From India Indian Airlines has daily flights between Kathmandu and Delhi (US$142/£89) or Varanasi (US$71/£44) and less frequent flights from Calcutta (US$96/£60) and Bombay; anyone under 30 is entitled to a 25% discount. Royal Nepal also flies daily between Delhi and Kathmandu. Soon privately owned airlines will be allowed to fly between the countries, increasing the destination choices.

From Thailand Since the border with Burma is closed you have to fly. There are direct flights but the cheapest way is to fly from Bangkok to Calcutta and then travel overland.

From Myanmar (Burma) It is rumoured that scheduled flights between Yangon (Rangoon) and Kathmandu may begin sometime.

From Tibet The overland route is the more interesting, but between mid-March and mid-November you can fly between Kathmandu and Lhasa. The cost is US$190/£119.

From Bhutan If you have a pre-arranged tour, it is possible to use Druk Airways' limited international network to stop at Paro en route to Kathmandu.

OVERLAND

From India By train from Delhi or Varanasi the most convenient border crossing is Sunauli (India)/Belahiya (Nepal), three hours by bus from Gorakhpur. The Delhi to Gorakhpur overnight train is approximately US$4/£2.50 in a 2nd class sleeper. Despite what touts in Gorakhpur say, there is no direct bus to Kathmandu. The Delhi to Kathmandu bus journey is for masochists and can take up to 60 hours. Most 'through' buses still mean a change at the border.

Immigration is staffed from dawn to dusk, although the border does not physically close at night; if you arrive late simply walk across and stay at the better hotels on the Nepalese side and visit immigration the next morning. Without a visa and entry stamps you'll encounter many problems in Kathmandu. Buses to Kathmandu (US$2.50/£1.50, 10 to 14 hours) leave between 5am and 9am for the day service and between 4pm and about 8pm for the night buses. For much of the way the route follows the Trisuli River and the scenery is an impressive introduction to the hills of Nepal.

From Calcutta the usual route is via Patna to the border at Raxaul/Birganj. The border crossing at Karkabhitta, near Darjeeling, entails a particularly tortuous 18 to 24 hour journey because, like that from Birganj, the road loops close to Pokhara before almost cutting back on itself to Kathmandu. A new eastern highway direct to Kathmandu is under construction but is unlikely to be completed before 2000.

There are several border crossings in west Nepal. Crossing at Nepalganj means a 16 to 18 hour night bus to Kathmandu; add another eight to 12 hours to that from the Banbassa-Mahendranagar border.

From Tibet When leaving, be sure to get your passport stamped by the Chinese. The couple of kilometres of hillside between the immigration posts is prone to landslides; note that it often has to be walked. From the border settlement of Kodari to Kathmandu takes seven to 12 hours by bus, depending on the condition of the road.

Visa Requirements See p65.

When to go

*Mainly fair throughout the Kingdom – **Rising Nepal** newspaper's delightfully general standard daily autumn forecast.*

One of the many joys of Nepal is that its weather is almost always reliable. It rains heavily during the summer monsoon, then is mostly fine for the rest of the year. The temperature pattern follows the northern hemisphere seasons.

While the monsoon is a blessing for the people of the Himalaya, for the trekker summer has little to recommend it. Mountains play hide and seek amid the cloud and the drizzle is annoying. However, the rest of the year makes up for this. By October the days are long and mostly fine. The royal blue skies display crystalline mountains to perfection and the villages are in the midst of the picturesque harvest – perfect trekking time. By the time autumn turns to winter the endless sunny days have dried the highlands golden. Temperatures cool at altitude, while in the lower middle hills they turn pleasant and occasional irrigated winter crops are sprouting. Although the real winter, January through February, is mostly fine, at altitude the cold and possible snow are troublesome to all but the most determined trekkers. March and the arrival of spring awakens the rhododendrons and trekkers; the weather is more variable and the atmosphere hazy down low but above 3000m/9850ft it's still sometimes staggeringly clear and a fine time for trekking, right up to the end of the balmy month of May.

❑ **Trekking statistics**
Entry to Langtang National Park from all entry points (94-95 season, Nepali calendar months; middle of the first month to middle of the second).

Jul-Aug	230
Aug-Sep	320
Sep-Oct	1360
Oct-Nov	1820
Nov-Dec	570
Dec-Jan	460
Jan-Feb	350
Feb-Mar	780
Mar-Apr	1360
Apr-May	770
May-Jun	275
Jun-Jul	100
Total	8400

SEASONS

The approach of winter (mid-October to late December)

This is classic trekking time, famed for clear skies and fantastic weather. By mid-October the harvest is finishing and the hillsides are drying from green to brown. Early October through to late November is also the busiest period. Most lodges and camp sites are brimming with trekkers. Commercial teahouse groups sometimes book out entire lodges, unfairly adding to the logistical crush. This is the best season for exploring and climbing. The long fine periods are occasionally broken for a day or two by a front which causes high cloud or cloud banks that roll up the valleys and then usually clear at altitude with the sunset. The odd stronger front may bring a spot of wet weather as well but it is impossible to tell (even the locals can't) whether a front contains rain. Barring unusual conditions during this trekking season, two or three periods of showers and drizzle or short-lived snow at altitude, can be expected. December is still a pleasant

❏ Rainfall & temperature

Average precipitation (mm) Kyangjin over six years. Average daily temperature in Kyangjin 3900m/12,800ft, ie the middle of the maximum and minimum, over six years.

	mm	°C
January	14	-3.5
February	24	-4.2
March	30	-1.7
April	26	1.3
May	65	4.1
June	74	6.8
July	147	8.0
August	178	7.7
Sept	83	6.5
October	6	2.1
November	4	-1.5
December	8	-3.4

if cool time for trekking. Statistically, it is the driest month of the year and the majority of trekkers have already headed home. Christmas/New Year is a good time to return to Kathmandu where the Nepalese help the poor foreigners who only have one festival a year to celebrate in style.

Trail conditions

	Perfect time to trek
	Good but conditions are variable
	Frequent cloud and rain make conditions less than ideal
	Possible snow can make trekking challenging
	Impossible to trek except in unusually good conditions

Winter (January to mid-March)

Early January often brings a week or so of disturbed weather. At higher altitudes this semi-regular snowfall is followed by more winter storms which break the long fine periods. Some years the light snowfall melts in the sunny spots, making winter and the early spring cold but pleasant. In others frequent heavier falls make trekking the alpine-like valleys challenging and sometimes impossible. A thick snow carpet may last into April. Snow can fall at altitudes as low as 2000m/6500ft, but below 3000m/9850ft it rarely lasts the day out. This is a pleasant time to trek the middle hills.

Spring and early summer (mid-March through May)

The spring rain, sun and warmth spark a flourish of growth. Rhododendrons paint the hillsides, beginning in late February at lower altitudes and blooming ever higher during March and April. Flowers enliven the forest floor and alpine areas are carpeted by wildflowers. Even fir and pine trees sprout fresh green needles.

The second trekking season commences at the end of March and continues to the end of May. The weather tends to move in cycles; absolutely fine for a few days to a few weeks then afternoon cloud and showers move in for a few days to a week. This is also considered a good time for climbing, providing you hit some long fine patches.

In the cloudy part of the cycle the morning often begins fine then cloud wisps form on random ridges and peaks. Slowly they build up and eventually the cloud rolls up the valleys during the afternoon, sometimes bringing drizzle or snow that often clears during the evening. Some mornings are cloudy but it often clears up later. During April and May you should expect the odd spectacular thunderstorm, hail shower and strong winds among the fine periods.

Below 4000m/13,100ft, longer days and a hotter sun hammers the snow so that by late March south-facing slopes are snow-free. In a light snow year, winter snow disappears quickly. In a bad year sugary corn snow persists on high passes to the beginning of the monsoon, although tracks are made through this. To beat most of the weather's vagaries begin very early in the morning.

Below 3000m/9850ft the atmosphere becomes increasingly hazy. This isn't all bad as it often takes the heat out of the sun and trekking at low altitudes becomes pleasant. Rice-planting time, late-March into April, is especially beautiful.

The monsoon (mid-June to mid-September)

The monsoon, with its life-giving rains, sweeps up from the Bay of Bengal and arrives in Kathmandu and the Langtang in the middle of June, although it is often a week or two early or late. It is heralded by a few days of spectacular thunderstorms and strong gusts of wind then it usual-

ly rains heavily for the first week. Following this the rains are more inter-
mittent until July, the month with the highest rainfall. The rain pattern is
not regular. It might be misty and rain every day for a week, then partially clear for days. Slippery trails are a problem, particularly for porters. In
the forests short leech-infested patches terrorise trekkers but porters
escape largely unscathed. Cloudbursts occasionally create dangerous
flash-floods and mud slides which can mean the end of that day's walking.

By September the monsoon is in retreat; officially it stops by mid-
September but it can cease as early as the beginning of the month or as
late as early October. The rain actually stops a few weeks after the monsoon is over.

The almost perpetual cloud cover is more of an annoyance than the
rain, particularly in July and August. The views are stunning when they
clear but you often wait days or even weeks for this to happen.' The mists
keep the temperatures surprisingly cool. The rewards of this season are
lush green valleys awash with a colourful sea of flowers. The usually barren high altitude fields fill up with crops and yaks are taken to the highest valleys.

Early autumn (mid-September to mid-October)
The monsoon has dwindled but some afternoon cloud and showers (or
short-lived snow above 4500m/14,750ft) must be expected. Take an
umbrella and dive into the nearest teahouse to wait a shower out. The risk
at this time is that the monsoon may not quite have ended, staging a return
with a few weeks of blanket cloud. Additionally, every few years the rem-
nants of a Bay of Bengal hurricane unload in a torrential downpour or
snow, down to 3000m/9850ft, for a day or two. This can occur as late as
November as in the huge 1995 storm but it is not common.

Dawn starts beat the gathering clouds, and long lunches beat the
fierce sun. Higher up it's pleasant during the day with cool but mostly
frost-free nights. With hillsides still green from the monsoon and since it
is harvest time, the villages are at their most picturesque.

THE KATHMANDU CLIMATE

At 1350m/4429ft, the capital's climate is quite mild. Monsoon showers
keep the temperature in the high 20°C/80°F during the summer, although
it's often sticky or uncomfortable if it doesn't rain. By the end of
September the tropical temperatures cool and by late October the
evenings are a little cold for just a shirt. Expect warm sunny days in
November but the evenings require a thick jacket and there's the occasional mild frost. From mid-December through January a morning fog
often settles on the valley making rising early a challenge. By mid-March
it's back to a single layer for the evening and by May the days have

---

❑ Kathmandu rainfall and temperature

Kathmandu	Rainfall mm Average	Days with rain Days min	Days with rain Days max	Daily average °C min	Daily average °C max
January	15	1	3	2	18
February	17	2	5	1	20
March	27	0	5	8	25
April	54	1	9	11	28
May	111	7	17	16	29
June	226	15	23	19	28
July	366	22	25	20	28
August	296	21	23	20	28
September	190	10	14	18	28
October	41	0	5	12	27
November	4	0	3	6	22
December	7	0	2	2	18

Notes: Days with rain, over five years 1991-5. This is indicative of what can be expected in the Langtang as well. Daily average maximum and minimum °C is averaged over the month, not the peak temperature in any one month; subtract around 3° for lowest possible minimum in that month and add around 5° for highest possible maximum in that month. The figures for average rainfall are over many years. (Falls in 1991-5 approximate this.)

become hot and the evenings balmy. Visiting Kathmandu is pleasant during any of the seasons although spring and autumn are the most popular, and most crowded, times.

How long to go for

If time is the ultimate luxury then a trekking holiday should be a decadent one. The more time you have in the mountains the better. It takes a day or two to leave the road culture behind and to adjust to the trekking lifestyle and exercise. It's usually only in the last couple of days, whether on a two-week trek or a two-month trek that several realisations dawn: 'I'm dirty and simply everything I'm wearing is filthy beyond belief; I'm thinner and always hungry and I'm dying for a huge steak or real salad; loved ones might be missing me'. Many people put in a couple of tough but satisfying days to get out.

If you only want to sample trekking rather than eat the whole pie, a week to ten days is a good length. Anything less is just a walk.

❏ **Mental Preparation**

Never been to a developing country before? Then some mental preparation is in order. Compare washing powder advertisements at home and in Nepal; a Nepali man is wandering along the trail, steps into a huge buffalo poo, slips and splat – he's covered from head to toe! Naturally his wife, waiting at the door for him, takes his cloths down to the nearest water tap in a bucket, and washes them to perfection. A lot of details will strike you as being vastly different.

Another good example is arrival at Kathmandu's airport. All airports are busy but in Kathmandu once you step outside, they are all interested in you, and more specifically where you will stay. Hotel touts fast-talk, taxi drivers don't take no for an answer and boys rush off with your luggage to stow it in another taxi (then demand dollars for the favour). Rs10-20 is enough as a tip; Nepalis can live on Rs100, less than US$2, a day. Many of the touts really are nice people but the situation means a high-pressure approach. From the most budget-minded trekker to someone heading to the Yak and Yeti hotel, you are all incredibly wealthy by local standards.

Once in Thamel little boys trail 'Shoeshine, shoeshine?', tiger balm sellers ply 'Tiger balm, Swiss army knife?' (actually fake Chinese ones), and every wayside carpet salesman tries to attract your attention, 'Namaste, hello, change money? Good rate'. After a polite but firm 'no', ignore them, rather than taking a Khukri (a large Gurkha army knife) from the nearest pestering khukri knife seller and taking off someone's head..

Time planning

Arriving in Nepal, it's best to allow a minimum of two whole days in Kathmandu (ie three nights). Don't under-estimate how long it takes to adjust to the different time zone and climate. If arranging a trek on arrival, three or four full days are better. Note that government offices are closed on Saturdays (but open Sundays) and there are numerous public holidays. Try to have at least one day in Kathmandu at the end of a trek in order to clean up and do last minute shopping. More time is all too easily filled by exploring the Kathmandu Valley.

For the trek itself allow a day or more than the quickest itineraries suggest. Getting to the starting point of a trek can take a day or just a couple of hours and buses do sometimes breakdown. Once on the trail, especially on a longer trek, allow a day or two for inclement weather or a gloriously lazy day for eating and reading. Although many people have never been hiking for more than four or five days at home (or indeed never been hiking at all) two weeks in the mountains of Nepal fly by all too quickly. Avoid the trap of planning a whole itinerary down to the last minute.

Allow four days to a week between treks if you're doing more than one. You'll need time to wash everything, organise yourself again and have a couple of lazy café days.

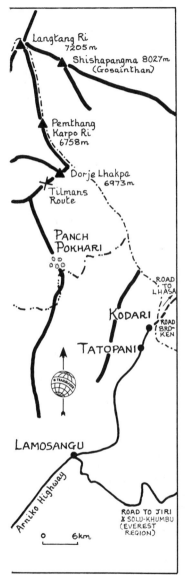

Route options

The mountains north of Kathmandu have something special for everyone, from those who wince at the word trekking to the expectant Himalayan first-timer and the veteran trekker whose face glows at the thought.

The area can hardly be called crowded and tourism is still in the development phase. In 1978, less than a thousand foreigners visited the park and now around 8400 trekkers are spread between the three main routes. Compared with the Langtang area, the Annapurna region receives more than five times as many trekkers and Everest receives double. The park is most popular with Germans and British, followed by trekkers from the USA and groups from France.

Many trekking routes in Nepal are based on ancient trading routes but the Langtang is an exception. All the tracks described here see little local traffic, just trekkers and trekker-generated porters.

The following notes give a basic outline of the treks in the region. For detailed route planning and transport options to the beginning of each trek see the sections at the beginning of the route descriptions in Part 5. Itineraries are covered in Appendix A.

The number of days quoted for each trek includes transportation time to and from Kathmandu.

SHIVAPURI (3-5 DAYS)

If you don't rate yourself as a trekker the Shivapuri walk might be best for you. The sophistication of Kathmandu is quickly replaced by rural Nepal. The route follows the ring of hills that circle Kathmandu so transport time is minimal and logistics are easy. From Nagarkot it is two easy days to Chisopani then one more to Sundarijal. Finishing at Kakani brings the total to four days. Spending a night in Bhaktapur before heading to Nagarkot gives time to explore this quaint city. Despite its proximity to Kathmandu it is not possible to teahouse this route. Most trekking companies have staff who know this trek well.

HELAMBU (7-9 DAYS)

On Kathmandu's back door step, the Helambu Circuit is a relatively easy cultural trek that bridges the Hindu region of the low country and the Tibetan culture of the north. In the almost tropical low country, the subtle lines and vivid colours of the rice paddies provide the perfect backdrop for the bright reds and gold of the Brahman women. Lean, sunparched men drive ploughs pulled by bulls, their off-white shirts and mud-coloured trousers matching the turned earth. Children skip out from homes of white and red ochre, past thatched cattle byres and through endless fields to school. Glancing up it is hard to imagine the cooler country above, where children traipse across grey flagstones and past flowerringed vegetable gardens on their way to school, their clothes of indeterminate colour matching the stone houses with their dim but welcoming interiors. Nearby, prayer flags flutter in front of a gompa and somewhere the haunting rhythmic chanting of lamas drifts across, broken by the sudden beat of drums, clash of cymbals and the tinkle of a clear bell. Terraces are replaced by forest and in the distance the occasional frozen peak sparkles.

The most popular trek is the Helambu Circuit. Unlike the quest to see Everest or crossing the Annapurna Circuit's Thorung La, this trek has no

---

❏ Helicopters

At present there are no scheduled flights to anywhere in Langtang. Part of the problem is the lack of a telephone in Langtang village and Kyangjin, so essential for planning and weather conditions. This may change in the next few years with a company offering flights during October and November to Langtang village and Kyangjin. Kathmandu trekking companies and travel agents will be in the know.

Helicopter charters are easy to arrange. Using the Russian MI-17 the 50 minute return flight to Kyangjin is US$1666.50. They take up to 21 people or a maximum payload of 3200kg up and 2300kg down. Four to six seat choppers cost around US$600-900.

goal other than to experience the region. It is often called the oldies' trek since the average age of guests in the lodge guest books is decidedly late prime. Despite this, it is a more strenuous walk than most people anticipate. There are a surprising number of hills between villages, another reason for taking it slowly. Basically the trek climbs onto a long ridge, follows this for a few days before dropping to cross a (rather deep) valley, then climbs again to follow another pleasant ridge descending off this to the road back to Kathmandu.

The circuit can be walked in either direction, but if you're teahouse trekking beginning from Sundarijal allows for a more gentle introduction to the local style of lodges. The alternative Sankhu or Nagarkot starts are outlined on p206/210 and the several route options from Melamchighyang and Tarkeghyang are outlined on p177.

Seasonal factors

In winter, when many treks become impossible, the Helambu Circuit comes into its own. At the circuit's highest point, Tharepati, snow lingers into March but the forested trail rarely holds much snow and so is usually passable. However, beginning from Melamchi Pul allows the option of returning there via an alternative route if snow is a problem at Tharepati. During the warmer times of the year it's still a pleasant walk although the midday sun can be hot. In the monsoon, thick cloud blankets the area and the trek is best avoided.

Helambu winter loops (4-6 days)

If you don't fancy snow fights at Tharepati or would like an even easier trek than the standard Helambu Circuit you could begin and end in Melamchi Pul. It is easier to trek up the valley via Timbu first and save the long descent down the Sarmathang ridge for the last day.

❏ Altitude sickness

Acute mountain sickness (AMS), often termed altitude sickness, is caused by going higher into thinner air faster than the body can adapt. Normally it is not a problem below 3000m/9850ft but when trekking above this it should be taken into account. Everybody adapts to altitude at different rates, however, this rule of thumb should ensure a safe trek; spend a minimum of two nights between 2000-3000m/6560-9850ft then from 3000m take a minimum of three nights, and preferably four nights to climb each 1000m/3280ft higher. The important altitude is sleeping elevation; during the day trek as high or low as you like.

Safety is the first issue and comfort the second. By exceeding the guidelines many people will suffer needless mild AMS symptoms – who wants to spend a night with a splitting headache? Accordingly, groups especially should plan conservative itineraries. Don't assume that foreign or local trekking companies have planned a sensible acclimatisation schedule; the reality is that most won't. See p236, for itinerary planners and p341 for more details on AMS.

THE LANGTANG VALLEY (MINIMUM 9 DAYS)

With Tamang and Tibetan villages, magnificent forest, steep hillsides, powerful glaciers and formidable ice castles, this is the big Himalaya at its best. Its proximity to Kathmandu has barely rubbed off on the inhabitants and even the influx of trekkers has brought surprisingly few changes. Women still chat in the sun weaving and drinking salt-butter tea or laboriously weed fields in animated groups. Men murmuring Buddhist mantras spin coarse wool while yaks graze, proudly oblivious to the admiring stares of trekkers.

The Langtang is basically one long, deep valley with only two main villages and a few smaller settlements. The forest and feeling of peace begin immediately. For the most part the trail follows the effervescent *khola* upwards darting in and out of beautiful forest. At 3000m/9850ft the forest fades to alpine scrub and, higher up, celestial rock and ice replace all life. The valley bears a striking similarity to the restricted Rolwaling Valley (near Everest). It can also be compared with the Annapurna Sanctuary trek; to be sure the mountains aren't about to fall on your head in quite the same way, but then you don't have to break your neck looking at them. The mountain panoramas are dramatic and compare surprisingly well with the magnificent ranges seen in the Annapurna and Everest trekking regions.

Beginning from the Dhunche road you have a choice of three fairly similar starting points for the trek. These are covered on p122. After exploring the valley the quickest way out is to head to Syabru Bensi and catch the bus.

The Langtang trek also combines well with Gosainkund (which in turn treks part of Helambu). There are two alternatives; walking out to Sundarijal or Melamchi Pul via Gosainkund or, marginally quicker, visiting Gosainkund then returning to Dhunche. See the itinerary planners on p236.

Seasonal factors

The Langtang Valley can be trekked just about year-round. In winter, snow is sometimes limiting, but trekking at least up to Kyangjin is usually possible.

During the monsoon it can still be pleasant enough if you hit a fine weather window. Certainly it is a better bet than mist-shrouded Helambu or Gosainkund. With no flights to be delayed, transport is less troublesome than to Lukla (Everest), west Nepal or Jomsom (Annapurna), and Langtang receives less rain than around Pokhara. However, if you have time, heading behind the main Annapurna range or Dolpo still might be better options (don't be fooled, despite the rainshadow tag – it still drizzles plenty in these regions and flights will be delayed).

In October or from April to early June the partially bare ridges of Helambu and Gosainkund swelter in the sun while the shady forest of the lower Langtang valley provides delightful walking and the coolness at altitude is refreshing.

Free camping

The last lodges are at Kyangjin, yet the valley stretches up another 20 walkable kilometres with many pleasant small side valleys. The only way to explore this area is to camp. Rather than camping all the way to Kyangjin, it's easier to stay in the lodges for the first three to four days and take a porter to carry the supplies. Then make Kyangjin a base and head up-valley for three to six days at a time, depending on how much you want to carry. There is enough terrain up there for a couple of forays. Once acclimatised and fit why waste it? The Kangja La beckons.

Free-camping in Gosainkund isn't so worthwhile since there are conveniently located lodges.

GOSAINKUND (MINIMUM 8 DAYS)

Nestled amid the lesser peaks of the Jugal range are a surprising number of high altitude lakes (*kund* or *kunda*), the holiest of which is Gosainkund. The crystal lakes, surrounded by rock and tussock, are stark in their beauty but the panoramas from the hike there are expansive and

---

❑ **Shiva's Lake, Gosainkund**

Shiva had descended from his normal abode, Mountain Kailash, the centre of the universe, to meditate in the foothills. Meanwhile the other gods were churning the ocean of existence to find *amrit*, the nectar of immortality, but they accidentally extracted a poison that threatened to kill everyone in the world. They begged Shiva, lord of all the gods, to contain the poison, so he drank it. This severely burned his throat (hence its blue colour). To quench the pain he rushed to the Himalaya and thrust his trident into the ground. Three springs formed, one from each prong, and he drank to cool his throat. These are now the lakes of Gosain, Bhairab and Saraswati.

Faithful devotees maintain that Lord Shiva visits the area during Janai Purnima and lies at the bottom of the lake in the form of a rock. Most pilgrims and many high caste Hindus climb up to Gosainkund for this festival (see Janai Purinuma p170). Also at this time colourful Jhankris (Shamans, or witch doctors) flock to Gosainkund (and other holy lakes high in the mountains of Nepal) to renew their powers, for Shiva is their patron. In a power place such as this, visions of events for the coming year are common.

A HRA (Himalayan Rescue Association) study proposed another reason for visions; hallucinations. Most of the 8,000-10,000 pilgrims now make a three to four day round trip from Dhunche to Gosainkund. This, of course, exceeds all altitude advice, and with serious consequences; around one in a thousand die and at least 5% have worryingly severe AMS. Symptoms reported include hallucinations.

include the huge Ganesh, Manaslu and Annapurna ranges. The trek follows an ancient Hindu pilgrimage route from Kathmandu and the relatively new Dhunche road provides a quicker exit.

While the Laurebina La isn't as high as Annapurna's Thorung La or the high passes in Everest, it's more accessible and requires only eight days, not two or three weeks – and 4600m/15,100ft is still impressively stratospheric.

The Gosainkund trek can be walked in either direction but, if you're not combining it with another trek, starting from the south and walking north makes more sense acclimatisation-wise. From Kathmandu the route first passes through Helambu with the options of starting from Sundarijal or Melamchi Pul. From Tharepati the routes converge to cross the Laurebina La to the lakes.

When combining Gosainkund with the Langtang Valley trek, visiting Langtang first is slightly more sensible. Most people spend several days exploring around Kyangjin and so gain considerable acclimatisation whereas the standard crossing of Gosainkund allows the bare minimum of time for acclimatising.

Gosainkund up and back
The crossing of the Laurebina La has a lot to recommend it but, especially if snow conditions are challenging, you could visit Gosainkund from Syabru then return to Dhunche. Note that Syabru is often called Thulo Syabru.

Seasonal factors
It is only possible to teahouse trek in Gosainkund for part of the year. Winter snow blocks the route and it is not usually reopened until March. During spring the conditions are quite variable. Snow can dust the pass at any time, even into May, although it only rarely stops trekkers crossing. Once the monsoon hits, the lodges mostly close. Gosainkund is particularly cloudy during the monsoon. By September a lodge or two reopens but waiting until mid-October avoids the cloud. See p167.

WILD TREKS

Over the Kangja La 5122m/16,804ft (minimum 2 weeks)
Say that a pass crossing is difficult and provide little information, and trekkers are intrigued, prompting many to talk about it and even a few to do it. That has been the situation until now.

The Kangja La, sometimes spelt Gangja La, is the highest pass over the Jugal Range which can be trekked. (The other pass is Gosainkund's 4600m Laurebina La). The crossing is spectacularly alpine; you can literally touch the glacier ice and a bit of scrambling is involved, so it definitely deserves the wild label. If this doesn't unsettle you a successful crossing is immensely satisfying. Sitting on the top, prayer flags flutter-ing, the Langtang (north) side panorama is a rough sea of the most mag-nificent mountains near and far. On the Helambu side, crinkled hills stretch further than the eye can see and some fascinating glaciated peaks beg your attention. Heading down, the route is still rough; this is no easy valley walk. Instead the lumpy path traverses a never-ending ridge, roller-coasting with abandon. Then within sight of villages on the short cut, you wonder if you'll even get there because the terrain is so rough.

For a long time it has been a camping route but it won't always be. During the October-November season only two days' food is now required – down from four – and some can survive without a tent. This is still no ordinary teahouse trek but things are changing – at least for the autumn season. In spring it is a full camping route and the amount of snow lying around determines your chances of success, which are by no means assured. Even in September, when every other pass in Nepal is open, groups have been turned back by unfavourable snow. This route is too rough and dependent on the weather for it to become wildly popular but with more information available undoubtedly the pass would be used more frequently.

Although it is possible to cross alone, it is not recommended. In fact for many people the most difficult choice will be between crossing with a guide or without. Acclimatisation is critical for this trek. For a discus-sion of the factors see p236.

Langtang Circuit (3 weeks)
This is the Gosainkund trek beginning at Sundarijal combined with the Kangja La and ending at Melamchi Pul. Beginning at Gosainkund is far more sensible unless you were at high altitude less than 10 days ago. Giving a name to this combined trek may give it more appeal in the long run, even if the name isn't particularly accurate.

In comparison the Annapurna Circuit is slightly shorter and gentler and better all round although it is also busier and needs a larger budget. Everest has even more hills but the high Khumbu valleys beg for explo-ration so if you have four weeks plus a trekking wanderlust, Everest is hard to beat. To its credit, adding some camping above Kyangjin does mean the Langtang Circuit is different in flavour and certainly a great trip. At the end of the day go with your instincts. Wherever you go you will have a great trek, Nepal's like that!

Yala Peak 5520m/18,110ft
From Kyangjin, in the Langtang Valley, the best trekking view point is Cherko, 4984m/16,351ft. Above is the even better Yala Peak, a minor mountaineering foray. The peak is so named because from Yala Kharka it looks like a mountain but it isn't really a peak at all, rather it's a bump on

a long ridge. The climb isn't difficult – it just involves walking on a crevassed glacier. With good conditions, a guide and ski pole it is easily within the reach of acclimatised ambitious trekkers. The summit views are superb and include the 8027m/26,335ft Shishapangma in Tibet. More details on p154.

TREKKING PEAKS (MINIMUM 3 WEEKS)

These are better called 'limited bureaucracy' mountains because you can't just trek to the summit – these all require real mountaineering. The Langtang has only the 5846m/19,180ft Naya Kanga (p223) which is beside the Kangja La. Close by in the Ganesh Himal is the other trekking peak in the area, the 5928m/19,450ft Paldor (p224). While both are under the magic 6000m/20,000ft level (and therefore the permit costs US$150) they have spectacular summit views that look over the hazy middle hills to the south and to the north, into Tibet, including fine views of Shishapangma.

Naya Kanga is generally considered the easier, with snow/ice slopes to 45°, while climbing Paldor involves a 55° slope, more glacier travel and a rocky ridge. Many groups have failed on Naya Kanga or Paldor, indeed even failed to reach the climbing base camp, because of inadequate acclimatisation. The second set of factors is the weather and snow conditions. Mid-October through to the end of December is the best time (but a large dump of snow during this period can upset the most carefully-made plans). Spring snow conditions are more variable, and usually more wading is required, unless there is already a trail. Also clouds often form early, requiring dawn starts. On the plus side, temperatures can be warmer and the whole region greener, at least by May.

For the discreet (or the well-heeled) mountaineer Langtang has surprising potential. There are peaks ranging from 5800m/19,000ft to 6900m/22,650ft that would be nice propositions; they're all classed as expedition ('unlimited bureaucracy') peaks. However, with luck, the number of trekking peaks may soon be expanded to include a couple of them. Also see the box 'Ultimate water-ice', p147.

TREKS IN NEIGHBOURING REGIONS (NOT COVERED HERE)

Ganesh Himal (2-3 weeks)
The Ganesh Himal is a 7000m+ range of mountains and hills lying roughly between the Langtang region and the Manaslu-Annapurna region. Despite the great mountain views and being readily accessible from Gorkha, Dhading, Syabru Bensi or Trisuli, little information can be found and consequently few trekkers visit the region. It is probably this oversight by trekking guide book writers (myself included) that has held this

region back from the attention that it deserves. The lack of facilities make it ideal for a fully catered two to three week trek organised in Kathmandu. The adventurous could get away with lightweight camping equipment and a guide, but need to carry plenty of supplies and be prepared for simple meals in the villages. There are several route choices, all involving hill climbs. The highest crosses the 4000m/13,123ft Singla Bhanjyang (difficult or impossible during spring). All options start and finish in low altitude areas. A fraction of the Ganesh Himal region is covered in the section for Paldor.

Jugal Himal (minimum 2 weeks)

South of the Jugal Himal are a series of valleys and ridges similar in geography to Helambu. However, the distances are longer, the hills higher and there are few facilities – and none specifically for trekkers. A guide is essential. Despite its proximity to Kathmandu, the area sees few trekkers. Lonely Planet's *Trekking in the Nepal Himalaya* has coverage of one of the possible routes.

Tilman's Pass (minimum 3 weeks)

Not to be confused with Tilman's Col, this is a challenging alternative exit of the Langtang Valley. It's an isolated route for mountaineers only, and perhaps a group a year crosses this way. After crossing the heavily glaciated pass the difficulties don't end; you still have to find your way down on steep and rough terrain to Panch Pokhari (five lakes). There's a summary of the trickiest bits beginning on p222. This is not the only other potential pass. Up the Pangrima Valley are three other possible points to cross the Jugal range but, again, the critical section is getting down the other side to trails. Study the Alpenvereinskarte Langthang Ost map (Austrian Alpine Club) for an appreciation of the difficulties.

Exploring

The Austrian Alpine Club maps reveal a number of possibilities. One of the most intriguing is Ganesh Kund (lake). There are vague trails up to kharkas above Melamchi, but is it possible to reach the lake itself? Note that at least one person has died trying to descend from around there to Changdam on the old trail marked on the Schneider map. Exploring the lakes around Gosainkund is another possibility. Be aware that it only takes a three-metre vertical wall to block a route. Also avoid the temptation to take a few risks and push on hoping that it will get easier – the chances are that it won't.

OTHER ACTIVITIES

Nepal now offers a lot more than just trekking. Unless your schedule is tight, these activities don't need to be planned in advance, just remember to allow some extra time.

Chitwan National Park wildlife safari (3-4 days)

Fancy shaking trunks with an elephant or sipping exotic cocktails under a crimson sunset? How about wildlife spotting by dugout canoe and elephant-back or watching rhinos forage in the savannah from the breakfast table? Royal Chitwan National Park is one of Asia's premier game parks, a mix of jungle, grasslands and river plains teeming with wildlife, including the endangered **royal Bengal tiger**, the rare **Gangetic dolphin** and the much more common **one-horned rhino**. It is well managed with buffer zones and the local people are beginning to see the long-term benefit, essential if they are to protect their own resources. Safari Asian style is quite different from Africa. The game, although abundant, is often more elusive. Also it is better hidden in the long elephant grass and jungle undergrowth, hence the advantage of spotting by elephant-back, from canoes and from machans (hides or blinds). However, you will see lots of game and there's a special thrill finding it in its natural environment.

There are two distinct ways of enjoying Chitwan: staying inside the park or outside. Sauraha, the travellers' haunt outside the park, is the cheaper but less satisfactory alternative; the elephant ride to go rhino spotting is short so most game spotting is done on foot (and by climbing trees if a rhino charges) or by jeep. And in the cosmopolitan village, you miss the absolute serenity of the morning and evening jungle. So, while the experience is good, there is better.

Inside the park, scattered all over the place, the wildlife resorts provide a secluded, peaceful, relaxing and comfortable place to stay. The activities are well-planned and the service is superb. Each has its own fleet of dugout canoes, jeeps and elephants who are handled by guides who know the wildlife's habits and who can usually spot the game long before you do. The resorts make the Chitwan Experience a brilliant way to begin or end a holiday in Nepal.

Bardia National Park (4-8 days)

Lost in Nepal's Wild West, Bardia is almost undiscovered compared to Chitwan, only because it is either inconvenient or expensive to access. Here four or five-day safaris penetrating well into the park are better. Access is from Nepalganj, a US$99 flight (one way) or a gruelling 14-18

❏ **Polo**

If polo is a gentleman's sport, elephant polo must be the sport of kings. Tiger Tops hosts an annual tournament at its Chitwan Jungle Lodge. It is a fun social occasion well attended with teams sponsored by liquor companies and adventure companies. The 1998 tournament will be held 3-9 December. Contact Tiger Tops (Nepal fax 1-414 075 or email tiger@mtn.mos.com.np).

hour night bus journey. From Pokhara, flights cost US$60 and the bus journey is the same length.

Other more remote parks are **Kaptada National Park**, a middle altitude forest plateau which can only be trekked into (seven to 14 days total) and the **Royal Suklaphanta Wildlife Reserve** which is close to Mahendranagar. The reserve is a grassland area with the occasional tiger and wild elephant, and is rich in rare swamp deer. It is a staggering 30 hours by bus or US$142 flight from Kathmandu.

Rafting (2-12 days)

While Nepal is famous for its mountains it should also be world-famous for its white water. Huge mountains mean big, steep rivers which are perfect for rafting and kayaking. For thrill-seekers no trip to Nepal would be complete without a white water expedition. Believe it or not, almost every trek in Nepal could be rounded off with a rafting expedition.

For a cheap and gentle introduction try the Trisuli. Almost every rafting company run trips on this river (two to four days) for most of the year. If you know you will enjoy the thrills and spills go straight for a river with a higher scare factor. The Bhote Kosi (two days) and the Marsyangdi (five days) are steep, technical and fun. For the ultimate experience, try the massive waters of the Karnali (eight to nine days plus three travelling) and the Sun Kosi (eight to nine days plus two travelling), which have rapids that will make even the coolest cucumber gulp in disbelief. Another world-class river is the exhilarating Tamur (Kanchenjunga region) with its magic trek in and approximately 130 rapids in 120km. For a shade off full throttle consider the cultural Kali Gandaki (five days, out of Pokhara).

Do you want to learn how to kayak? Kayak Clinics come highly recommended – just ensure the instructors are qualified.

The high water season, for those with no fear, is late September-early October and May. Trips run into November then begin again in March and taper off by late May. Wherever you go, safety should be paramount. Take a look at Peter Knowles' *Rafting: a consumers' guide*, available in Kathmandu. There are only three Thamel companies to run big rivers with; **Ultimate Descents**, **Equator Expeditions** and **Himalayan**

❑ **Addiction warning**

The nervousness, no, the plain fear of being committed to a rapid, then the sheer exhilaration of running and surviving the huge white water make rafting one of the most thrilling life experiences. Between the roller-coasters are peaceful stretches, chances to splash around and relax, letting the adrenaline highs give way to that priceless inner glow. Also special is the warmth and fun of being an integral part of the team.

Encounters. For more information on all the rivers of Nepal read Peter Knowles and Dave Allardice's delightfully written *White Water Nepal*.

Mountain biking (1-4 days)

The hills around the Kathmandu valley have many roads. Most of these should be called four-wheel drive tracks, though for some even this title is fanciful. However they are perfect for mountain biking. Trips can be organised through **Himalayan Mountain Bikes** or **Dawn till Dusk** in Thamel. A minimum of two, sometimes four people is required.

Biking/motor-biking around the valley

Cycling used to be the most pleasant way to see Kathmandu but now with the dust and pollution few people cycle there for pleasure. However, once outside the city limits it's a different story; see a detailed map of the valley for ideas. Clunky Indian mountain bikes (better kept on tarmacked roads) cost US$2-4 a day while motorbikes go for around US$10 a day plus petrol.

Mountain flight

If you've just got to see Everest but don't like the idea of the high altitude trek, take a breathtaking close-up of the Khumbu from a mountain flight. During the autumn peak season highly rated mountain flights around the Annapurna Circuit also operate out of Pokhara. Taking any other domestic flight is, if the weather's perfect, also spectacular.

Balloon flight

The latest adventure activity to lift off in Nepal is hot air ballooning. Piloted by a colourful Australian, the hour or so flight is exhilarating, peaceful and somewhat random; you land where the gods have taken you.

❑ Costs for other activities	
Chitwan – inside the park	US$140 up (plus US$80 by car)
Chitwan – outside the park (Sauraha)	US$65 up
Bardia National Park	US$220 up (plus US$200 if flying both ways)
Rafting	US$15-65 a day
Karnali	US$400-600
Sun Kosi	US$300-450
Kali Gandaki	US$150-250
Marsyangdi	US$180-300
Bhote Kosi	US$80-100
Trisuli	US$25-80
Mountain biking	US$25-45 a day
Mountain flight	US$99
Balloon flight	$195

Pokhara

Beside a lake gazing up at the huge Annapurna range, the delight of Pokhara is that there's nothing to do besides enjoying the cafés. It is also a good base to begin or end Annapurna treks and ties in well with trips to Chitwan National Park and rafting the Trisuli, Seti and Kali Gandaki.

Visiting Tibet

If you already have a Chinese visa, you can usually cross the border as an individual. On the other side, since there are (officially) no buses, you often have to hire a landcruiser (minimum US$60 per person) to Shigatse. This also gets around random permit problems.

The easier and quicker way is to book one of the eight-day fixed departure tours in Kathmandu. These drive to (or from) Lhasa stopping at most points of interest along the way. The budget versions cost US$480-600, including the US$190 flight back, with departures Saturdays and Wednesdays. They run from March through to mid-November. There are four or five operators in Thamel with little to distinguish them. Most trekking and travel companies organise through them too.

Visiting Bhutan

The Land of the Thunder-dragon is a particularly rewarding destination. The friendliness of the people and the smooth organisation come at a price; around US$200 a day whether trekking or travelling. Visits take time to arrange; a minimum of two weeks but starting at least three months in advance is better.

A second trek

Trekking can be addictive! Around 20% of trekkers do it again in the same holiday. Trekkers also have one of the highest tourism return rates in the world; an amazing number of people just keep coming back year after year.

After a first trek you should know how the teahouse system works and be more comfortable with the way Nepal is in general. The rest of the country is now wide open. Teahouse trekking is still only easy in the three main areas of Annapurna, Everest and Langtang, but based out of tea-houses some wild routes with plenty of exploring are still possible. On a more generous budget (US$20-50 a day, plus flights), heading away from the main areas and camping makes sense. This could be full service trek style or a mixed approach; using local teahouses where possible and camping where not, taking lightweight camping gear and a minimum of porters. During the October-December season or late spring, the more ambitious may want to throw in a 6000m/20,000ft trekking peak too. Looking through picture books in Kathmandu can give a better idea of the differences in the areas.

The number of days required for a shorter cultural and lower level trek (shorter) and the minimum and normal number of days for a standard trek (standard) are given where relevant.

Eastern Nepal

A friendly, relatively developed area where it is generally possible to find rough accommodation in villages. In the Everest region the teahouse accommodation is highly developed. There's an incredible concentration of big mountains, each with a pleasant walk in.

Kanchenjunga 10-12 days (shorter) 21, 28+ (standard)
A classic trek, with plenty of variety, which can be teahoused (simple style!) at lower levels with camping in the upper mountain-surrounded sections.

Makalu 14, 18+ (standard)
Tea-house trekking is possible part of the way – until you reach the wild uninhabited region. Route options are limited and you may experience problems with adequate acclimatisation but there are incredible neck-cricking mountain views.

Jiri walk-in to Namche (then Khumbu-Everest) 7-9 to Namche (shorter) 18, 21+ (total, standard) There are many hills on the route in to Namche but the teahouses are pleasant and not crowded. The trek forms part of the famous 'expedition' route in.

Everest via Arun 8-12 to Namche (shorter) 20, 23+ (total, standard)
A longer route in which offers more variety. Teahouses are fairly basic.

Everest fly in 7 (shorter) 10, 14+ (standard)
You can get too Tengboche in six days but going higher is rewarding. The area is busy

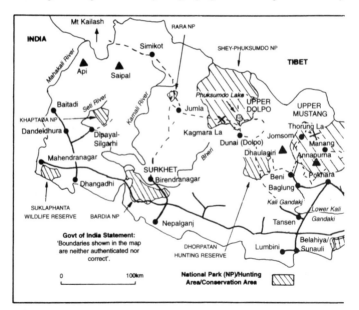

during the high season but getting flights in and out is no longer a problem.

Exploring nearby 9, 14+ (standard)
Dudh Kund, Pike Peaks and Lumding Kharka are rarely visited but magnificent destinations.

Everest trekking peak 16, 21+ (standard)
A variety of 6000m+ peaks and the chance to see the region as well. Island Peak and Mera are overrun during the October season.

Rolwaling 10 (shorter) 12, 15+ plus Everest (standard)
You must get a trekking peak permit for this route. The area is similar to the Langtang valley but bigger and there are incredible mountaineering exploration possibilities.

Central Nepal
The middle hills are densely populated which means interesting cultural walks are possible. The Annapurna region is heavily trekked and blanketed with teahouses. Shorter treks are popular from September to May (ie except in the monsoon season). Access is quick and easy from Pokhara.

Low trade route 4-8 (shorter)
This route goes from Trisuli to Pokhara (or Gorkha or Besi Sahar road) and it is hot at any time except during the winter. The road means this route is no longer trekked but there are simple teahouses for those who can live rough.

Manaslu 18, 21 (standard)
A special permit is required for this route and you must go with a group but this circuit is a classic offering lowland and highland cultures as well as a 5000m+ pass. However it is busy in October.

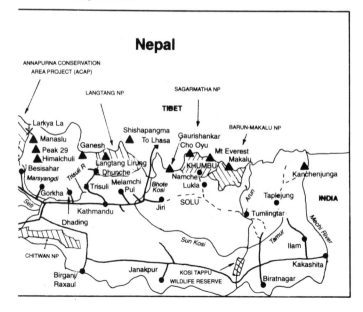

Ganesh Himal 12-18 (shorter) 12-21 (standard)
There is next to no information on this region between Kathmandu and Pokhara. Groups do venture there; as long as you have a guide teahousing/camping is another rough option. A cultural experience but there are plenty of hills. See p224.

Annapurna Circuit 14, 18+ (standard)
A classic and popular trek with teahouses all the way. The trek can be shortened by flying out of Jomsom. There are plenty of areas to explore but nothing has been written about these.

Annapurna trekking peak 16, 20+ (standard)
Near Manang are five trekking peaks all of which should be within the capabilities of an experienced trekker with a climbing guide.

Jomsom trail 7-14 (shorter)
A popular route which can almost be trekked using one and two star lodges.

Poon Hill/Ghandruk 3-7 (shorter)
This is popular because the trek is short and sweet though there is a large hill to climb.

Annapurna sanctuary (Annapurna Base Camp) 9-12 (standard)
Dramatic mountain scenery but the route requires some backtracking and part of the trek isn't cultural because there are no traditional villages – only lodges catering for trekkers. Beware of AMS, particularly on organised treks.

Upper Mustang (Jomsom to Jomsom) 10-12 (shorter)
A US$700 permit is required to visit the last functioning walled city in the world. The Tibetan desert landscape on this route is wonderful.

Dhorpatan 9, 12 (shorter), 13-18 (standard)
The teahouses are simple and some camping is required. Jaljala at 3250m/10,660ft is the highest point and you should camp here. Churen Himal Base Camp is an undiscovered sanctuary which is similar to, but not quite as grand as, the Annapurna Sanctuary. Tansen is a beautiful and quiet hill station.

Around Dhaulagiri (Marpha to Pokhara) 12, 15 plus acclimatisation (standard)
One of the wildest, coldest and possibly most dangerous treks in Nepal. You must acclimatise properly first and take a guide who has been there many times. Porters shouldn't be taken; groups do, of course, take them and there have been many deaths.

Western Nepal – Nepal's Wild West
All treks require either several days on buses plus a flight or two, or expensive flights. Crew costs add up quickly. The area is remote and much less developed than east Nepal – sometimes shockingly so. District headquarters have shops and food but elsewhere little is available for trekkers and their crew. The mountains are less spectacular but the terrain is more varied. Flights are difficult to arrange; if RNAC (Royal Nepal) can't take you, head to Nepalganj and hope to get on a helicopter. For larger groups chartering a helicopter is definitely best.

Dolpo walk in 16, 21+ (standard)
The variety on this trek makes it a new classic; begin with the cultural Dhorpatan Circuit then cross a series of 4000-4600m passes into the Tibetan area of Dolpo. See also below.

Dolpo fly in 12-18+ (standard)
Do-Tarap, Kagmara La, Phuksumdo – there are lots of possible routes. The higher regions are pure Tibetan areas with dry rugged scenery while the barren middle hills

are the domain of poor Chetris. Many groups visit in September and early October. November-December and May-June are still good months.

Quick Dolpo 8-10 (shorter)
You get up to Phuksumdo Lake. Flights in cost US$300+ but you get the very best of Dolpo.

Upper Dolpo 17+ (standard)
A US$700 permit is required but essentially this offers a taste of trekking in old Tibet.

Rara Lake (fly to Jumla or walk in) 9-11 (shorter, 11+ (standard)
There are two semi-standard routes (neither of which are busy) and many exploration possibilities. You can end in Simikot.

Kaptada 7-10 (shorter)
A route which is rarely trekked. Kaptada is a beautiful 3000m forest plateau.

Api-Saipal 22, 26+ (standard)
Out there! And long! The West Seti hydro project may mean there's a road into this area soon.

Mt Kailash 16, 20 (standard)
This involves crossing into Tibet west of Simikot and returning via Simikot or Lhasa. Asian Trekking charges a minimum of US$2400.

What to take

The basic essentials

What you need depends very much on your trek and the season. The shorter the trek the less you need and the longer the trek, the less you want to carry.

For all treks you need a comfortable rucksack and a sleeping bag. You'll want mainly cool loose clothes for the days in the lower country, even in winter. Typically you'll wear a shirt/blouse and trousers/pants or a skirt, cotton socks and a sun hat. A windproof jacket or fleece might come out if the afternoon is windy. At higher altitudes the days are cooler and a set of interchangeable warm/windproof layers is best. A thermal

---

❑ **The art of staying warm**
'Even though it was summer (May), bring a sleeping bag and some warm clothes as it gets bloody cold up there'. **Robert and Marina** (Australia) – about the Langtang trek but it is also applicable to Gosainkund.

It takes more than good clothes to stay warm. The critical period is when you stop walking, especially at the end of the day. Avoid suddenly getting cold by changing damp clothing for dry and perhaps having a hot drink as soon as you get in. It is preferable to stay warm rather than get cold and try to warm up afterwards.

top, perhaps covered by a shirt/blouse is typical wear and a fleece or windproof jacket is useful at rest stops or if the weather is less than perfect. Trousers/pants alone are fine for during the day but in the evening longjohns/fleecepants are also necessary. Several synthetic or wool layers will do for sitting around in high altitude lodges from late April to October but at other times a thick down jacket for cold mountain tops and fridge-like lodges is essential.

Most people tend to take too much. During the main trekking season, October to December, it is nearly always dry so you need one set of hot weather clothes; it's not necessary to have two pairs of walking trousers/pants. For cold weather, take only what you can wear at the same time (plus an extra shirt and changes of underwear). From late winter into April, clothing may get wet so an extra thermal or light fleece might be appreciated, but no more, and if going high you should be prepared for snow.

Don't skimp on your sleeping bag during the cold months; sleeping warm is an important key to staying healthy.

It is possible to buy or rent many items in Kathmandu, see p96.

Group trekkers

Most companies supply a kit bag for your equipment. Porters simply loop a *namlo* (a rope with a head strap) around two or three bags (yes, 30-45kg in all) and away they go. Normally they do the same if given rucksacks.

Porter-guides prefer to carry a rucksack. Leave some room in the top for their equipment.

Dress standards

These vary considerably around the country. Kathmandu is the most liberal and culturally diverse place though Western women will find dressing modestly attracts far less attention. The well-off (locals and foreigners) are expected to dress conservatively.

Along the regular trekking routes the Nepalese are used to (though have never understood) the comparatively odd and occasionally indecent

---

❑ **Who's offended?**
After a pair of well-exposed female Western legs walked past trailed by the group's drooling crew, we asked the female lodge owner what she thought. She didn't ask us if she was a prostitute or to our surprise, berate her at all: 'She has wonderful fat legs so she can be proud of showing them.' And how we laughed!

Well, we ended up staying at the same lodge as the pair of legs and, after some raksi, couldn't resist repeating the story. Naturally it went down like the proverbial ton of bricks: 'How dare she call me fat,' was the offended reply. Sulky and insulted, unfortunately, she didn't bare her legs again.

Back in Kathmandu we could understand why the sari-clad women revealing a roll of fat were so proud and caught the occasional admiring glance...

ways in which Westerners dress but in less frequented areas locals may still be shocked. Being dressed in a culturally acceptable way gains you much greater respect among the local people, a fact that many trekkers have commented upon.

For men, baggy shorts are more or less acceptable and a T-shirt OK, but singlets, running shorts or cycle pants, despite the fact that some porter-guides wear them, are going too far; bare chests are rude.

For women double standards exist. Long baggy shorts are worn although a skirt that falls past the knee, or light baggy trousers, are definitely more appropriate. A T-shirt is the minimum for modesty and Lycra trousers/pants invite unwarranted attention. Another practical local option is the *kurta surawal*, baggy trousers/pants that narrow around the ankle, and a knee-length shirt.

EQUIPMENT LIST

• **Sleeping-bag** Essential; a down bag is lighter and more compact than a synthetic one of the same warmth. From May to the end of October a three season bag is adequate. For the cold months, November to March, take particular care to choose a warm (four season) bag. When buying or renting a down bag look for good and even thickness; the down should be fluffy and light. A muff around the top of the bag makes a big difference to overall warmth. Trekking companies often provide bags but if you already have a good one it's worth bringing it instead. Sleeping bags of variable quality can be rented in Kathmandu for US$1 or less a day.

• **Sleeping-bag liner (cotton or silk)** Having one of these saves washing your sleeping-bag and adds warmth. In Kathmandu, these can be made up cheaply and easily from light cotton. Light-weight silk is difficult to find and the readily available imitation silk is not as good.

• **Rucksack/backpack** It's important to have a comfortable one. The feature that will help most in this respect is a good waist band. Small backpacks are neat and look trendy but a larger pack is preferable since gear does not have to be tightly compressed and packing is easier. Group trekkers will need only a day pack but once you put a jacket, camera and water bottle in, plus more odds and ends you need a big one – 30 litres or slightly more – preferably with a proper waistband to make it as comfortable as possible. You can rent or buy these in Kathmandu; renting full -sized rucksacks is not easy but there are plenty of shoddy ones for sale.

• **Boots** One of the most important things for ensuring a happy trek is having comfortable feet. Carrying a backpack places a greater load on your feet than normal so rigid supportive boots will feel more comfortable in the long run. It's possible to trek in running shoes but the new generation light-weight trekking boots are far superior. Trekkers seem to get away with these boots even in winter but this can be dangerous during a snowfall. Sturdy but light all-leather boots are better in cold weather. Don't forget to take some water-proofing goo.

When choosing boots look for good ankle support, plenty of toe room (essential for the long descents), a stiff sole (helps prevent tired feet by lessening twisting), and boots that aren't too heavy. Check the inner lining – leather is good but Cambrelle (which can destroy some of the bacteria that cause foot odour) is even better. Light-weight trekking boots generally have good shock-absorbing qualities but some foams can actually be crushed if they are too heavily loaded. Boots are better worn in before trekking; the process should include walking up some steep hills.

For independent trekkers weight and space are of prime importance so a single pair of comfortable boots is generally enough. If trekking with a group, a pair of shoes for relaxing around camp can be useful.

Your feet will be doing far more work than they're used to so take great care of them. The rest of your body has the luxury of changes of clothes but your feet are confined to a single pair of boots that must cope with the extremes of heat and cold. Air them, and your socks and boots, frequently – lunch is an ideal time. Consider changing your socks more than once during the day and wash your feet and socks, if nothing else, at least every few days. If you feel a hot spot or a blister developing, stop immediately and treat it before it's too late to prevent damage.

• **Socks** Most of the time your feet will be warm or even hot while walking so quality cotton-mix sports socks are fine. Three to four pairs are enough. For colder conditions bring a couple of pairs of thick walking socks; four pairs of these would be better if you're trekking in the wetter months. Light-weight trekking boots generally fit snugly so wearing two pairs of socks at the same time (originally used in stiff boots to prevent blisters) is not practical.

• **Down jacket** A big, thick down jacket is essential above 3000m/9850ft during the cold months. Find one of bum-warming length with hand-warming pockets and a hood. During the warmer months a hat and a jersey or fleece combined with a rain jacket will be adequate.

• **Wind/rain jacket** Another essential. High up, if the sun is shining, it can be wonderfully warm but when a breeze picks up the true air temperature becomes apparent and wind protection is a necessity. Since it rarely rains all day – or even at all in peak season – having an expensive, totally waterproof jacket is not necessary. When it starts raining everybody simply takes cover in the nearest shelter. Plastic ponchos are of use only during the monsoon.

• **Jersey/fleece jacket** Opinions vary; when it's cold people with down jackets consider them essential but those with only fleece say they are adequate. Fleece is no substitute for a down jacket in real winter, however. From May to October, the wet times, fleece is a better choice. Kathmandu is a great place for buying luxuriously thick wool jerseys but they are heavy.

• **Shirt/blouse** T-shirts are popular but thin long-sleeved cotton shirts/blouses are more versatile; the collar protects the back of your neck and the sleeves can be rolled up or down. Take two so that you have a dry one to change into after trekking.

• **Underwear** Four to five pairs of what you usually wear are plenty. If you frequently wear a sports bra bring two, otherwise what you normally wear is fine.

• **Thermal underwear** Longjohns and a top are essential above 3000m unless substituted by fleece for the warmer seasons. Thermals should be used with fleece in winter at altitude.

• **Pants/trousers** These are easily bought in Kathmandu. Loose, lightweight, dark-coloured cotton/polyester travel trousers/pants or rock-climbing baggies in nylon or cotton/nylon mixes are best. Jeans are not practical.

• **Mid-calf length skirt/Kurta surawal** Longjohns or leggings complement a skirt in the cooler country. Also bring some long trousers/pants if trekking above villages where the dress code isn't as important. Kurta surawals are readily available in Kathmandu.

• **Fleece trousers/pants** These are not needed during the warm seasons since longjohns with walking trousers/pants over the top will do. In winter they are almost a necessity, though.

• **Windproof/waterproof trousers/pants** If your trekking trousers/pants are partly windproof an additional pair isn't needed. A pair may however be useful during winter.

• **Warm hat** A warm hat is essential if your jacket doesn't have a hood.

• **Sun hat** You need something to protect your head in hot sunny weather, particularly from April to the end of October. A light hat with a wide brim is good, as is a cotton scarf with a visor.

• **Mittens/Gloves** These are essential above 3500m/11,500ft except during the monsoon. The hand-knitted gloves available in Kathmandu are fine.

• **Gaiters** Leggings that protect from the ankle to the knee are useful in Nepal only when it has snowed heavily. On the main trails, a path is cleared quickly after a large snowfall so, if you can wait, you can survive without gaiters. Off the main trails or when climbing, they are essential. Three or four metres of cheap cord to wrap around the toe of your boots to increase grip on icy snow is also useful.

• **Towel** This doesn't need to be big; quick-drying sarongs are the best.

• **Water bottle** Essential for adequate hydration. Bottles should be leak-proof, tough and able to withstand boiling water (partly in order to make a comforting hot water bottle). On a teahouse-only trek, a one litre bottle between two can do.

• **Sun screen** is vital. The ultra-violet (UV) concentration increases around 4% for every 300m/1000ft gain in altitude and snow reflects 75% of UV. Apply sunblock frequently and liberally at higher altitudes.

• **Sunglasses** It's important to have a good pair of sunglasses – they must be able to protect against UV. For prolonged high altitude sojourns side pieces are useful but ski goggles are not needed. If you wear glasses it's best to get a pair of prescription sunglasses made. Alternatively detachable dark lenses have proved adequate. **Contact lens** wearers report problems with grit and pollution in Kathmandu but few problems in the hills except cleaning them in cold conditions. To prevent the cleaning solution from freezing it's best kept in your sleeping-bag on very cold nights.

• **Torch/flashlight** A necessity. It's worth getting a good quality torch and using Western batteries. Head torches are particularly handy for group trekkers in tents. Independent trekkers may get by with a cheap Kathmandu torch. Don't dispose of alkaline batteries in the hills.

• **Walking stick** On long descents a stick lessens the shock to your knees. Hack yourself a bamboo one or get one from a lodge; they often have a recycled collection of staves. More convenient is a telescoping ski pole that easily ties onto your backpack for the flatter sections.

• **Binoculars** A small pair is great for eyeballing monkeys and close-ups of the staggering mountains. Nikon, Pentax and Minolta brands are cheaply available in New Road, Kathmandu. Nikon 7 x 20s (seven times magnification, 20mm diameter lenses) sell for around US$80.

• **Umbrella** This is particularly useful from late spring through the monsoon season to the end of September but they also provide great protection against the sun. Umbrellas are available in Kathmandu.

• **Pack cover** It's worth having something to cover your backpack between January and the end of September. A large, carefully cut plastic bag is a reasonable substitute. Both are available in Kathmandu; you can also buy plastic bags at roadhead villages.

• **Toiletries** This is where you can really save some weight. There is no need for a half litre bottle of shampoo; the chances are you will only wash your hair a few times. Sachets and petite bottles are readily available in Kathmandu. There are no plugs for electric razors. The smallest size of toothpaste sold is perfect for a month. Don't forget deodorant ('the trekkers' shower'). Natural, anti-bacterial mineral crystals (as used by Indian barbers after shaving) are available and cheap, but are hard to find.

• **Toilet paper** This is available on main routes so start with only one roll.

• **Candles** are essential for late night bookworms. Most hotels use a bright kerosene lantern in the dining room and some supply a candle or small kerosene lamp for the sleeping rooms. Having a few candles saves hunting around. Thicker candles are better. Be aware of the fire risk.

• **Lighter or matches** Either or both are handy for lighting candles and are considered essential for burning used toilet paper by those who haven't tried to burn pink Chinese toilet paper – it doesn't burn well.

• **Moisturiser** A small tube for sensitive or well cared for skins is useful as the air is dry and the sun harsh.

• **Lip balm with sunscreen** is essential to prevent chapped and blistered lips and should be used frequently above 3000m.

• **Sanitary napkins/towels** These are available in Kathmandu but you may have to search a bit for tampons.

• **Pre-moistened towelettes** ('Wet-ones') are handy for group trekkers but bulky for individuals.

• **First aid kit** See the medical section, Appendix B.

• **Water purification kit** An essential, see Appendix B.

• **Reading matter** Bring several books for the long afternoons.

• **Diary** Many people like to write a diary while they trek. The fresh air, stunning scenery and uncluttered days are inspiring.

• **Money pouch/belt** Most people find wearing one while trekking a hassle and keep it buried in their pack until they stop for the evening.

If you plan to stay exclusively in lodges or are trekking with a group then a tent, foam pad, stove, cutlery, plate and mug are not needed.

Camera
If you bring one always keep it with you. Thieves are well aware of the value of cameras so check your insurance policy to ensure your camera is fully covered. A modern compact, especially with a zoom lens, is light and convenient. Today's auto-everything camera places high demands on

---

❑ Getting the best pictures isn't always easy, even in a readily photogenic country like Nepal. When shooting people in bright sunlight, shadows often turn out black; try using a fill-in flash (often automatic on the better compact cameras). Better still, portraits taken in a shaded area near bright sun come out wonderfully subtle.

Too many wide angle scenery shots are boring; with a zoom lens you can focus on details – a particular mountain or a couple of houses in a village – rather than trying to cram them all in. Telephoto landscape shots often look more dramatic if there is no sky showing; this is an especially useful trick if the sky is cloudy and likely to appear washed out.

---

batteries which sometimes give out in the cold so take a spare set. Bring some cleaning equipment as lenses get dusty.

While compacts are good, bigger cameras are better. Bring several zoom lenses (or a 28-200mm) for complete flexibility; a telephoto lens (to 200mm or more) is essential for close portraits and landscape detail and a wide angle lens (from 24mm) is great for getting it all in. A polarising filter is useful and learning its tricks can be fun. It can significantly cut down reflection giving skins, landscapes (tree leaves in particular) and the sky a deeper, richer colour. It does this best when used in bright sunlight at 90° to the sun. It should not be used for every shot and it's possible to overdo the effect.

Cameras with zoom lenses mostly have smaller apertures so faster 200ASA or even 400ASA film makes it easier to take shots in lower light. Disposable cameras are a last resort, even the ones with a panoramic lens.

Film Kathmandu stocks a wide variety of print, black and white, and slide films (Kodak, Fuji, Konica, Agfa) at competitive prices. The Kathmandu laboratories do a reasonable job developing print film and blow-ups are exceptional value. Unfortunately the quality for black and white and slide film developing is not so good.

RENTING OR BUYING EQUIPMENT IN KATHMANDU

There's a great variety of rental equipment here which saves buying expensive specialised gear. Easy-to-rent items include down jackets, sleeping-bags, insulating pads, plastic boots, ice-axes and crampons.

Many items can also be bought here for less than in Europe or Australasia. Buying in the States is usually cheaper. You can rely on finding lightweight trekking boots (mainly HiTec brand but the choice is limited), thick down jackets, locally-made rucksacks, inferior down sleeping bags, quality head torches and their batteries, Maglite torches, new MSR stoves, Blue Gaz stoves and bottles, fleece jackets, woollen mittens, gloves, socks, hats, jerseys, low quality longjohns, umbrellas, large 'porter' or duffel bags, telescoping ski poles and sunglasses. Climbers can find all the alpine (but not rock) hardware they need.

The items that are better brought from home include high quality socks, boots, thermal underwear, liner gloves, stylish fleece and quality rain gear.

Increasingly, equipment is being made in Nepal. While much of it is serviceable, the quality is much inferior to outdoor equipment from home. Disturbingly, local manufacturers have chosen to copy Western labels but these fakes are generally easy to pick out from the originals. The stitching is uneven, the webbing and fabrics feel inferior and are less colour-coordinated, logos are on plastic labels and the designs are less innovative. All locally made Gore-Tex jackets and trousers/pants are definitely not made from Gore-Tex; and you can be sure that all *The North Face*, *Lowe* and *Wild Country* labelled backpacks and sleeping bags are fakes – the real gear has the name on zip rings and pops, and machine-embroidered logos and labels that are difficult to duplicate. If using a locally-made rucksack, take a sewing kit. Dental floss (with several large needles) is the strongest and easiest to use thread.

The fleece of locally made garments comes from Korea. The quality is not far off the American-milled fleece but it can hold smells after time. The range of colours is limited and only one thickness is available, but you can't complain about US$25 for a jacket or pair of trousers/pants.

Chinese or Hong Kong-made sleeping bags compete with locally-made ones which either use Russian or Korean down; these are all of passable quality, although since the down is untreated it often smells after a while. Local down is not worth buying.

CAMPING AND ADVENTURE TREKKING EQUIPMENT

Group trekkers are provided with extensive lists. Climbers need a tent, plastic boots and all the paraphernalia for glaciers.

While camping, except between May and October, a substantial down jacket, thin balaclava and thick longjohns or fleece trousers/pants are virtually essential.

The brave could get away without a tent if camping above Kyangjin and crossing the Kangja La during the October-December season but you should have a survival blanket or plastic sheet. A bivvy bag would be useful although not necessary, but a four or five-season sleeping bag is needed. Above Kyangjin there are plenty of roofed *kore* (small, rough shelters which are used in summer by herders; although not at Pemthang Karpo) and the chances are it won't rain anyway. Note that some of these kore might still be occupied. Once over the Kangja La the first roofed kore are at Keldang, a long day from Base Camp even in good conditions. Taking a tent, or at least a fly sheet does, of course, increase your security.

During spring and into the monsoon season a tent is essential because the kore are full of snow and thick, impossible to remove, ice. Bring an alarm clock for early starts and a few novels for long snowy afternoons. Tents and clothing should be waterproof; fleece clothing is perfect. Note that even during May it can be surprisingly cold.

Along with a stove and pots don't forget plates, mugs and cutlery. Extra water containers (three or four litres per person) save water trips while cooking. Kerosene is available at Kyangjin but petrol isn't.

If using a Thermarest self-inflating mattress, an ultra-lite with a very thin back-up pad is a comfortable, safe combination on the bare grass; otherwise a thick foam pad will suffice.

Don't neglect your crew's equipment
While you may have the latest and best equipment your crew certainly will not. Sirdars usually have reasonable gear. The sherpas and kitchen hands are less well-equipped and generally appreciate cast-offs, perhaps a Kathmandu fleece or a good piece of clothing as part of the tips. Porters have nothing and appreciate clean serviceable clothes of any sort, especially old running shoes or boots. See p96 for more information.

RECOMMENDED READING

While much has been published on Nepal, little of note covers Langtang. The exception is the delightfully written *Nepal Himalaya* by the indefatigable explorer HW Tilman. This book is included in the remarkable volume *Seven Mountain-Travel Books* (The Mountaineers, Seattle, USA and Diadem, London 1983). It is usually available through libraries.

Guidebooks
There's a wide range of books to help you explore the Kathmandu Valley and the rest of the road-accessible country; all of them are cheap and are available in Kathmandu. Apa's *Nepal Insight Guide* has beautiful coffee-table photos and an informative text but is of limited use as a practical guide. Apa also have a Pocket Insight Guide featuring self-guided tours which is perfect for a flying visit. Lonely Planet's *Nepal – a travel survival kit* is comprehensive and good on practical information while Moon Publications' *Nepal Handbook* is a literate, sensitive and in-depth guide. The *Rough Guide to Nepal* offers stiff competition to both, with its comprehensiveness and enthusiastic chatty style; all could be called Bibles.

When it comes to trekking the choice thins. The *Nepal Handbook* and *Rough Guide* are good for deciding how to and where to go, but that's it. Lonely Planet's *Trekking in the Nepal Himalaya (6th edition)* is thorough in many ways but lacks detailed trail information, such as the times between places. Stephen Bezruchka *Trekking in Nepal* (long-awaited 7th edition due soon) has trail times and interesting cultural and environmental discussions. *Trekking Peaks of Nepal* by Bill O'Connor is the standard but dated reference for climbing these 'limited bureaucracy' mountains. Trailblazer also produces detailed guides to Everest and Annapurna.

MAP RECOMMENDATIONS

This guide includes simple maps that cover all the trekking routes. For an overview and to identify peaks, a large map of the area is invaluable. Note that most maps of the Langtang Region are out of date (even updated 1997 versions), with the trails drawn as they were in the 1960s. These present day inaccuracies have caused trekkers trouble and have even taken a few lives, so believe trail information from this guide first.

Maps of the region may be expensive and hard to find at home but are readily available in Kathmandu. The variety of cheap one and two colour maps are copies of each other or the more expensive maps. For general trekking they are OK. The Ganesh Himal and Jugal Himal are covered in modest detail only by the Mandala dyeline maps.

The best topographical maps are part of two related series. The *Helambu-Langtang* 1:100,000 Schneider map, commissioned by Nelles Verlag, covers most of Helambu and the Langtang Valley to the glacier but, maddeningly, the peaks to the north aren't shown. It was partly compiled from the ancient Indian, one inch maps and from surveys in the early 1970s so the trail information and size of villages is well out of date. It is these inaccuracies that have been widely transferred.

The matching *Kathmandu Valley* 1:50,000 Schneider map (eight colour, 2nd edition 1989) covers the last day or so of the Helambu trek and the treks around the Kathmandu Valley rim but doesn't show any dirt roads. Both maps can be found in Kathmandu for around US$15.

❏ **Useful Web sites**
Sites which can be helpful for planning a trip include the following:

• The Nepal section at http://www.south-asia.com.
• Check http://www.bena.com/nepaltrek/index.html for links to many Nepal sites.
• The best online health information can be found on CIWEC Clinic's section on Kathmandu's concise page at http://www.bena.com/nepaltrek/ciwec/immune.html.
• At Lonely Planet's site (http://www.lonelyplanet.com), you can leave messages for other travellers on their 'Thorn Tree'.
• Also see Himalaya Trekking's site at http://www.webfoot.co. nz/nepal-treks

The best maps for exploring and climbing around the Langtang Valley are the more up to date Austrian Alpine Club maps *Alpenvereinskarte Langthang Himal Ost* (East) and *West* 1:50,000 sheets. They cover a tempting distance into Tibet, including Shishapangma. In Kathmandu, these are available only at Pilgrims book store, for around US$11 each.

A general map of Nepal holds endless fascination for trekking and map addicts. Locally available cheapies are Mandala's *Map of Nepal* (1:800,000), with a useful inset of district, regional and zonal headquarters while the Himalayan Booksellers *Map of Nepal* features ridge line diagrams of the main trekking areas on the reverse.

❏ **Western doctors in Langtang?**
The Himalayan Rescue Association (HRA) (see p99) and the government have discussed the idea of setting up a trekkers' aid post in Kyangjin. It would be modelled on the very successful aid posts in Manang and Pheriche. If the project does go ahead it should be up and running during the main trekking season in 1998. The services provided will include daily altitude sickness lectures (free) and consultations by Western doctors for around US$18.

Medical
Appendix B is a guide to the most common afflictions of trekkers. It is always worth consulting a doctor if possible, or other sources; the medical section in Lonely Planet's *Trekking in the Nepal Himalaya* is particularly detailed. For more extensive coverage of diseases and coping with injuries the delightfully concise pocket guide *The Himalayan First Aid Manual,* by Jim Duff and Peter Gormly 1994, is perfect for trekkers heading off the beaten track and is light enough to be carried anywhere. This should be (but isn't) carried by every sirdar. It is available in some Kathmandu book shops and from Kathmandu Environmental Education Project (KEEP) (p104). The weightier doctor-style *Medicine for Mountaineering,* published by The Mountaineers, is a must for mountaineering expeditions and is also available in Kathmandu.

Budgeting

Currency
US, Canadian, Australian, Hong Kong and Singapore dollars are accepted, plus all the main European currencies, cash and travellers cheques (any major brand although only American Express has an office in

Kathmandu). Major credit cards are accepted by star-class hotels, by some trekking and rafting companies and in some shops; they can also be used to get cash advances at banks. Eurocheques and Post Giros are not accepted. As in the rest of Asia, some US$ cash is always handy. Nepal's once thriving black market is slowly being eroded by more realistic exchange rates and currency regulations. There are, however, still plenty of touts who will take you into a shop and exchange dollars (even travellers cheques) for rupees at marginally more favourable rates. You should be aware that exchanging money on the black market does nothing to help the country's balance of payments.

COSTS IN KATHMANDU

Your choice of hotel will largely determine the amount spent on basics. A spartan double room with communal bathroom facilities goes for US$2-5/£1.25-3 a night, and with attached bathroom US$5-15/£3-9.50. A pleasant one or two-star room is about US$20/£12.50. The four to five star hotels range from around US$90-180/£56-112.50.

Food is of a more uniform price. If you avoid the ten most expensive restaurants, you can have a meal for US$1-5/£0.60-3; US$5-8/£3-5 a day is plenty. What you spend on drinks depends on your poison; large bottles of beer and double nips of cheap spirits are around US$1.50-2/£1-1.25, while soft drinks cost less than US$0.50/£0.30.

For a budget traveller, around US$100/£65 a week is adequate for cheap hotels, good food, sightseeing, visa extensions/trekking permits, and other necessities such as chocolate, bicycle hire, newspapers and a quick call home. It is the avoidable one-off expenses such as flights, rafting trips and quality souvenirs that will have a large impact on your budget plans. With much less than US$100/£65 per week, careful budgeting is required.

THE TREKKING BUDGET
Independent trekkers
Once it was difficult to spend even US$5/£3 a day but extensive menus and luxuries tempt trekkers to spend more. Around US$10/£6 a day per person gives you good food and accommodation plus a few treats. Lodges charge under US$1/£0.60 for accommodation, and main courses are around US$1/£0.60. Chocolate, beer and Coke are not so cheap but even with an excess of these luxuries spending more than US$15/£9.50 daily would be a challenge. At the other end it is still possible to trek on US$5/£3 a day.

There are other things to allow money for – extra films, souvenirs and emergency situations (a porter to carry your backpack if you twist an ankle) – so it's best to take perhaps US$100-200/£60-125 more than your budget. A trekking permits costs US$5/£3 per week and the National Park entrance US$12/£7.50 (although this may rise). If you're planning to organise a guided trek on arrival or to hire a porter see p98 for costs.

Commercial treks
With the basic costs paid up front, it's simply a case of following company guidelines and allowing for the few extras. While trekking there are no expenses bar the odd bottle of beer and tips for the crew, so just allow for souvenirs, extra film and snacks.

Health precautions and inoculations

The physical aspects of trekking
Trekking means walking almost every day for four to seven hours, often for two weeks or more. Despite the breaks, it adds up to being strenuous exercise. Many people begin only moderately fit but generally cope well and end the trek feeling amazingly healthy. A few find the reality of continuous walking difficult. If you lead a sedentary life plan an exercise programme well before you go. Brisk walks are a good start, building up to include walking up and down hills in whatever boots you plan to wear in order to introduce your body to the rigours of hill walking. Jogging and aerobics are reasonable substitutes. Muscles strengthen fairly quickly, although painfully, if you overdo exercise. Stretching should be included in your training programme; once you've warmed up stretch gently, without bouncing, holding each pose for 20-30 seconds.

MEDICAL CONDITIONS

Anyone with heart, lung and blood pressure abnormalities or a continuing medical condition should have a check-up and get a medical opinion before setting off.
• **Older people** Age is no barrier. However, the older you are the more important prior fitness preparation is.

• **Children** Caution should be exercised when taking children trekking. Younger people can be slower to adapt to altitude, and very young children have difficulty in communicating exactly how they feel. The generally considered safe maximum for pre-teenage children is 3000m/9850ft, although many have been higher. Within the limitations, trekking with children can be very rewarding and bring you even closer to the locals; there are few people without children in Nepal. Little legs are easily carried by a porter when tired and Sherpanis (female Sherpas) are good babysitters. Teenagers have more chance of succumbing to the effects of altitude than adults so school groups should allow an extra day or two over the most conservative itineraries and be particularly watchful.

• **Asthma** is no reason to avoid trekking. Except in polluted Kathmandu, there are fewer irritants in the air so most asthmatics actually feel better while trekking. Look after your medication – wear your inhaler on a chain around your neck or keep it in a pocket. There is still the normal risk of a serious attack so brief your companions on what to do.

• **Diabetes** There is no reason for diabetics to avoid trekking but you cannot afford to lose the medication so keep it with you at all times and warn your friends about the procedures in case there's an emergency. It's very important to monitor your glucose levels frequently and carefully and to keep blood sugar levels well controlled.

• **High blood pressure** Blood pressure will fluctuate more and be higher than usual while on a trek. You should seek the advice of a doctor who is aware of the history of your condition.

• **Previous heart attacks** Studies have yet to be conducted but it is likely that the level of exertion required on a trek is more significant than the altitude factor. Seek the advice of your doctor.

• **Pregnancy** It is not a good idea to trek when you are pregnant. Complications, even in the early stages, occasionally occur and can require immediate expert attention.

INOCULATIONS

The majority of Nepal's population has no access to doctors or modern medicines so the health situation is poor. Disease and malnourishment are rife and even sickness which is easily cured by medicine often leads to death without it. Visitors arriving with immunisations, healthy bodies and access to clean water are much less at risk. A bout of diarrhoea, however, is almost inevitable, no matter how careful you are.

There are no official immunisation requirements to enter Nepal but the following should be considered. The best people to consult about the vaccinations currently recommended are clinics specialising in travel medicine. They will have access to more up-to-date information than a normal general practitioner. The best online information can be found on http://www.bena.com/nepal trek/ciwec/immune.html.

• **Hepatitis A** is usually passed on in contaminated water; immunisation is considered a must by most doctors unless you have had hepatitis A before. The vaccine is *Havrix* or new to the market *Vaqta* and a full course will give up to ten years' protection. A cheaper alternative is a gamma globulin injection which should be given just before departure and be repeated every four to six months while travelling. Although this is a blood-based product there is no chance of contracting AIDS from this immunisation.

• **Hepatitis B** is a disease which is avoidable since, like AIDS, it's passed on by unsafe sex or contaminated blood products. A vaccine is available.

• **Meningitis** Occasional cases of meningococcal meningitis occur in Nepal. It is an often fatal disease but the vaccine is safe and effective and should be obtained.

• **Cholera** The World Health Organisation no longer recommend this vaccination. It is only partially effective and often causes a reaction. The risk of travellers acquiring cholera in Nepal is extremely low.

• **Typhoid** is prevalent in Nepal. There are now a variety of vaccines and one should be obtained.

• **Tetanus-Diphtheria** This vaccine is recommended if you have not had a booster in the last 10 years. Many doctors advise a tetanus booster every time you intend to travel for any length of time.

• **Polio** If you escaped immunisation as a child a series of vaccinations is recommended. If you have not had a booster as an adult, one may be required. Check with your doctor.

• **Measles, mumps and rubella** If you did not have these diseases (or the vaccinations) as a child you may need a vaccination.

• **Japanese Encephalitis B** This disease is transmitted by mosquitoes and there have been sporadic outbreaks in the Terai (lowland Nepal) and India. Western doctors based in Kathmandu suggest the vaccination only for people visiting the Terai for extended periods.

• **Rabies** This deadly virus is transmitted by the bite of an infected animal, usually a monkey or dog. The risk of being bitten is minimal but is probably greatest in Kathmandu since some of the street dogs are certainly rabid. A thorough 15-minute washing of the wound with soap has a high chance of removing the virus. A vaccination is available but even if you've had it you'll need a follow-up course of two further injections. If you've not been vaccinated and are unlucky enough to be bitten, a series of injections is available only from the CIWEC clinic in Kathmandu, and should be started within a week.

• **Malaria** Carried only by the lowland Anopheles mosquito, malaria exists in pockets of the Terai in Nepal and across much of the rest of rural Asia. There's no risk in Kathmandu or while trekking in the Langtang. GPs at home are often unaware of this. The risk while visiting Chitwan or going rafting is extremely low but consider taking medication during, or close to, the monsoon season. The drug of choice for different areas changes as resistance builds up in the parasite. If you have just visited a malarial area, for example India or Thailand, then it's vital to continue taking your medication for the recommended length of time.

The first line of protection, however, is to avoid being bitten. The Anopheles mosquito is active only between early evening and dawn so you should cover up well between these times and use mosquito repellent on any exposed skin.

If you are behind on any of the immunisations listed above, they can be safely obtained at clinics in Kathmandu.

MEDICAL INSURANCE

A combined travel/medical insurance policy is a sensible choice for any traveller and a requirement for most tours booked in your home country. Since trekking may require helicopter rescue, which is not always covered by general travel schemes, many trekking companies offer special-ly-tailored policies. Independent trekkers should register with their embassy in Kathmandu which will be contacted if helicopter rescue is required. Forms are available at the Himalayan Rescue Association in Kathmandu. Note that a rescue mission does not take place unless there is a guarantee of payment by a trekking company or your embassy (see p89).

On the other hand medical care is not expensive (nor always of a high standard) in Nepal so many travellers use their return ticket as insurance knowing that parents will also help out if necessary.

It is important to realise that while trekking you can be a long way from help. Sometimes you will have to be your own doctor, there is no other choice. For clinics in Kathmandu see p89, and see Appendix B for a detailed discussion of staying healthy on the trek.

PART 2: NEPAL

Facts about the country

GEOGRAPHICAL BACKGROUND

Perilously placed between the Asian superpowers of India and China, Nepal is a land-locked rectangle roughly 800km by 200km (500 miles by 120). It straddles the hills and mountains between the enormous Ganges plain and the high Tibetan plateau. In the south is a narrow strip of flat land known as the Terai. Rising abruptly from this are the small Siwalik hills and the Mahabharat range. Between are broad valleys, the Inner Terai, which were once infested with a deadly malaria. Thanks to DDT spraying in the 1950s that threat has largely been eradicated and this rapidly developing area is now the fertile bread basket of Nepal. The wide band of steep middle hills shelters the older centres of population – Kathmandu, Pokhara and smaller towns like Trisuli. To the north are the majestic Himalaya including Kanchenjunga, Makalu, Lhotse, Everest, Cho Oyu, Manaslu, Annapurna and Dhaulagiri – eight of the ten highest peaks on the planet.

The Himalaya

Although they are the world's highest mountains, what fascinated early explorers was the fact that they did not form a continental divide. This is, in fact, to be found further north on the Tibetan Plateau.

The Himalaya were formed by the collision of two continental plates; the Indian plate was forced under the edge of the Asian plate which in turn pushed part of the Tibetan Plateau up into jagged mountains. However, as quickly as the Himalaya rose, the rivers to the north cut their southern paths faster, which accounts for the great depth of many of the valleys in the region.

CLIMATE

Nepal is on the same latitude as Florida and Cairo so the climate in the lowland areas is hot and the winters temperate. The trekking areas are, however, well above sea level and consequently temperatures vary considerably. The climate comprises distinct seasons but with an important additional feature; the monsoon. This moisture-laden wind gathers in the Bay of Bengal and sweeps up across India to spend its force on the Himalayan mountain chain between mid-June and mid-September. The climate is mainly dry and sunny for the remainder of the year.

Autumn is renowned for clear skies and pleasant temperatures. By winter the high hills take on dry brown shades and the mountains are occasionally dusted with fresh snow. Spring – March to May – is a colourful season which is punctuated by the odd shower of life-giving rain but the heat gradually builds until the monsoon relief arrives. The trekking seasons are detailed on p20.

HISTORICAL OUTLINE

Facts and fables

Nepal's early history is clouded in folklore and legend. One story relates how the Kathmandu Valley, then a huge sacred lake, was emptied through a channel cut by the stroke of a god's sword. The Chobar Gorge, which drains the valley, indeed fits the description and geologists maintain that the soil in the valley gained its renowned fertility as a lake bed.

At the time of the Buddha, in the second half of the 6th century BC, the Kirati ruled the Kathmandu valley. They were a Mongol race whose descendants include the Rai and Limbu people who are now settled in east Nepal. Buddhism spread slowly and the arts and architecture developed under the 28 successive kings. Around 300AD, the Indian Licchavi dynasty invaded Nepal and introduced the caste system and Hinduism; since then both faiths have co-existed. Around 900AD power struggles enveloped the valley and it was not until 1200AD that the Indian Malla dynasty became established. The caste system was rigidly defined and trade, cottage industries and the enduring Newar culture blossomed, although there was occasional infighting that laid the towns of the valley to waste. The 1400s brought the wealth of architecture, carving and sculpture that still surround the Durbar Squares in Kathmandu, Patan and Bhaktapur. Known then as Kantipur, Lalitpur and Bhadgoan respectively, these three cities divided into separate flourishing but quarrelsome kingdoms in 1482 on the death of Yaksha Malla.

Unity, treachery and extravagance

In 1768 Prithvi Narayan Shah of Gorkha (a princely kingdom between Kathmandu and Pokhara) conquered the Kathmandu valley and began the Shah dynasty that continues by direct blood line to this day. He started by consolidating the many individual kingdoms that now form the basis of Nepal. His successors, although 'honourably defeated' in the 1814 war with British India, were able to resist colonial domination; a fact that the Nepalese are proud of to this day.

Overall control by the Shah dynasty was undermined by the rich nobles whose constant struggle for power often led to violence. However, in 1846, unequivocal control was seized by Jung Bahadur Rana who slaughtered all the ministers and high officials in what became known as the Kot Massacre. He declared himself Maharajah and the founder of a second line of Nepalese kings. To ensure continuity of the line his family married into the Shah dynasty and other high caste families; Jung Bahadur Rana alone fathered over 100 children. He and his heirs effectively ruled the country although the King, kept in seclusion, was the highest authority. The Rana family amassed incredible wealth, visible in the numerous European-style palaces (inspired by Jung Bahadur's visit to Europe), which now house various government departments in Kathmandu. This feudal dynasty held Nepal in its grip for over a century until 1950, when the puppet king Tribhuvan escaped to India.

The post-war period

Following the end of the Second World War much of Asia was in turmoil. Both newly independent India and China seemed to have their hungry eyes on the tiny neighbour that divided them. At the same time political discontent and fear were growing in Nepal.

Now known as the father of democracy in Nepal, BP Koilara managed to undermine the Ranas' control and India assisted in engineering the return to power of King Tribhuvan in 1951. Keen to establish its independence as a country in its own right and not as an Indian vassal, Nepal quickly invited foreign countries to open consulates in Kathmandu. Thus ended more than a century of isolation.

The panchayat system

In 1955 King Tribhuvan died and he was succeeded by his son, Mahendra. The constitution was reformed and in 1957 the people of Nepal voted in the Nepal Congress Party with a decisive majority. However, bribery and corruption played a large part in the country's first elections and continued in the new government. This gave King Mahendra the excuse to step into power and at the end of 1959 he arrested the entire cabinet. He took direct control himself, later instituting the panchayat system. Under this system the locally elected leaders of village councils nominated the candidates for higher posts, all ultimately under the King. In theory, this was quite a reasonable system and it was endorsed by the new Eton-educated King Birendra (still the reigning monarch) when his father died in 1972.

Democracy established

Corruption and self-interest prevailed and popular discontent spread again, erupting in 1979 with violence (a rare event) in Kathmandu. The panchayat system was put to the test by a public referendum and survived, but only just. Its days were numbered and the government's inability to solve a serious trade dispute with India in 1990 and its continued persecution of the opposition caused public protest. Meetings dispersed with bullets became riots and the palace was surrounded by machine-gun toting soldiers.

The soldiers were supposedly there to protect the King but soon let it be known on which side their sympathies lay, as did the foreign aid donors. Cornered, the King lifted the ban on political parties in April 1990. He agreed to become a constitutional monarch and a temporary government was formed.

In 1991 the promised elections were held. The Nepal Congress Party (symbol; a tree) won, putting the Communist Party (the sun) in the role of opposition party.

Congress versus communists

After the elections the new government announced considerable changes. The price of subsidised foods, such as rice, was freed to stimulate production. Development became a catchword and a goal, with many sectors being targeted, including tourism.

Expecting the promised improvements and a rise in living standards to come quickly once the democratic machine was in place, Nepalis soon lost confidence in their new government. The opposition parties were much to blame, stirring up riots in which several people were killed. The government itself was torn by internal dissent and Nepal's second general election was called 18 months early, in November 1994. The communists took power, ruling in a coalition government under the leader of the United Marxist-Leninist Party, Man Mohan Adhikari.

Nepal's experiment with soft communism lasted until September 1995 when Adhikari's party lost a vote of no-confidence in parliament. A tripartite coalition government composed of the Nepal Congress Party, the right-wing Rastriya Prajatantra Party (RPP) and the Nepal Sadbhavana Party, was sworn in under prime minister Sher Bahadur Deuba. Allegations of large-scale corruption have plagued the government and it will probably be replaced by a communist-led coalition. One can only hope that the credibility of the democratic system isn't destroyed by the vindictive and often directionless political bickering.

ECONOMY

Nepal's rural backwardness may be attractive to tourists but the medieval way of life is not easy for most Nepalese. In the past, tenant farmers – the majority of the population – paid crippling taxes to landlords in a vicious semi-feudal system. The 1964 reforms sought to redress this by land redistribution, reducing rental to a (still unbearable) 50% of the crop and by formally abolishing the caste system. They were only partly successful. Even now 90% of the population live off the land with the majority existing at subsistence level. It's a simple, hard life virtually without money; which is one reason why the average annual per capita income is so low – around US$150. (The other reason is this figure includes only government related income and expenditure so, in effect, the non-tax paying rural economy is excluded).

This legacy means the prospects for farmers' children are bleak. Nepal's astronomic birth rate and a lack of new arable land are the main problems. The ever-expanding population has been partly absorbed by the Inner Terai but the amount of arable land available per person continues to drop. Crop yields have increased but a lack of technology and mismanagement has meant Nepal has become a net food importer. There are dire predictions about the decline of land fertility and the destruction of the forests; already there are food and firewood shortages. However in the 1970s many developing countries were faced with similar predictions, very few of which have eventuated.

Nepal is barely industrialised. Demand for jobs far outstrips supply resulting in exploitative wages and working conditions. With no manufacturing base, all machinery and construction materials must be imported which means paying hard currency or Indian rupees, and earning these is difficult. Of the few exports, the majority go to India since reliable and cheap shipping is problematic for greater distances. The hard currency earners are carpets, tourism (250,000 Westerners, 125,000 Indians a year), and Nepalese working overseas, particularly the Gurkha soldiers. Foreign aid programmes are, however, big business in Nepal and a third of government funding comes from this source.

DEVELOPMENT

There is no doubt that considerable development is needed in Nepal, if only to avert tragedy. The root of the problem is the spiralling population growth. Nature's harsh natural balance was upset by the introduction of a few simple life-saving measures such as oral rehydration salts and basic hygiene principles. The five million people that lived in Nepal in 1950 have multiplied to 20.8 million, and this population is expected to double in the next 30 years with unpredictable results.

It's difficult to get the message of birth control across to Nepal's peasant farmers when to them more hands are an asset and extra children are an insurance against others that may die. Obviously education and health care are a good start. If you are secure in the knowledge that your children will live (their health being better protected by vaccines and clean water) and believe that their quality of life may be better (with education) you will be more interested in trying to limit the size of your family. Electricity and roads provide opportunities for diversification from agriculture and a move to a more cash-orientated society where the benefits of birth control become more obvious.

Such massive changes don't happen overnight, certainly not in Nepal, despite vast quantities of foreign aid and a huge number of programmes.

Practical information for the visitor

VISA AND TREKKING REGULATIONS

Visas
All visitors require a visa for Nepal; this is easily obtained at the airport or border on arrival (one passport-sized photo is required) or at Nepalese embassies abroad – sometimes the more expensive option.

At the airport a single entry visa valid for 15 days costs US$15 and a 30-day visa costs US$25, payable only in US$ cash. A double entry visa costs US$40 for an initial 30 days for the first visit and provides another 30 days on re-entry. Similarly, a multiple entry visa for US$60 is valid initially for 60 days. The fees change occasionally. Visas can be extended in Kathmandu, Pokhara and Nepalganj and cost the equivalent of US$1 a day. Tourists are allowed to stay for four months in a calendar year with a further one month possible at the discretion of the Director General, Department of Immigration. Visas for children under 10 years old are free. If your visa has expired by more than one day Immigration officials fine you US$3 a day.

Trekking permits
To go trekking you need a permit from the Department of Immigration in Kathmandu. If you've booked through a trekking agency the relevant permit, national park entrance fee and visa extension (if required) will be organised for you. See p96 for more details.

LOCAL TRANSPORT

• **Air** Nepal has an extensive domestic network to make up for the lack of roads. There are at least seven competing airlines who have divided the profitable routes among themselves. In the hills the STOL Dorniers of the private companies compete with Royal Nepal's 18-seat Twin Otters. (The Ml-17 Russian helicopters are now only for charter use). Since radar is not used, bad weather can postpone flights, sometimes for several days. While Royal Nepal's pilots are excellent the management is a shambles – try to avoid the airline. Tickets can be bought direct from airline offices but travel agents get them for the same price, saving a taxi trip. Fares must be paid in hard currency, cash, travellers' cheques or plastic, not rupees. Any change or refunds are returned in rupees.

• **Long distance buses** Services are run using sturdy Indian buses that cope well with the rough roads, destroying you rather than the bus. Night coaches are for masochists who prefer bumping and banging to sleeping. Day buses are often filled to bursting point and feature a variety of seating and standing room, mostly unsuitable for long legs. The spectacular scenery and experience can, however, make up for the lack of comfort.

There are regular tourist buses between Pokhara, Kathmandu and Chitwan. These cost a little more but are much less crowded with no standing passengers allowed. They also leave from close to Thamel, saving a taxi fare to the bus station. See p94 for more details.

● **Local buses** Around Kathmandu these are large Mercedes vans that have seen better days. Services are cheap and unbelievably crowded. There is a route numbering system that is hard to fathom. Pickpockets are an occasional problem.

● **Taxis** are plentiful and cheap. All have meters and can usually be coerced into using them. Extra charges, if any, come on an officially stamped sheet. Don't accept any stories about meters being broken or needing recalibrating. Expect to pay more only at night.

Hiring a vehicle for the day is best organised directly with a taxi driver, or through a travel agent for mini-buses.

● **Tempos** are small three-wheeled vehicles. There are two types; small auto-rickshaws which are black and yellow, and fixed-route blue tempos with enough space in the back for eight Nepalis, or a single foreigner with a backpack!

● **Cycle-rickshaws** are found in all major towns. Bargain before you get in.

● **Bicycles** are a cheap way to get around Kathmandu; the place would make a perfect bicycle city if it weren't for the appalling pollution and the lack of road rules. Standard and mountain bikes are easily hired in the Thamel and Freak Street areas.

LANGUAGE

Nepali, a Sanskrit-based language similar to India's Hindi, is the country's official language. Nepali is not the mother tongue for approximately half the population; ethnic languages such as Sherpa and Newari being widely used in local areas. Nepali is the medium for schools but English is also taught and you'll meet a surprising number of children who know at least a few English words (cynics would comment that they know enough to be annoying but not enough to be useful). In the tourism industry English is the main language, although it is by no means fluently spoken. In the main trekking regions it's quite possible to get by speaking only English.

It is handy to learn a few phrases if trekking without a guide (see Appendix F). Learning more is rewarding and will provide many amusing reactions. Simple spoken Nepali is not difficult and most Kathmandu bookshops sell compact phrase-books.

ELECTRICITY

The electricity grid covers only the major towns and cities, and power cuts are frequent. The supply is 220V and 50Hz using old-type round-pin sockets (two-pin and three-pin, small and large). Rural Nepal has no electricity, apart from a few very small-scale private or foreign aid hydro schemes. On a trek it is impossible to recharge batteries for video recorders – other than with a solar panel – because even if a village has electricity, the power is rationed to a few bulbs per house and turned on only for the evening.

TIME

Nepal is 5 hours 45 minutes ahead of Greenwich Mean Time (GMT), and 15 minutes ahead of India (as a show of independence). There is no special summer time.

MONEY

The Nepalese rupee (Rs) comes in banknote denominations of 1, 2, 5, 10, 20, 50, 100, 500 and 1000 rupees. The rupee is divided into 100 paisa but as a tourist you will seldom have to deal with anything less than a rupee. There's a nickel coin worth a rupee, a brass one worth two and some aluminium coins for lesser denominations.

❑ Rates of exchange	
US$1	Rs58.50
UK£1	Rs94.26
Can$1	Rs42.50
Aus$1	Rs42.50
NZ$1	Rs38.00
DM1	Rs33.30
FF1	Rs10.00
CHF1	Rs40.50
IndRs1	Rs1.60

Changing money
Prior to the 1990s, most tourists changed money on the black market since nobody had thought to put banks where they were needed. This has changed now that there is a bank in Thamel and many hotel receptions can change money; ensure you are given a receipt. There's still a black market where you may get up to 7% more for your money. Small denomination notes, in particular Rs100 notes, and some change are useful.

Tipping
Once virtually unknown in Nepal, this custom is spreading through the tourism services. Tipping hotel and restaurant staff is not necessary but if the service was good a 5% tip or small change would be appreciated.

Tipping trekking crews is normal providing the service was good – overseas companies offer guidelines. For a locally-organised crew, the amount is entirely up to you. Minimum tips could start from Rs100 for each porter, for the sherpas and cook boys double this, and for the cook and sirdar double again. Alternatively, somewhere around 5% of the total trek cost divided up is reasonable; it is up to you how this money should be distributed. If you leave the distribution to the sirdar it is possible the porters will get nothing.

POST AND TELECOMMUNICATIONS

Once all letters were carried by sweating runners whose small bell warned of their approach. The mail was considered so important that everyone had to get out of their way. Now the postal system is rather less efficient. Letters to or from Europe, USA and Australasia usually take around two weeks but can take up to a month and surface mail three to six months. The best addresses to have mail sent to are star-class hotels, American Express or communication centres in Thamel. The Poste Restante service in the GPO consists of large boxes for each letter of the alphabet that contain hundreds of letters and anybody can look through them so occasionally letters do go missing.

Kathmandu is blessed with a good telephone system and international calls and faxes can be sent and received with ease. The international dialling code for Nepal is +977 followed by 1 for Kathmandu (01 within Nepal). In the hills, telephones are few and far between although more are being installed.

E-mail services have arrived and it is easy to set up a temporary address. Rates are around US$0.45 per kilobyte for sending and receiving.

TV, NEWSPAPERS AND MAGAZINES

Kathmandu has TV news in English at 9.15pm followed by the BBC TV World Service. Satellite TV on the Star TV network from Hong Kong is available in larger hotels. At 8pm on the national AM radio channel there's a mountaineering weather forecast in English.

The local English-language dailies are the *Rising Nepal,* the (rather better) *Kathmandu Post* and *Everest Herald.* The *Rising Nepal* decorously informs the general public whom the King has felicitated (usually fellow rulers on their national days) or who has received an audience. It also gives a rosy but vague outline of what the government is currently debating and gleefully declares the millions given in aid or soft loans and also includes odd titbits, like the state of the New Zealand economy. The international news is usually confined to a few columns. The *International Herald Tribune, USA Today,* and the *Asian Wall Street Journal* are sold everywhere as are magazines such as *Time*, *Newsweek*, *Far Eastern Economic Review*, *Asiaweek*, *Business Week*, *The Economist*, *Stern* and *Der Spiegel*. There's a plethora of Nepali magazines, many advertising tourist orientated services and interests. One that is worth looking out for, although its views are rather negative, is *Himal* – a quarterly Himalayan development and environmental discussion magazine. The British Council has a reading room with a variety of magazines and papers.

HOLIDAYS AND FESTIVALS

Government office and business hours are 10am to 5pm, Sunday to Friday. On Saturday government offices (including the Department of Immigration for trekking permits) and banks are closed but you can still change money in larger hotels. Embassies are closed on Saturdays and Sundays. Souvenir shopping and sightseeing are possible every day although museums are closed on Tuesdays.

Nepal is a land of colourful festivals and these are celebrated with fervour, especially by the less well-off masses. Dates are generally determined by the lunar calendar and so fall on a different day each year. The following will be of particular interest to visitors:

• **Indra Jatra** signifies the end of the monsoon (September) and the beginning of the harvest. Masked dances are performed and the giant Seto Bhairab in Durbar square spouts chang (local beer).

• **Dasain** (Durga Puja) is a 10-day festival (held in October) which is the most important in the Hindu year; it commemorates the victory of good Lord Rama over Ravana, the demon king of Lanka. Rama, an incarnation of Vishnu, is venerated by Hindus as the paragon of all virtues so the victory symbolises the ultimate triumph of good over evil. This is a time of family reunion and consequently results in total chaos as everybody heads home. On days eight and nine there's a mass slaughter of buffaloes, goats and chickens. Vehicles are blessed by having their wheels doused in blood. Government offices are closed for at least three days. This has the equivalent importance of Christmas.

• **Tihar** (Diwali) is the five-day Festival of Light that takes place in late October or early November. Amongst the symbolism is an acknowledgement of the value of brothers and sisters, dogs and cows. Children go from house to house singing and dancing and are given a little food or money. At the height of the festival on the third day people light their homes with candles to welcome Laxmi, the goddess of wealth.

• **Janai Purnima**, the date of which is dictated by the August full moon (8 August for 1998), is the day when high caste Hindus change their *Janai*, the sacred thread. The two most favoured pools for the sacred bathing ceremony are Gosainkund (lake) and the more easily reached Khumbeswar in Patan. Buddhists celebrate this as the day Buddha attained enlightenment.

• **Gai Jatra** or **Saparu** is a Newari festival which is celebrated the day after Janai Purnima by families who lost a member during the year. Rather than being a day of sorrow it is a day of light-hearted merriment. Men strut around in saris and kids dress as saddhus or cows. The cow is the holy vehicle who on this day help departed souls cross the cosmic ocean to the after world.

Buddhist festivals

In Kathmandu these are mostly celebrated at Boudhanath (Baudha) and Swayambhunath. They are also celebrated in the hills by the Buddhist Sherpa, Tamang and Tibetan peoples.

• **Losar** (Tibetan New Year) is celebrated in mid-February. It is a time to receive new clothes (making them is a winter job) and put up new prayer flags. The two main Buddhist sects celebrate separate Losars.

• **Buddha's birth** and death are celebrated on the May full moon. Everything is cleaned and stupas are whitewashed.

• **The Dalai Lama's birthday** on 6 July is particularly celebrated by Tibetans.

FOOD

Despite the ethnic mosaic the local cuisine is not particularly inspiring. Standard Nepalese fare, dal bhaat, consists of rice, lentils and a few vegetables. It can become monotonous but is certainly cheap and filling – your plate is topped up until you've had enough.

In response to trekkers' requests the restaurants of Kathmandu and Pokhara (and along some trekking routes) experimented with foreign dishes with surprising success. There's now an incredible variety of non-Nepalese cuisines at these places. Authenticity is not a strong point but you can eat passably Mexican, Italian or Thai food. There are excellent restaurants in Kathmandu specialising in tandoori and other styles of Indian food. 'Buff' (buffalo) steaks are a feature on many menus (beef being outlawed in this Hindu kingdom, although some restaurants import it from – India!). The range of Tibetan food includes *momos* (meat or vegetables encased in dough and steamed or fried), and meat soup known as *thukpa*.

Cakes and pies can be a real delight; these vary from restaurant to restaurant but are wholesome and just as Mum would make them. The vast choice includes apple pie, apple strudel, cheesecakes, chocolate cakes, lemon meringue pies, cinnamon rolls and banana cream pie.

DRINK

All water should be treated (see Appendix B) before it is safe to drink. Plastic bottles of mineral water are available but from an environmental point of view drinks such as Coke are better since the glass bottles are recycled. Several types of beer are brewed here, some under licence from foreign companies (Tuborg, Carlsberg, San Miguel and Singha). Chang is locally brewed beer produced by villagers, tungba is fermented millet served in a wooden mug over which boiling water is repeatedly poured and raksi (fermented and distilled anything - rice, wheat, corn, millet, barley) is their fire-water.

THINGS TO BUY

In Kathmandu and along trekking routes, shops selling souvenirs and handicrafts abound. They offer Newari art, Tibetan thangkas (paintings of religious symbols and figures on cloth), jewellery, bronze Buddhas and Hindu deities. Boys wander around the streets of Thamel pestering you to buy khukri knives, chess sets, hash and tiger balm. Carpets come in a great variety, many with modern designs in vegetable-dyed pastel shades. Luxuriously thick, they are made from a blend of New Zealand and Tibetan wool. When buying jewellery finding quality silver is not easy and you should beware of glass 'rubies'. Most 'turquoise' is dyed concrete-dust.

Hand-knitted jerseys/sweaters and clothing are made in the distinctive styles of the regional cultures and are popular with travellers. In Kathmandu, embroidered T-shirts are a speciality. There's a wide range of motifs to choose from and designs look good on fleece jackets too.

Bargaining

As with the rest of Asia, bargaining for many things is the norm. Rates at budget hotels, especially off season, can be negotiated. Souvenirs definitely require bargaining, although there are no hard and fast rules as to how much. As a foreigner (incredibly wealthy in comparison to most Nepalese) you start at a disadvantage and this will be utilised. Many people are afraid of being ripped off yet in some cases the amounts are trifling. Also you can be sure that in a country where most people spend everything they earn on basic food and accommodation any extra is put to good use. Bargaining need not be aggressive – it's better to treat it as a game with smiles and jokes. After a price has been agreed it must be honoured. Once the transaction is complete that is the end of the matter, all is forgiven and forgotten. Harbouring resentment comes across as a small-minded Western attitude.

Trekking exposes you to few situations that require bargaining. Most lodges have a menu with fixed prices that really are fixed – where you eat or stay is your choice. Buying at markets or from a farmer or hiring a porter, however, requires some negotiation.

SECURITY

Kathmandu is safer than most Western cities. Violent crime is virtually unknown and it is generally safe to take taxis, cycle and walk the streets and alleys at night, although women may be more comfortable in a group. Despite the relaxed atmosphere in hotels, staff are honest, rooms have barred windows and managers are security-conscious, keeping an eye on who goes in or out. In the cheaper hotels other travellers are a greater risk, if anything. The better hotels have security boxes for valuables and all will store luggage safely while you trek.

Around town adept pickpockets work crowded local buses. The usual ploy is to distract you with conversation or by pretending to be interested in your watch. Pickpockets also have a field day at busy festivals – as the queues of foreigners outside the American Express office the following day testify. Use a hotel security box or keep your travellers' cheques and money in a pouch or money belt and never let your camera or other valuables out of your sight.

The trekking regions were once crime free but as the population has been exposed to the wider ways of the world occasional cases of theft now occur, especially from luggage on bus roofs. This risk is easily minimised by taking tourist buses where nobody is allowed to ride on the roof and on local buses by buying an extra seat for luggage, or putting it in the dusty locked compartment at the rear; alternatively you could ride on the roof with it – see also p123. A couple of violent attacks have occurred on the Kangja La route and occasionally tents of trekking groups are slit during the night and valuables disappear. Trekking crews are trustworthy, although if you lend gear you will have to ask for it back. In the crowded lodges during high season occasionally the odd thing goes missing, generally a camera or valuable trekking equipment, but in a quiet lodge things are safe. When free-camping it would be tempting fate, especially if there people around, to leave everything at camp unattended while on a day trip. The other risk is birds who wreak havoc looking for food so stash everything and, if leaving a tent up, leave the door partially open so that they don't have to tear their way in.

You are incredibly wealthy by local standards so don't flaunt your gear or openly display large quantities of money and camera equipment. You should show that you value and care for all your belongings.

PART 3: KATHMANDU

Kathmandu

The bloody roads are bloody bad, The bloody hash is bloody mad, It makes the sad-dest bloody glad in bloody Kathmandu Adapted from Captain Hamish Blair's **Bloody Orkney** poem, circa 1967.

Nepal's capital city is a fascinating mélange of medieval and modern that combines astounding beauty with appalling squalor and poverty.

Time has stood still in parts of Kathmandu. In the narrow alleys, around the numerous temples and shrines and along the banks of the Bagmati River people go about their daily lives in much the same way as their ancestors did hundreds of years ago. Yet the contrasts between old and new become ever more bizarre. A porter struggles under the weight of two colour-television sets, carrying them in the traditional fashion – supported only by a *namlo*, the strap around his forehead. A young Tibetan monk in ochre robes passes on his way to the great stupa at Baudha, his shaven head in the grip of walkman head-phones.

For first-time Asian visitors, Kathmandu is a visual feast but for long-term travellers who've journeyed up from India it's also a feast of a more basic nature. The city has some of the best budget restaurants on the sub-continent dishing up everything from pepper steaks to enchiladas, chocolate cake to apple crumble. Accommodation too is excellent and can be better value than in India. Communications are good and you can make international phone calls, send faxes and e-mail with the minimum of delay. It's well worth setting a few days aside to see something of the city.

HISTORY

Origins
The name Kathmandu is believed to be a corruption of Kasthamandap ('square house of wood'), the thousand year old *dharamsala* (rest-house) that still stands in Durbar Square.

The first identifiable civilisation in the Kathmandu Valley was that of the Kirats who occupied a number of sites in the region in the second half of the first millennium BC. They were succeeded by the Licchavi in the second century AD and the Thakuri in the ninth century. The settlements were centred around religious sites known as piths or power places, and were usually on the tops of hills.

Early urban planning

Kathmandu was a town of almost 2000 houses by the beginning of the Malla period (13th century), centred on Pashupatinath. Like the other two large towns in the valley, Patan and Bhaktapur, it was an independent kingdom. Religion controlled not only the lives of the people but also the layout of these towns. Wandering through the chaotic maze of streets and temples in modern Kathmandu, it's difficult to believe that there has ever been any town-planning here; but, in fact, centuries ago Hindu philosophy determined the design of whole towns based on the Vastupurus Mandala, a complex layout in the shape of a square. This was composed of many smaller squares assigned to different deities and their temples. The main temple and palace, the centres of spiritual and temporal power, were symbolically placed at the very centre. Rich agricultural land surrounded each town.

Newar architectural heritage

The dominant culture in the Kathmandu Valley until the unification of Nepal by the king of Gorkha in 1768 was that of the Newars. They are best known for their spectacular architectural legacy – the temples and palaces that surround the Durbar Squares in Kathmandu, Patan and Bhaktapur. They built with brick, wood and tiles and are said to have invented the pagoda. Until the introduction of reinforced concrete in Nepal just 40 years ago, Kathmandu was truly the Florence of the East. Visiting in 1959, Michel Peissel, in *Tiger for Breakfast*, described the city as 'simply one vast work of art, from the humblest of the peasant's rectangular brick homes to the most impressive of the two-thousand-odd pagodas whose gilt roots rise above the neat rows of houses. Each house, each temple, each shrine is decorated with delicately carved beams representing gods and goddesses, or animals drawn from reality and from fantasy, carved in dark wood that stands out against the background of pale pink bricks.'

Rigid town planning did not allow for the enormous growth that has taken place in the area. Satellite towns were developed to house the growing population and these often became associated with a particular industry – Thimi, for example, is still a pottery centre. Most of the towns in the Kathmandu Valley did, however, manage to conform to their original plans, at least until the time of the Ranas. Jung Bahadur, the first of this line of prime ministers, visited Europe in 1850 and introduced the bizarre neo-classical style of architecture exemplified in the vast whitewashed edifices that can be seen in various stages of dilapidation in the city. Large areas of agricultural land were taken over for their construction.

Modern Kathmandu

The real attack on the strongly inter-related cultural, social and religious framework of the valley's urban centres did not, however, really begin until the 1950s, after the restoration of the monarchy and the opening up of the country. The effects have been dramatic, though, and many parts of Kathmandu have degenerated into an urban sprawl of unsightly concrete block buildings. The district of Thamel looks little different from tourist ghettos in the other Asian capitals on the backpackers' route but twenty years ago it was largely fields. The Kathmandu Guest House, opened in 1968 to house Peace Corps volunteers, was the first hotel here.

Kathmandu today is plagued with the problems that beset all rapidly expanding third world cities; overcrowding, severe pollution and traffic congestion to name but a few. The population of the Kathmandu Valley now stands at 1.3 million; the growth rate is almost five per cent per year. None of these problems seems to tarnish the allure of the city as far as the tourist is concerned. Nepal draws a paltry quarter of a million tourists – less than a third of whom, you'll be glad to know, go trekking. For all its problems there are many enchanting temples and colourful festivals and an evening wandering around the old alleys and squares can be magical.

ARRIVAL AND DEPARTURE

By air

• **Arrival** The modern airport buildings of Tribhuvan International Airport were opened in 1990. In the arrival hall there's a small duty-free shop with limited choice – sample goods and prices: 200 Marlboro cigarettes US$9, French wine US$5-9, J&B whisky US$13, Baileys US$16 – and a foreign exchange counter. Across the hall at the Immigration counters visas are issued to those who don't have them. A 15-day visa costs US$15 and a 30-day visa US$25; a double entry visa (allowing 30 days plus another 30 days) is US$40 and a multiple entry 60-day visa will set you back US$60. Visa fees are payable in US cash only. If you don't already have US cash you can get it, with some hassle, from the foreign exchange counter. Downstairs are the luggage carousels, staffed by predatory porters who expect at least Rs20 if you use their services.

You pass through **customs** into the main hall. Pick up a free city map at the **tourist office** here and a copy of *Traveller' Nepal* magazine. There's also a **post office, communications agency** (for telephone calls and faxes), **bank** and **hotel reservations counter**. If the airport bus is running (unlikely), tickets are sold at the booth here. Some hotels (and even some of the budget places) offer free transport from the airport.

To get out of the airport you need to push your way through an enthusiastic mob of hotel touts and taxi drivers crowding round the entrance. Taxis to the city centre (a twenty-minute ride) and Thamel cost Rs150-200 (US$2.50-3.30) if you get your own outside or Rs200 if you arrange one with the pre-paid taxi desk in the main hall. If you're really counting the pennies you can go to the bus stop for the crowded local bus (Rs4) by walking to the end of the airport drive and turning left.

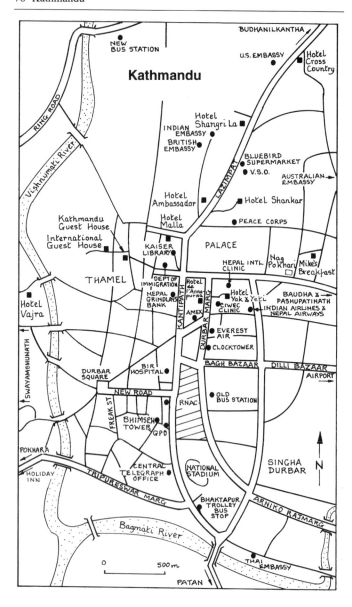

Kathmandu

• **Departure** A hefty airport departure tax of Rs700 (Rs600 for neigh-bouring SAARC countries including India) for international flights is payable, in local currency only, before you check in. At the bank here you can convert into hard currency (usually US$) only up to 15% of the rupees for which you have encashment certificates. Alternatively you can dispose of surplus rupees at the shop in the corner of the departure hall; this sells gift packs of tea and Coronation Khukri rum in exotic khukri knife shaped bottles. If flying with a cheap airline check in early as late arrivals are sometimes bumped off the flight. Due to the short runway and the altitude, large jets must leave approximately 20% of the seats empty.

By land

Some of the tourist buses take you to Kantipath, a couple of minutes walk from Thamel. Most go to the new bus station about 3km north of the city on the ring road. Buses from Sundarijal and Melamchi Pul still use the old Ratna Park bus station in the centre of town. Frequent shuttle buses (Rs2) link the two, passing along Sora Kothay by the northern end of Thamel. A metered taxi should be around US$1.

The blue-and-white Sajha buses usually stop at the GPO which is close to Freak St and a 15-minute walk to Thamel.

ORIENTATION

Greater Kathmandu, which includes Patan as well as Kathmandu itself, lies at about 1400m/4593ft above sea level. The Bagmati River runs between these two cities. The airport is 6km to the east, near the Hindu temple complex of Pashupatinath; the Buddhist stupa at Baudha is 2km north of Pashupatinath. The other major Buddhist shrine, Swayambhunath, is visible on a hill in west Kathmandu. The third city in the valley, Bhaktapur, is 14km to the east.

Within Kathmandu, most hotels and guest houses and the Department of Immigration (for trekking permits) are to be found in Thamel, a 15-minute walk north of the historic centre of the city, Durbar Square. Freak Street, the hippie centre in the '60s and '70s which still offers some cheap accommodation, is just off Durbar Square. Some of the top hotels and the international airline offices are along Durbar Marg which runs south from the modern royal palace.

WHERE TO STAY

Hotel areas

• **Thamel** Most travellers find Thamel the most convenient area in which to stay, although it's now largely a tourist ghetto. Everything you could want is available here: a vast range of accommodation (from $1/£0.62 to $90/£56 per night), good restaurants, souvenir shops, book shops and travel agencies. It's also close to the Department of Immigration for trekking permits and visa extensions.

• **Freak St** In the halcyon days of the '60s and '70s when Kathmandu was a major stopover on the hippie trail, Freak St, just off Durbar Square, was the place to hang out. Although the hash dens are now all closed it still retains a quaint, almost timeless charm. Its 15 or so hotels and restaurants are all in the rock bottom to cheap bracket.

• **Other areas** Although the above alternatives are probably the most convenient areas in which to stay there are other options. In Patan, there are a couple of budget hotels off Patan's Durbar square and also a few good three to four-star hotels. At Baudha, there are several cheap hotels; Westerners studying Buddhism often rent rooms from Tibetans here.

Prices

The prices given here are for the high season (October-November/March-April) for single/double rooms, with common (com) or attached (att) bathrooms as indicated. You may be able to get a discount of anything up to 50% outside the high season, depending on the length of your stay. Many hotel owners quote their prices in US dollars (so they are also used here); you pay in rupees, though. The dollar/pound exchange rate hovers around US$1.60=£1.

Budget guest houses (US$5/£3 or less)

In Thamel there are around 40 places to choose from in this price bracket, and in some you'll even get an attached bathroom for this price. A few hotels have triple or quad bedrooms. Check that the hot water works and try to get a room that faces away from the roads – Kathmandu is plagued by noisy dogs and honking taxis. The cheapest hotels tend to be in Narsingh Camp (behind Pumpernickel Bakery), in Chetrapati – a suburb adjoining Thamel – or hidden in the outskirts of Thamel.

Freak Street is one of the few places in the world where it is still possible to find a room, admittedly small, for US$1 a night. A slightly larger budget widens the choice considerably. The majority of hotels are on the main street but looking down alleys nearby yields more.

Cheap hotels in Thamel

Most Thamel hotels offer a range of rooms, the majority falling in the US$6-15/£3.75-9.50 price bracket. The hotel should provide clean sheets, blankets and a desk while the better ones will supply towels and toilet paper and perhaps be carpeted. Little features to check are: is there a vent or window in the bathroom; a clothes line; and a rooftop garden? Features aside, when choosing a hotel, go by the reception staff – are they friendly and helpful or lackadaisical? Most people new to Kathmandu begin looking at hotels in the heart of Thamel. However, there are plenty of hotels in every direction, none of which are more than a few minutes walk from the centre.

The best known of the cheap hotels in Kathmandu must be the long-running *Kathmandu Guest House* [82] (☎ 413632, 418733), a Thamel landmark. Popular with groups, it's bursting in the high season. They have a few rooms from US$6-8/8-10 (com) but most accommodation here is US$17/20 (att) or more in the new wing.

Moderately-priced hotels
There are numerous reasonable hotels in the US$15-30 price range. Most have attached restaurants. All rooms have attached bathrooms with hot water and, in the more expensive rooms, a TV and perhaps and air-conditioner/heater. Some of the cheaper hotels have a few de luxe rooms that fall into this price range too.

Three-star hotels
Around the three-star standard are two well-managed traditionally built hotels. *Hotel Vajra* (☎ 272719, fax 271695) was conceived and paid for by a Texan billionaire and built by Newar craftsmen, with wall-paintings by Tibetan and Tamang artists. Rooms are US$14/16 for singles/doubles with wash-basins, US$33/38 with attached bathroom and US$53/61 for the new wing; it is located near Swayambhunath. The traditionally decorated *Summit Hotel* (☎ 521894) in Patan is popular with expeditions seeking peace; prices range from US$20 to US$75. Both hotels have a pleasant atmosphere, nice gardens, restaurants and thoughtful amenities.

Close together in north Thamel are the recently constructed *Hotel Marshyandi* [137] (☎ 414105) and *Hotel Manang* [137] (☎ 410993). Some of the cheaper hotels in Thamel have rooms that are just as good but their lobbies and restaurants are a cut above.

Four- and five-star hotels
Until its unfortunate demise in 1970, the top place to stay was the Royal Hotel. Its success was largely due to its proprietor, the legendary White Russian émigré, Boris Lissanevitch. It was the country's first Western hotel; it opened in 1954 in a wing of the palace that is now the Bahadur Bhavan. Virtually everything for it had to be imported from Europe, shipped to India and then carried in by porters. Staying here you'd be guaranteed to meet interesting people and many of the mountaineering expeditions made it their Kathmandu base.

Now the most popular is *The Yak & Yeti* (☎ 413999, fax 227782), with rooms from US$130/160 to US$450 for a suite. Centrally located, it has everything you'd expect from a five-star hotel, although the modern wings don't exactly blend with the old Rana palace which forms part of it. The Yak & Yeti Bar with its excellent Chimney Restaurant was moved here from the Royal Hotel when it closed. Close by is the new *Hotel Durbar*, rated four star since it lacks a pool. The *Soaltee Holiday Inn Crowne Plaza* (☎ 272550, fax 272205) is probably the best of the big

Thamel Accommodation In **ascending order by price** for singles/doubles with common (c) or attached (a) bathroom. Prices in US$ but payable in rupees.

01 **Frugal GH** $1.50/2 (c)
02 **Norling GH** (221534) $1.50/3 (a)
03 **MK GH** (212866) dbl: $2 (c), $3 (a)
04 **Pheasant Lodge** (417415) $2/2.50 (c)
05 **Cosy Corner** (426467) $2/2.50 (c) $5 (a)
06 **Continental GH** (221446) $2/3 (a)
07 **Fortune GH** (411874) $2/3 (c & a)
08 **Hotel Potala** (419159) $2/3 (c)
09 **Friendly GH** (414033) $2/3 (c)
10 **Mini Om GH** (229288) $2/3 (c)
11 **Buddhist GH** (241456) $2/3 (c), $5 (a)
12 **Hotel Silk Rd** (212224) $2/3 (c), $4/6 a
13 **White Lotus GH** (224563) $2/3(c)$3/5 (a)
14 **Hotel Star** (411004) $2/3 (c) $6/8(a)
15 **Everest GH** (222231) $2/3 (c), $3/4 (a)
16 **Hotel Kathmandu Holiday** (220334) $2 (c), $3/4 (a)
17 **Pooja GH** (416657) $2/3 (c), $3/5 (a)
18 **Mt Blanc GH** (222447) $2/3 (c), $4/5 (a)
19 **My Mom's House** $2/3 (c), $4/5 (a)
20 **Guest Palace GH** (225593) $2/3c, $5 a
21 **Plover Nest** (220541) $2/4
22 **Souvenir GH** (410277) $2/4 (c), $8 (a)
23 **Chitwan Tulasi** (410203) $3/4 (c)
24 **Hotel The Earth** (229039) $3/4 (c), $7/8 (a)
25 **Htl Yeti** (414858) $3/4 (c) $7/8 (a)
26 **Kunal's** (411050) $3/4 (c), $5 dbl (a)
27 **Fishtail Home** $3 dbl (c), $4 dbl (a)
28 **Green Peace Ktm GH** (426817) $3 (c), $5 (a)
29 **Yak Lodge** (224318) dbl: $4 (c) $5 (a)
30 **Htl Florid** (416155) $5 (c), $8 (a)
31 **Hokkaido GH** (426051) $4/6 (c)
32 **Skala** (223155) $2/4 (c), $4/6 (a)
33 **Gurkha Soldier GH** (230666) $2/3 (c)
34 **King's Land GH** (417129) $3/4 (c)
35 **Blue Sky GH** (426550) $3/5 (c)
36 **New Orleans** (425736) $3/5 (c)
37 **Polo GH** (242356) $3/4c, $4/5a
38 **Namaskar GH** (421060) $4/5 (a)
39 **Orange GH** (410182) $2/4 c, $4/5 (a)
40 **Pumori GH** (424270) $2/4 (c) $4/6 (a)
41 **Fuji GH** (229234) $4/5 (c) $6/9 (a)
42 **Gorkha** (214243) $3/5 (c), $4/6 (a)
43 **Rainbow GH** (417157) $3/5 (c), $3/6 (a)
44 **Bharati Home** (224986) $4/6 (a)
45 **Tourist GH** (418305) $4 (c), $6 dbl (a)
46 **A-One GH** (229302) $4 (c), $6 (a)
47 **Tibet Peace GH** (415026) $3/4 (c), $4/7 (a)
48 **Marco Polo** (227914) $4-10 (c,a)
49 **Tara GH** (220634) $3/4 (c), $5/8 (a)
50 **Htl Puska** (228997) $3/5(c),$4/6(a)
51 **Ktm Peace GH** (415239) $4/5 (c), $6/12 (a)
52 **Holy Lodge** (416265) $3/5 (c), $7/10 (a)
53 **Dolpa GH** (224367) $4/5 (c) $6/7 (a)
54 **Shangri-La Guest House** (250118) dbl: $5 (c) $10 (a)
55 **Earth House** (418197) $4/6 (c), $6/12 (a)

56 **Base Camp Hotel** (212224) $4 (c), 7(a) dbl
57 **Valentine** (425051) $4/6 (c), $8 dbl (a)
58 **Deutsch Home** (415010) $4/5 (c), $7/10 (a)
59 **Shiddartha Guest House** (227119) $5(c), $7/10/12 (a)
60 **Hotel Shakti** (410121) $5/7 (c), $16/18 (a)
61 **Htl Iceland View** (416686) $8/12 (a)
62 **Lhasa GH** (226147) $5/6 (c), $8/12 (a)
63 **Hotel Horizon** (220904) $6 (c) $20 (a)
64 **LP GH** (412715) $6/7 (c), $8/10 (a)
65 **Down Town GH** (224189) $5/10(a)
66 **Thahity GH** $5/10 (a)
67 **Mustang GH** (426053) $5/8 (c), $10/15 (a)
68 **Hotel Elite** (227916) $4/8 (c), $12/20 (a)
69 **Mt Annapurna GH** (255462) $5-15 dbl (a)
70 **Htl Jagat** (227701) $5/10 (a)
71 **Htl Mt Fuji** (413794) $8/12 (a)
72 **Htl Himgiri** (250048) $6/10 (a)
73 **Acme GH** (414811) $4-10 (c) $6-20 (a)
74 **Holyland GH** (411588) $6/10 (a)
75 **Hotel Namche Nepal** (417067) $3-8 (c), $5-20 dbl (a)
76 **Universal GH** (240930) $8 (c), $8/10 (a)
77 **Damaru GH** (240945) $4 (c), $6/12 (a)
78 **My Home**(231788) $10/14 (c) $14/18 (a)
79 **Capital GH** (414150) $4/5 (c) $7/8 (a)
80 **Tibet Rest House** (225319) $6/9 (c), $8/12 (a)
81 **Hotel White Lotus** (249842) $4/8 (c), $10/14 (a)
82 **Kathmandu Guest House** (413632) $6/8 (c), $17/20 (a)
83 **Hotel Bikram** (417111) $6/10 (a)
84 **Trans Himalayan GH** (214683) $7/15 (a)
85 **Sagarmatha GH** (410214) $4-8 (c), $10/20 (a)
86 **Potala Tourist Home** (410303) $6/10 (c) $12/15 (a)
87 **Villa Everest** (413471) $7/16 (c), $30 (a)
88 **Shakya GH** (410266) $7/10 (c), $10/12 (a)
89 **Htl Nana** (418633) $8/10 (a)
90 **Mustang Holiday Inn** (249041, fax 249016) $8-20/10-30 (a)
91 **Potala GH** (220467) $8-10/15-20 (a)
92 **Pilgrims Htl** (416910) $8/10 (c), $15 (a)
93 **Tibet Cottage** (226577) $8 (c), $12 (a)
94 **Yeti Guest Home** (419789) $4/6 (c), $8/12 (a)
95 **Thorong Peak Guest House** (224656) $8/12 (c), $14/18 (a)
96 **Tibet GH** (214383) $9/10 (c), $13/15 (a)
97 **Newa GH** (415781) $12/17 (a)
98 **Prince GH** (414456) $7/10 (a)
99 **Hotel Shree Tibet** (419902) $10/15 (a)
100 **Khangsar GH** (216788) $8/10 (a)
101 **Sherpa GH** (221546) $8 (c) $10/15 (a)
102 **Hotel Lily** (414692) $8/12 (a)
103 **Htl Greeting Palace** (417212) $10/15 (a)
104 **Hotel New Gajur** (226623) $12/16 (a)
105 **Hotel Pisang** (220097) $12/15 (a)

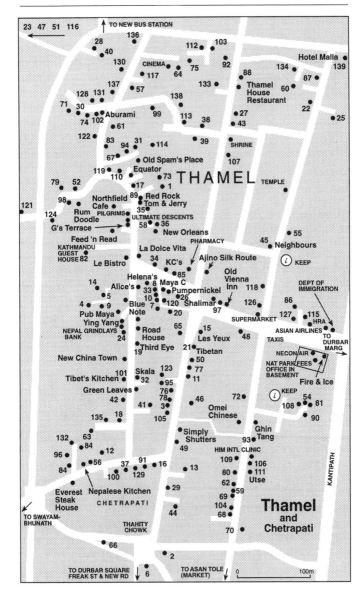

23 47 51 116

TO NEW BUS STATION

28
40
136
130
CINEMA
117
64
75
112 103
92
88
Thamel
House
Restaurant
134
67
139
Hotel Malla
137
57
128 131
71
30
74 102 Aburami
61
122
83
94 31
67
119 110
52
79
98
124
Rum
Doodle
G's Terrace
Northfield
Cafe
PILGRIMS
35
58 36
ULTIMATE DESCENTS
New Orleans
Feed 'n Read
KATHMANDU
GUEST
HOUSE 82
Le Bistro
La Dolce Vita
34
KC's
85
PHARMACY
Ajino Silk Route
Old
Vienna
Inn
118
14
Alice's
Helena's
8
33
Maya C
Pumpernickel
10
26
120
Shalimar
97
126
86
127 115
HRA
DEPT OF
IMMIGRATION
5
4 9
Pub Maya
Ying Yang
NEPAL GRINDLAYS
BANK
24
Blue
Note
7
20
65
15
48
Les Yeux
Road
House
Third Eye
19
21
Tibetan
50
77
11
SUPERMARKET
ASIAN AIRLINES
TAXIS
NECON AIR
NAT PARK FEES
OFFICE IN
BASEMENT
Fire & Ice
TO
DURBAR
MARG
KEEP
New China Town
Tibet's Kitchen
101
Skala
32
123
95
76
78
3
46
72
Omei
Chinese
54
108
81
90
Green Leaves
42
41
105
135
18
132
63
84
96
84
56
12
37 91
100
129
16
13
Everest
Steak
House
Nepalese Kitchen
CHETRAPATI
29
Simply
Shutters
49
Ghin
Tang
93
HIM INTL CLINIC
109
80
62
69
104
68
59
106
111
Utse
Thamel
and
Chetrapati
KANTIPATH
70
TO SWAYAM-
BHUNATH
THAHITY
CHOWK
66
2
TO DURBAR SQUARE
FREAK ST & NEW RD
6
TO ASAN TOLE
(MARKET)
0   100m

THAMEL

TEMPLE

SHRINE
107

Old Spam's Place
Equator
73
17
1
89
Red Rock
Tom & Jerry

45
55
Neighbours
KEEP

New Orleans

99
113
38
27
43
39
114

60
22
25

30
137
57
138

106 **Hotel Norling** (240734) $10/20 (a)
107 **Hotel Sonna** (424806) $5/11 (a)
108 **Imperial GH** (249339) $12/15 (a)
109 **Htl Blue Diamond** (226320) $12/15 (a)
110 **Hotel Garuda** (416340) $9-20/13-25 (a)
111 **Hotel Utse** (226946) $13/20 (a)
112 **Htl Gauri Shankar** (417181) $14/19 (a)
113 **Hotel Karma** (417897) $10/15 (a)
114 **Htl Tashi Dhargey** (415378) $15/20 (a)
115 **Hotel Tilicho** (410132) $15/25 (a)
116 **Htl Moonlight** (419452) $10-25/14-35 (a)
117 **Hotel Buddha** (413366) $15/20 (a)
118 **Htl MM Internatl** (411847) $20/30(a)
119 **Hotel Mona** (422151) $15/20 (a)
120 **Hotel Excelsior** (411566) $18/22 (a)
121 **International GH** (410533) $16/19
122 **Hotel Mandap** (413321) $18/24 (a)

123 **Htl Tashi Dhele** (217446) $15/25 (a)
124 **Hotel Shikhar** (415588) $10/14 (a)
125 **Hotel Lantipur** (414850) $10/15 (a)
126 **Hotel Tridevi** (416742) $12/15 (a)
127 **Tibet Holiday Inn** (411453) $10/15 (a)
128 **Hotel Rimal** (410317) $15/20 (a)
129 **Hotel Tayoma** (244149) $15/30 (a)
130 **Hotel Tenki** (425905) $15/20 (a)
131 **Hotel Blue Ocean** (418499) $15/25 (a)
132 **Nirvana Garden H** (222668) $18/25 (a)
133 **Hotel Thamel** (417643) $18/25 (a)
134 **Htl Norbu Linka** (414799) $20/30 (a)
135 **Hotel Pyramid** (246949) $20/30 (a)
136 **Hotel Manang** (410993) $50/60 (a)
137 **Htl Marshyangdi** (414105) $30/40 (a)
138 **Htl Vaishali** (412968) $90/100
139 **Hotel Malla** (410320) $110/132

five-star hotels, although it's not as well located, being in the west of the city, in Kalimati. Rooms range from US$150-675. It's popular with Indians, mainly because it has the best casino on the sub-continent.

Back on Durbar Marg is the ***Hotel de l'Annapurna*** (☎ 221711, fax 225236) with rather ordinary rooms from US$125/135-300, a large pool and seedy casino. Opposite the Annapurna, a better hotel with similar prices, US$105/115, is ***Hotel Sherpa*** (☎ 227000, fax 222026). The ***Hotel Malla*** [139] (☎ 410620), one minute north of Thamel, is pleasant with rooms from US$100/110. It has a new fitness centre and a swimming pool. In the same price range is the ***Hotel Kathmandu*** (☎ 418494) along Maharajganj, in the far north of the city. The best value in this group is the ***Hotel Shangri La*** (☎ 412999, fax 414184), in Lazimpat, with rooms from US$100/115. All five are popular with groups.

The quietly located Indian-owned ***Hotel Vaishali*** [139] (☎ 412968, fax 414510) is Thamel's first four-star hotel. Rooms are from US$90/100 although travel agents can offer substantial discounts.

Probably the best hotel in Kathmandu is ***Hotel Dwarika*** (☎ 470770, fax 471379), which has opted out of a star classification. If Kathmandu is a living museum, this is the ultimate place to experience it. The red brick buildings are lavished, inside and out, with ornate panels painstakingly restored from old Kathmandu houses. Every room (US$110/125) is an individual work of art, and the restaurants' offerings are similarly exotic.

Note that all star class hotels add a 10-14% government tax to the bill.

❑ **Water alert**
Kathmandu has an ongoing water shortage. Most tourists won't notice this since hotels have huge tanks to get around times when supplies are low. However to help ordinary Kathmandu-ites who aren't as lucky:
When it's yellow, it's mellow, when it's brown, flush it down
Sue Behrenfeld (USA)

WHERE TO EAT

Kathmandu's restaurants are renowned amongst travellers throughout South Asia for their ability to serve passable approximations of Western dishes. You will, however, probably be more appreciative of Kathmandu's apple-pie and enchilada cuisine after a trek rather than on arrival direct from the West. It's surprising how quickly you forget how things are really supposed to taste! The cost of meals in restaurants doesn't vary as greatly as hotel prices. Most main courses cost less than US$3/£2, often much less.

Be especially careful about what you eat before you set out on your trek; you're more likely to pick up a stomach bug in a Kathmandu restaurant than in the hills. A test on the quality of the tap water in Thamel showed it to contain more than ten times the World Health Organisation's recommended safe maximum level of faecal matter. The better restaurants are serious about hygiene but don't believe all restaurants that tell you their salads are washed in iodine. If they're busy they may not have time for Western 'idiosyncrasies' such as this. Similarly filtered water is not reliably clean; stick to bottled or hot drinks. Unless otherwise indicated the restaurants described are in Thamel (see map p81).

Breakfast

Even the smallest guest houses now offer breakfast and snacks either as room service or in their own snack bars. Most of the Thamel restaurants have set breakfasts that can be good value but there are a few places worthy of special mention.

The *Pumpernickel Bakery* does a roaring trade in cinnamon rolls, bagels and other pastries and cakes. There's a pleasant garden behind it and the noticeboard here is a good place to track down trekking partners. *Brezel Bakery's* roof-top café offers competition especially with its quick service.

For many years the place to go for a long, relaxing start to the day has been *Mike's Breakfast*. You breakfast on authentic American (hash browns, pancakes and syrup, fresh coffee with free refills etc) and Mexican fare in a garden, serenaded by the sounds of the ex-Peace-Corps owner's classical record collection. The main branch is in Naxal (north east of Thamel) but there's a second branch, the *Northfield Café*, near the Kathmandu Guest House.

Lunch and dinner

• **Western** The cheapest restaurants in Kathmandu serving Western fare are in and around Freak St. although a slice of hippie history died in 1996 with the closure of the infamous Lunchbox. The long-running *Snowman* has be renovated too, leaving it sterile, although the desserts are still astounding value at Rs20. The cream caramel is still the best in

Kathmandu. *Jasmine Restaurant*, just off Freak St, still has a nice mellow atmosphere and does vegetable fried rice for Rs25. The *New Mandarin* (in reality almost as old as the hills) is as popular as ever, breakfast costs Rs28. In the Annapurna Lodge, the *Diyalo Restaurant* offers main courses from Rs35-60 and shows free videos in the evening. *Oasis Garden* is more expensive but does, as the name suggests, have a pleasant garden; steak and chips are Rs80. Opposite, the *Paradise Vegetarian Restaurant* is probably the best place to eat in Freak St. Their crêpes with garlic cheese are recommended but will set you back Rs75.

Back in Thamel, restaurant prices can be much higher, but there are still places where you'll get a cheap meal that's reasonably filling. *Lips Café* at My Mom's Home offers chicken fried rice for Rs25. *Neighbours' Restaurant* in the Tourist Guest House does a filling egg curry rice for Rs27.

Helena's is a popular place, main dishes are Rs80-140 and there's good cappuccino as well as a wide range of cakes and pies. Nearby, the *Clay Oven* has outdoor seating in a small garden. Main dishes here range from Rs55 to Rs125. *Narayan's*, in Chetrapati, is also popular, especially for its desserts. The *Road House Café* is a rather self-consciously cool terrace-diner with a have-a-go-at-anything menu. The food's ordinary but the music, usually live, is mellow. For a refreshingly different menu and good music don't walk past *New Orleans*. Their authentic chicken burrito with chips and salad is Rs90 and a Mississippi-mud cocktail with real Baileys is Rs110.

Many places have steaks on the menu, usually (but not always) buffalo steak. It's often served as a 'sizzler' and arrives in front of you on a heated cast-iron plate doing just that. The *Third Eye* is a good place for a steak (around Rs200) and in the back room you can recline on the cushions while you eat. It's popular, however, so you need to come early. The enduring *Everest Steak House* is also good, with a wide range of real beef fillet steaks, from Rs140 right up to Rs600 for chateaubriand.

Now in its 20th year, *KC's Restaurant & Bambooze Bar* is as much a Thamel institution as the Kathmandu Guest House. The food's good but prices are distinctly up-market. A sizzling steak from the people who introduced the 'sizzler' to Kathmandu now costs Rs195 and if that doesn't fill you up you can round off your meal with their cheese board (yak, mozzarella and cottage cheese with wholewheat bread and pickles Rs100).

Another Kathmandu institution recommended for its food is the *Rum Doodle*. Enjoy a real fire without guilt; the logs are made from crushed rice husks. Lemon grilled chicken goes for Rs170 and their excellent rum raisin cheesecake or apple pie with custard is Rs50.

Most of the video restaurants around Thamel show Hollywood's latest but feature unmemorable food and low quality recordings. The exception is **Red Rock** near Old Spam's Place. **G's Terrace** is a Western-Nepali joint venture and authentic Bavarian cuisine is served in this pleasant roof-top restaurant. There's Bavarian home-made potato soup with sausage and specialities like French pepper steak in cognac and cream. Most main dishes are over Rs200. **Old Vienna Inn** serves Austrian cuisine for similar prices. In their attached delicatessen the salami rolls (Rs42) are delicious and can be eaten there or on the run.

There are several more delis and sandwich spots; try also **Titbit** in Hotel Garuda. The **Delicatessen Center** on Kantipath is distinctly upmarket, stocking a surprisingly wide range of imported cheeses and other delicacies at unsurprisingly high prices. The **Hot Shoppe** in Durbar Marg also has a selection of pastries. Good cheaper sandwiches can be found opposite Pilgrims Hotel.

Simply Shutters Bistrot (☎ 226015) is a recommended place for a special occasion. The menu is sensibly limited to a few choices on a set menu (Rs340) and the quality of the food is high. A sample menu might include chicken liver paté, boeuf bourguignon and vodka orange sorbet. The restaurant is closed on Tuesday; reservations are essential in the evening as there are only a few tables.

Many of Kathmandu's top restaurants are in the Durbar Marg area and in the five-star hotels there are some excellent Western-style restaurants, some run by Western chefs. The buffet lunch or dinner at the **Yak & Yeti** costs Rs537 including tax.

Lazimpat has a wide range of good if slightly expensive restaurants catering to the large expat community around there.

• **Nepali and Newar** Although some Thamel restaurants will serve dal bhaat, it's usually at grossly inflated prices. There's a cheap Nepali place (no name), serving dal bhaat for Rs30, by the entrance to the Acme Guest House, and another, **Nepali Foods Restaurant**, near the Tourist Guest House.

The **Nepalese Kitchen** has a range of dal bhaat specials (Rs80-165) that are far superior to the dal bhaat that most Nepalis consume twice a day. There's live music several times a week.

The up-market **Bhanchha Ghar** (meaning Kitchen House) in Bagh Bazaar offers wild pork or dried deer meat to accompany drinks and the dinner menu is similarly exotic. Imitating this is **Thamel House Restaurant** (☎ 410388) set in a renovated 100-year-old Newar house. Main dishes range from Rs80-130 and the nine-course set meal costs Rs450.

• **Tibetan** restaurants are amongst the cheapest places to eat in Thamel. The **Tibetan Restaurant** in the same building as the Lovers' Nest Guest House is excellent value and is run by friendly Tibetans. You can get a plate of ten momos here for Rs15; buffalo chowmein costs Rs20. Under the Kingsland Guest House, *Tashi Deleg* is popular and also does Western food that's good value. The best-known Tibetan place here is *Utse*, now relocated to the hotel of the same name. The pingtsey soup (meat soup with wontons) is excellent, as are their momos (vegetable, mutton, buffalo or pork) which cost Rs37 for ten. Given a couple of hours' notice, they will prepare a complete Tibetan banquet (Rs860 for four people).

• **Indian** Mughal/tandoori dishes appear on many menus but can be disappointingly unlike what you would expect in a good restaurant south of the border. Serving good Indian food has made the Third Eye popular but *Mandap Restaurant* compares well, even if the menu is limited. Delicious thick chicken tikka masala, with a nan bread or rice is Rs162. *Feed n' Read*, behind Pilgrims bookshop, turns out decent southern Indian dosas for Rs40-50.

The grimy *Shalimar Restaurant* does a good value chicken masala for Rs35; chicken tikka costs Rs75 and the chef is from India. There's Kashmiri food, including rogan josh, at the newly-opened *Hotel Mughal Darbar*. On Durbar Marg, there's the *Amber Restaurant* which is popular with local people.

The top Indian restaurant is the Hotel de l'Annapurna's *Ghar-e-kabab* (☎ 221711). It specialises in the rich cuisine of north India; main dishes are around Rs200 and there's live music in the evenings. You may need to book in advance.

• **Mexican** People rave about every meal at The Northfield Café; it's the only place for nachos (Rs100) or a tostada, and chocolate or dessert addicts – try the brownie sundae (Rs95) at your peril!

• **Italian** Many restaurants serve pizza and pasta but the *Fire & Ice Pizzeria & Ice Cream Parlour* stands way above the rest. Located just opposite the Department of Immigration, it has to be experienced to be believed. Run by an Italian woman who's imported her own computer-controlled Moretti Forni pizza oven, some of the best pizzas on the subcontinent are now turned out here – to the sound of Pavarotti. Prices range from Rs170-290 and there's wine by the glass for Rs130. It's very popular but is closed on Sundays.

• **Chinese** Most restaurants have spring rolls and chowmein on their menus although what appears on your plate is usually unmemorable. The *New China Town Restaurant* is the best in Thamel but the quality has deteriorated now that the Chinese chef has departed to begin a new China Town above the Bluebird supermarket in Lazimpat. However, main dishes here range from chicken fried rice (Rs55) to prawn in black bean sauce (Rs150). Probably the best Chinese restaurant is the *Mountain City* at the Malla Hotel, just north of Thamel.

• **Thai** Now in larger premises in Lazimpat, *Him Thai* still has a pleasant garden setting and a good reputation. Prices have risen though; chicken satay is Rs140 and most main dishes are around Rs160. Thai food is the speciality at *BK's* in Thamel, however their continental food compares well with its neighbours, KC's and Helenas.

• **Israeli** Catering to the large number of Israeli visitors that the country is now attracting, *Aburami* opened in 1992. The food is quite authentic and good value. Hummus with chapattis costs Rs48, Israeli salad and felafels with chapattis is Rs94, and they do some of the best chips (Rs36) in town. It's a popular place and they put on special meals for Jewish festivals.

• **Japanese** Catering to the ex-pats, there are a number of Japanese restaurants and some of the dishes are surprisingly authentic. The best place is said to be *Tamura*, in the south of the city off the Arniko Highway. The other places are nearer Thamel. *Fuji*, located just off Kantipath, is also good; assorted tempura costs Rs180 and set meals range from Rs230-550. *Koto*, on Durbar Marg, is slightly better value.

• **Vegetarian** All restaurants have some dishes for vegetarians who are sick of dal bhaat. *New Nirmala* has brown bread garlic toast (Rs8) and excellent cream of spinach soup for Rs35. Tofu lasagne al forno is Rs89. *Skala Vegetarian Restaurant* is set in a pleasant garden and has an imaginative menu (herb roulade with mushrooms and brown bread for Rs80).

If it's Indian vegetarian food you're after, try the *Foodsmen Maharaja Restaurant* near Hotel My Home. The owner, a Sikh, supervises the production of delicious Punjabi cuisine. A cheese paratha costs Rs18 and egg curry Rs35. On Freak St, Paradise Vegetarian Restaurant is quite an excellent place to eat.

• **American** Nepal isn't the place to suffer a Mac Attack; McDonald's hasn't arrived. The alternatives are *Nirula's* and the cleaner brighter *Wimpy*, both on Durbar Marg. Beefburgers are out of the question for Hindus, muttonburgers being the less tasty alternative. Suffering ice cream withdrawal? Try a banana split at Nirula's.

NIGHTLIFE

Pubs and bars

Kathmandu turns in early although there are a few bars in Thamel that stay open late for the tourists. In theory everything closes at 10pm but most bars simply close the door or gate and draw blackout curtains so, if you want to party late, enter before 10pm. *Rum Doodle Restaurant & 40,000ft Bar* is a Kathmandu institution, with yeti prints on its walls inscribed by members of mountaineering expeditions. It's named after the book, *The Ascent of the Rum Doodle*, a send-up of the mountaineering account genre. As well as a wide range of drinks (hot rum punch at Rs100, for example) the food here is good; main dishes are Rs110-180.

The Tom & Jerry Pub is noisy and popular, an old favourite. There are pool tables and satellite TV. *Pub Maya, Maya Cocktail Bar* and the *Himalayan Cocktail Bar* are all similar with loud music and deadly cocktails. The *Blue Note* is a jazz bar with a rooftop for balmy evenings.

Old Spam's Place plays live music most nights and has a pleasant garden with a café for snacks and dessert. English pub-style bar snacks include chip butties (Rs50) and almost Cornish pasties (Rs95). The latest addition to the Thamel scene is *Melrose Place* opposite Hotel Karma. It pumps out dance music and is developing into a local disco.

SERVICES

Banks
There are several bureaux de change in Thamel. Nepal Grindlays has a counter (open 9.45am-4.15pm, Sunday to Friday) south of the Kathmandu Guest House. Their busy main bank is on Kantipath and further down are several more banks. There's also a bureau de change in the Department of Immigration which is open during normal banking hours (10am-2.30pm, Sunday to Thursday, 10am-12pm on Friday). The Himalayan Bank has a branch in the large building almost opposite Immigration but, strangely, changes a maximum of US$100 per transaction.

The American Express office (☎ 226172, open Sunday to Friday 10am-1pm and 2-5pm) is by the Mayalu Hotel. You can get credit card cash advances on Mastercard or Visa at many banks.

If you want change on the black market (see p67) it'll find you soon enough if you wander past the carpet shops in Thamel.

Bookshops and libraries
Kathmandu has some excellent bookshops, including some second-hand shops where you can trade in your novel for another. You can catch up on what happened in Britain two weeks ago in the papers and magazines at the British Council Reading Room on Kantipath. The Kaiser Library, Kaiser Shamsher Rana's private collection, is worth visiting as much for the building as for the 30,000+ musty volumes. This Rana palace is now the Ministry of Education and Culture and is just west of the modern royal palace.

Communications
• **Telephone and fax** Kathmandu has an efficient phone system. Since the Central Telegraph office is inconveniently far from Thamel and charges a minimum of three minutes for international calls, it's easiest to

use one of the many communications agencies. You can make international calls and send and receive faxes at these places, for which you pay a modest premium.

• **E-mail** Many communications agencies now offer this service. Prices are around US$0.45 per kilobyte to send and US$0.35 to receive.

• **Post** The GPO is in the south of the city, a twenty-minute walk from Thamel. Poste Restante letters are held here; you need to show your passport to claim parcels. When sending letters you should try to get them franked or the stamps may be removed and resold. Alternatively, for a small commission, the Thamel communications agencies will handle this for you. The international courier companies – FedEx, DHL (☎ 222358) and TNT – offer standard door to door services. For import-export business cargo, talk to one the many specialist cargo companies in Thamel.

Embassies
• **Australia** (☎ 371678), Bansbari
• **India** (☎ 410900), Lainchaur
• **Israel** (☎ 411811), Bishramalaya House, Lazimpat
• **New Zealand** (Honorary Consul ☎ 412436), Dilli Bazaar
• **Sweden** (☎ 220939), Khichapokhari
• **Thailand** (☎ 371410), Bansbari
• **UK** (☎ 414588), Lainchaur
• **USA** (☎ 411179), Pani Pokhari

Left luggage
All hotels and guest houses are happy to store excess luggage while you go to Chitwan or off on your trek, although they expect you to stay with them on your return. Some also have safety deposit boxes for valuables.

Massage
To relax those après-trek and après-rafting aching limbs a number of places offer massage. Stated charges are from around Rs500 for an hour but if business is slack you could try to bargain this down a bit. The number of massage parlours has mushroomed in recent years and the women who purport to be masseuses have become younger and more attractive; the whole business appears to be taking its lead from Bangkok, something the government will actively discourage.

Medical Clinics
CIWEC (☎ 228531, open Monday to Friday 9am-12pm, 1-4pm) is the best place to go for medical treatment in Kathmandu. It has now moved to a more convenient location just off Durbar Marg, near the Hotel Yak & Yeti. Consultations cost US$40 or the equivalent in any currency. **Nepal International Clinic** (☎ 412842, open Sunday to Friday 9am-5pm) is

also excellent and consultations cost US$30 or the equivalent. It's opposite the Royal Palace, slightly east of Durbar Marg.

Cheaper but still good clinics in Thamel are **Everest International Clinic** (☎ 411504), on the square north of Les Yeux and **Himalaya International Clinic** (☎ 225455) near Hotel Utse. **Synergy**, Narsingh Camp, although heavily advertised, can't be recommended.

Supermarkets

Best Shopping Centre near Marco Polo Guest House has lots of imported goodies and the cheapest chocolate in town. **Bluebird Supermarket** in Lazimpat has a wider stock.

Swimming-pools

The top hotels all have swimming pools and allow non-residents to use them for a price. The largest is at the Hotel de l'Annapurna but it'll cost you Rs350 to swim here. Closer to Thamel the Malla Hotel's smaller pool costs Rs250 and is set in a pleasant garden. For doing laps the pool at Balaju Water Gardens is more practical, especially in the morning. The strength of the chlorine is reassuring.

TRANSPORT

Cycling used to be the best way to get around but traffic pollution problems have got worse each year. There are lots of rental stands around Thamel. No deposit is required; you sign the book and pay the first day's rental. Be sure you check the tyres, brakes, lock and bell before you cycle off. Lock the bike whenever you leave it as you'll be responsible for its replacement if it gets stolen. You can rent an old India Hero with patched tyres for Rs30 per day or a smart new Chinese Pigeon for Rs40. The Taiwanese or clunky Indian mountain bikes go for Rs80-100. If you're renting for more than one day (a good idea as you can keep the bike overnight at your guest house) you can usually negotiate a lower rate.

A number of places in Thamel now rent out **motorbikes**, mostly 250cc Japanese bikes made under licence in India. They cost Rs400-600 per day, plus Rs25 for a helmet; a cash deposit is sometimes required but usually they simply want to know where you're staying. You're supposed to have either an international driving licence or a Nepali one.

There are lots of **taxis** around Kathmandu. If they aren't willing to use the meter get out and try another. At night you have to pay more. If their meter needs recalibrating they will have an officially stamped conversion sheet, though sometimes this is only in Nepali. Going to and from the airport is the exception; you won't get away with paying less than Rs150.

There are also **auto-rickshaws** whose drivers use a meter but expect to pay a bit more than what is shown. Unless you know the fares, taxis generally cost about the same. Kathmandu's **cycle-rickshaw** wallahs understand just how your delicate Western conscience ticks, so bargaining is required if you're going to pay anything like local prices (but the money does go to a good cause).

There are extensive **bus** routes around the city and out to the airport but this is a slow and crowded option and there is no map to work out the system. Beware of pickpockets.

WHAT TO SEE

You could easily spend a week in the Kathmandu Valley, such is the rich concentration of sights here. UNESCO has realised this too and the valley is home to no less than seven World Heritage Sites, a fact that Nepalese are justly proud of. Several companies operate bus tours (ask in the larger hotels and travel agencies) but renting a bicycle and exploring independently is rather more rewarding – getting lost is all part of the fun. Wandering around the exotic temples shouldn't be limited to daylight hours. During full moons and festivals, worship and celebrations often continue well into the night.

Durbar Square

First stop on the Kathmandu sightseeing trail is Durbar Square, also known as Hanuman Dhoka. This complex of ornately carved temples and monuments includes: the old royal palace (closed Tuesday); the Kumari Bahal (the home of the Kumari, the 'living goddess', a young girl chosen as the incarnation of the Hindu goddess Durga); the Kasthamandap (the wooden pavilion from which the city's name is said to have derived); and the tall Taleju temple, built in the 16th century. The best time to be here is early in the morning when people are going about their daily pujas (worship) or during festivals. Evening time is also pleasant and tour group-free.

Baudha (Bodhnath)

This Buddhist stupa is one of the largest in the world. Seven kilometres from the city centre, it's a major place of pilgrimage – especially for Tibetans. There's a large Tibetan community here and several monasteries which are also worth exploring.

From dawn to dusk the faithful make their circumambulations (always in a clockwise direction) under the fluttering prayer-flags and the all-seeing eyes of the giant white stupa. It's a fascinating place to visit, especially at the time of a new or full moon, and at Losar when there are special festivities. The *Stupa View* has the best food (try 'Elephants feet') while nourishment of a more basic nature is available at the *Oasis Restaurant* and a number of other places nearby. There are also a couple of bars serving momos and tungba just around the corner from the Oasis; look for a curtain across a door – there are no signboards. Order a plate of *sukuti* (spicy fried dried meat) to accompany your tungba and momos. It's all ridiculously cheap but not terribly hygienic – so it's probably best enjoyed when you come back from your trek.

Swayambhunath

Visible from many parts of the city, this ancient stupa is the second most important Buddhist shrine in Kathmandu. It's a 40-minute walk west of Thamel. The steep climb up through the woods is certainly good practice for a trek and there's a good view from the top but Swayambhunath has little of the atmosphere of Baudha. It's also known as the 'Monkey Temple' on account of the troupes of macaques here. Don't feed them as they can get vicious when the biscuits run out.

Pashupatinath

Hindu pilgrims come from all over the sub-continent to this Nepalese Varanasi (Benares). It's an extensive complex of temples beside the Bagmati River and is 6km from the city centre.

Pashupatinath derives its fame from the metre-long linga, carved with four faces of Shiva, which is kept in the main temple (closed to non-Hindus). The whole complex is dedicated to Shiva and is a focus for sad-dhus, wandering ascetics, some of whom may have walked here from as far away as south India.

As at Varanasi, people perform their early morning ablutions from the ghats here. It's also the most auspicious spot to die and be cremated. The funeral pyres by the river have become something of a tourist sight, attracting coachloads of foreigners who display astounding insensitivity by taking endless photos of the burning bodies.

Patan

Also known as Lalitpur, the second of the three main city-states inside Kathmandu Valley is now just a suburb of the capital. Patan's Durbar Square is probably the best collection of late Malla architecture in the country and is rather less touristy than Durbar Square in Kathmandu. A taxi from Thamel should cost around US$2 using the meter.

It's also worth visiting Kumbeshwar Square which boasts the only five-storey temple in Patan. The water in the pond here is said to flow directly from the holy lake of Gosainkund in Langtang. At the north-east corner of the square is Kumbeshwar Technical School. Visitors are welcome at this school and orphanage which was set up to help the lowest castes in the area. Tibetan rugs and sweaters of considerably better quality than those on sale in Thamel can be purchased here.

Bhaktapur

The third city, Bhaktapur, is a medieval gem which is visited only fleetingly (if at all) by tourists. Fourteen kilometres east of Kathmandu, it's an almost entirely Newar city that is strongly independent of Kathmandu;

some of the people who live here can't even speak Nepali. An atmosphere of timelessness pervades this place – much more so than in Kathmandu or Patan. Bhaktapur's main attraction is its Durbar Square with the Palace of Fifty-Five Windows but here, as in the rest of the city, many buildings have been damaged by earthquakes.

The major earthquake in 1934 affected more than half the buildings. Much of the reconstruction work has been done by the Bhaktapur Development Project, a sensitive urban renewal programme sponsored by the German government.

It's a dusty hour-long cycle ride to Bhaktapur from Kathmandu or you can take the electric trolley-bus from Tripureshwor which will drop you across the river, a 15-minute walk from Bhaktapur's Durbar Square.

The city council collects a Rs300 entrance charge at the main entrance and trolley bus entrance area.

Thimi

This small Newar town is famous for its pottery and the streets and squares are lined with recently thrown pots drying in the sun. Ten kilometres from Kathmandu, Thimi makes a pleasant cycle-excursion and can be combined with Pashupatinath and/or Baudha.

Nagarkot

The most popular mountain-viewing spot near Kathmandu is Nagarkot, 32km from the city on the road that passes Bhaktapur. Most people spend the night here since the view, which includes Everest (just) and four of the other ten highest peaks in the world, is best in the early morning. There are lodges to suit all pockets from less than US$1 to over US$80. There are, however, tours that leave Kathmandu before dawn to catch the sunrise from Nagarkot. You can also get here by bus from Bhaktapur (hourly , the journey takes two hours), by mountain bike or motorbike. The view from Chisopani, on the Helambu and Gosainkund treks, is similar.

Other entertainment

Several of the top hotels put on evening **cultural shows**, some including dinner. There's a nightly floor-show in an impressive Rana palace theatre, now the **Naachghar** (dancing house) restaurant at the Yak & Yeti Hotel. It's expensive and you must book (☎ 413999).

Several of the best Thamel rafting companies put on slide shows with free rum n' coke to tempt you. **Chris Beall's slide presentations** offer good unbiased advice for trekkers about to head into the hills. The shows cost Rs250 and are held in the Kathmandu Guest House when he's in town

For many years the Soaltee Oberoi (now the Soaltee Holiday Inn Crowne Plaza) hosted Nepal's only casino; a place that is popular with visiting Indians. Now all the top hotels have casinos and foreigners who have arrived in Nepal within the last seven days are given Rs100-worth of chips free (show your air ticket). They're open 24 hours a day.

Everest Snooker has seven tables and charges Rs120 per hour for a table. Follow the winding road out past Holy Lodge and it's on the right almost opposite Hotel Shikhar. The Hotel Moonlight also has tables; there is no charge if you stay there.

MOVING ON

By air
Nepal's air transport system has expanded rapidly since the government allowed the formation of private carriers in 1991. It has, however, just been announced that the ML-17 helicopters used by some airlines for regular flights, are to be used only for private charter and cargo work from 1 Jan 1998. This will reduce Nepal's domestic air capacity almost by half, which will have a significant impact on domestic air services.

There are flights daily to major destinations. If possible avoid the less than reliable national carrier, Royal Nepal. All airlines charge the same rate for the routes they share. A return fare is double the one-way fare.

Route	Fare
Kathmandu-Pokhara	US$61
Kathmandu-Meghauli (Chitwan)	US$72
Kathmandu-Lukla	US$83
Kathmandu-Nepalganj	US$99
Pokhara-Jomsom	US$50

• **Everest Air** (☎ 253252, 241016, 222290; helicopter charters (☎ 473127).
• **Nepal Airways** (☎ 412388/9, 410052, 422846; helicopter charter ☎ 418214, 418652, 412158).
• **Necon Air** (☎ 472542).
• **Asian Airlines** (☎ 410086, 416116, helicopter charters 423315)
• **Gorkha Airways** (☎ 423137, 414039).

Phone lines are often engaged so either deal with a travel agent or go directly to the office.

By bus
• **Pokhara** The easiest way to get to Pokhara is on one of the tourist buses that run from Kantipath near Thamel, leaving at 7am. Sometimes there are also later buses at 11am and 2pm. Tickets can be bought at most travel agents for around US$4-5. The blue Sajha buses (US$1.25, seven hours) run from near the GPO at 7am. Tickets can be bought up to two days before departure from the kiosk there.

Buses from the new bus station well north of Thamel leave between 6.30 and 10am (US$1.50, 10 hours) and the minibuses (US$3, seven hours) at 7am.

• **Chitwan** Tourist buses are the most convenient because they go direct; they leave from Kantipath at 7am (US$3, five to six hours).

• **Other destinations in Nepal** From the new bus station there are buses to most towns in Nepal; many depart early in the morning. If you don't get a ticket for a seat take some patience pills. Surprisingly, even the roughest torture sessions can be fun with the right frame of mind.

To **Besisahar** (US$2) takes anything up to 12 hours. They leave at 6.30 and 8.30am. You should book one day before at the fourth window from the right at the bus station.

Buses for **Kodari** (the Tibetan border) and **Jiri** go to the old bus station in the centre of town.

• **To India** Watch out for travel agents' 'through' tickets. Since everyone has to change into an Indian bus at the border, there's actually no such thing; you are given a bus ticket to the border and a voucher to exchange with an Indian bus company with whom they've got an arrangement. Since things don't always run as smoothly as they might it's safer, cheaper and just as easy to buy the tickets as you go along. It also gives you a choice of buses and the option to stop off where you want.

The best crossing point for Gorakhpur, Varanasi or Delhi is via Belahiya/Sunauli. Buses to Belahiya (US$2, nine hours) leave between 6 and 9am and there are also night buses. Going via Mahendranagar (US$6, 24 hours) is an alternative route to Delhi, only another six to eight hours away. For Patna and Calcutta it's better to go via Birganj/Raxaul (US$2, 11 hours).

For Darjeeling you'll have to make the gruelling trip to Karkabhitta (US$5, 17-21 hours) on overnight buses leaving between 3 and 4pm. All leave from the main bus station, and, whether heading east or west, go via Mugling.

❑ **Tourist revenue**

When Kirkpatrick visited Kathmandu in 1793 the charge for seeing the inner sanctum of the Changu Nayaran temple (roughly between Nagarkot and Bhaktapur) was a tola (11.5g) of gold for the high priest. Thankfully trekking is cheaper than that but the Nepalese government still charges a surprising amount of cash for the privilege. One way of looking at this is that it's a tax but it's rather more visible than most taxes in your home country.

Nepal's government, like most, is short of money and getting foreigners to pay is considerably less painful than taxing the mostly poor local population. Virtually nobody pays income tax so Nepal's only significant tax bases are import duties, liquor taxes and some tourist taxes. Most hotels, restaurants, trekking, travel and rafting companies pay taxes but by cooking the books this revenue is far less than it should be. So as you pay these 'large' fees spare a thought for the government and especially the people of Nepal.

Trek preparation in Kathmandu

Trekking permits

These are obtained from the **Department of Immigration** (☎ 412331), located on Tridevi Marg, just east of Thamel. It's open for applications for trekking permits and visa extensions between 10am and 2pm from Sunday to Thursday and 10am to 12pm on Friday. The forms for the three main trekking areas are colour-coded; you need a blue one for the Langtang region. Two photos are also required (these are available instantly in several photo shops near by). The charge is the equivalent in Nepalese rupees of US$5 per week. Since the charge is per week even if you are only planning, say, an 11-day trek you might as well get a permit for the full two weeks. You also need to pay the National Park entrance fee (Rs650 but this may rise to Rs1000) in the National Park Office located in the basement of the shopping centre across the road. Visa extensions cost US$1 per day, paid in equivalent Nepalese rupees, and require one photo.

Permits and visas are usually ready the same day in the afternoon between 2pm and 4pm Sunday to Thursday, and between 12pm and 3pm on Friday. At the height of the season you may have to wait until the following day so make your application as soon after the office opens as possible. If trekking with an organised group the trekking agency normally takes care of the permit details.

Still can't decide where to trek?

Flicking through the many coffee-table books on Nepal can help. Rather than clogging Pilgrims' bookshops' corridors try the British Council, the Himalayan Rescue Association (HRA) or the Kathmandu Environmental project (KEEP) libraries first: all are marked on the map of Kathmandu, p81.

ORGANISING A GUIDED TREK IN KATHMANDU

If you're planning to organise a trek with porters, tents and a cook along a standard route it's worth pointing out that the lodges offer a service that is nearly as good. Another option to the full expedition-style trek is hiring a porter-guide or porter and using the lodges. Expedition-style

(Opposite) Kathmandu: The main stupa at Baudha being prepared for a festival.

trekking is pleasant and luxurious and worth considering for these reasons alone. It is also ideal for peak season trekking in a large group, remote area treks and for climbing trekking peaks.

Trekking companies
There are more than 200 trekking agencies in Nepal. The top outfits have offices on Durbar Marg but there are many other reputable companies based in Thamel. Despite the small offices, most trekking companies are well practised at organising treks. Some have been set up by sirdars who gained a particularly good name for themselves and had enough recommendations to secure steady business. Try to talk to other trekkers who have used a company's services. Contact and book directly with a trekking company, rather than with a travel agent or hotel tout who will collect an unjustly large commission – to the detriment of the quality of the trek.

Trek personnel
A **sirdar** (trekking guide) is an organiser rather than a trained specialist of history and culture; guides as such don't exist for the trekking regions. He (virtually never she) will speak basic English and carries only his personal equipment. The older Sherpa sirdars are generally more knowledgeable but few guides are expansive; displaying their country and culture is not a widely understood tourism concept.

The sirdar, who is often the leader as well when there is no foreign representative, hires and/or supervises the porters and the sherpas (who are not necessarily from the Sherpa clan), and is also in charge of the money. It is therefore a powerful position and a good sirdar will ensure the trek functions in a trouble-free manner. A lacklustre sirdar can cause endless minor problems. **Sherpas** are the sirdar's assistants – general helpers who erect and pack the tents, serve the meals and help in any way they can. They ensure nobody gets lost and carry the members' daypacks if they tire. Most speak some English. The **cook** is another key figure, heading a small army of **kitchen boys** (who are sometimes girls).

A **porter** is a load-bearer who generally speaks little or no English. The standard trekking company load is 30-40kg/66-88lbs but if you are doing the hiring then a more gentle 20-25kg/44-55lbs will leave a spring in a porter's step and flexibility about the stages.

Operating independently from the above personnel are the **guide** and the **porter-guide**; usually people who are not experienced enough to be a

---

(Opposite) Top: When you're trekking with a group the camp is set up for you, usually away from the village, as shown here (near Melamchi Pul, see p182). **Bottom:** The Yolmo people of Helambu pride themselves on having spotless, well-organised kitchen-dining rooms. This is typical of many lodges in Helambu (see p177).

sirdar but who speak some English. Guides consider that their job should not involve carrying your gear, while porter-guides will help out by carrying a modest 10-15kg/22-33lbs.

Costs At present the official minimum charge for a fully organised trek (all food, tents and crew) is US$20/£12.50 per person per day, for which you get a simple, often quite adequate level of service. US$30-40/£18.75-25 per person per day should provide a good standard of service. The top companies charge US$40-60/£25-37.50 a day (excluding domestic flights) for better food, better and more equipment and slicker service.

Ensure it is clear exactly what you are paying for and, more importantly, what is not included. Obviously the wages for the crew must be included as well as food and tents, but are bus tickets or a private bus, taxes and the National Park entrance fees? Decide also on the rates for extra days, for example if you decide to trek for longer or shorter.

HIRING GUIDES AND PORTERS

When choosing a porter or porter-guide, whether hiring through a company or independently, follow your instincts. A pleasant manner is more important than fancy clothes and older, scruffier porters are often the most reliable. Mutual respect is important so don't be afraid to show who's boss. They are being paid comparatively well and the working conditions are less demanding than a normal portering job. By hiring someone you take on the responsibility of an employer. One couple who had previously hiked a lot in the Rockies said, 'It was like having a child with you'. Others find the experience rewarding and at the very least it makes getting up the hills easier. Trekking personnel look after themselves in most situations, finding food and lodgings (and often assisting you in this task), but when it comes to snow conditions with the risk of frostbite and snow-blindness, porters are notoriously naïve. Usually it is you who will have to take preventative action and pay to hire boots, a jacket and sunglasses.

Hiring in Kathmandu Trekking companies are happy to arrange crew but be clear what the charges include. You normally pay a daily rate to the trekking company and then pay for the crew's food and lodging on the trail. A few guides are adept at running up huge bills so it's sensible to establish what they will be eating. Most, however, prefer dal bhaat, the standard cheap Nepali food. Setting a daily allowance for food is another idea; perhaps Rs150 to Rs200 outside the national park and Rs250 to Rs300 inside. An alternative arrangement to agreeing to pay for the crew's food is to pay a higher food-inclusive daily rate.

Since you will be spending a good deal of time together, talk with the guide beforehand and perhaps even go out for a meal with him; if you have doubts, ask for someone else. With porters, if they are going to high altitude, insist on knowing what equipment the company will provide for him but be warned that no matter what's agreed, once you're up there the crew often lack the right gear.

The daily rates for porter-guides are US$6-12/£3.75-7.50. Rates for porters are slightly less, around US$5-8/£3-5 but prices vary considerably between the many agencies. Some trekking companies exploit their employees mercilessly. The crew may often receive no more than standard wages but must hire cold weather gear themselves and pay for food which is progressively more expensive the higher up you go.

Hiring on the trail In Dhunche, Bharkhu, Syabru, Syabru Bensi and Melamchi Pul porters are easy to find. By asking around in Dhunche or Syabru Bensi you may be able to find a porter-guide.

Note that if you hire through a trekking company all staff are (in theory) insured while those hired independently on the trail are not. Also, many people have mentioned that hiring a porter-guide locally often costs a similar amount to one hired in Kathmandu through an agency.

MONEY FOR THE TREK

Other than in Dhunche, there are no banking services on any of the Langtang treks. So this means taking your entire trekking budget in cash rupees from Kathmandu. It is useful to have plenty of small change and Rs100 notes, especially if travelling alone. Out of the peak season most lodges have trouble breaking a Rs500 or 1000 note.

❏ **The Himalayan Rescue Association (HRA)**
Despite the name, the primary goal of the HRA is to prevent altitude sickness-related deaths. To this end during the main trekking seasons staff in the Kathmandu office, the Manang and Pheriche trekkers aid posts, and, if the project goes ahead, a new post in Langtang, give lectures. In addition to altitude sickness advice these cover other common medical problems (much the same as Appendix B in this book).

The aid posts also provide excellent medical services. During the main trekking seasons, Western doctors are on hand for consultations (Rs1000) and for medical emergencies (donations are expected) – services that have saved a lot of discomfort and lives. They also treat the locals and trekking staff for a much smaller fee.

The Kathmandu office is marked on the map on p81.

PART 4: THE LANGTANG REGION

Langtang National Park

Langtang National Park (created in 1971) was Nepal's first national park. The introduction of the national park system was significant because it marked the beginning of a slow change in attitude to conservation and wildlife. Previously, wild animals were hunted or were considered a pest; anyone who killed a leopard or tiger with a knife and lived to tell the tale was presented with a medal from the king.

> ❏ **Langtang Ecotourism Project**
>
> It is all too easy to be cynical about government institutions, what everybody does (or rather doesn't do) and development organisations in general. Luckily the reality is somewhat different to first appearances. It has always been a heartening experience talking with people in the many different organisations who are striving to help. One project that is making a difference is the Langtang Ecotourism Project. This is managed by The Mountain Institute (TMI) and the National Parks and Wildlife Service (HMG) and is funded by USAID. It's a small but well run three year programme to assist Langtang lodge owners in realising benefits from trekking tourism within a sound ecological and culturally appropriate framework. Much of the work involves getting locals to think about, plan and then actually organise what they need themselves, rather than handing everything to them on a plate.
>
> Of direct benefit to the trekker are the lodge management courses where, amongst other things, cooking and hygiene are taught. On the ecological front, for years the locals have been discussing using kerosene for cooking. With some extra motivation this is now becoming a reality with kerosene depots being set up and agreements made between all lodge owners to use it. Even the army has tentatively agreed to begin using it. The idea of kerosene heaters is also being considered, since half the wood lodges consume is used just to keep trekkers warm. Gas has also been suggested for some villages while in a few areas cooking on sustainably harvested wood may be the best answer.
>
> On the toilet front new methods, such as the composting toilets which are used in other regions to turn the waste into fertiliser, are being discussed. The National Park has also got around to asking that the worst-placed systems be moved, eg the ones over streams.
>
> Then there's the perennial problem of rubbish. Long ago the National Park established rubbish pits; the challenge is to motivate people to use them properly. Burnables should be regularly burnt while non-burnables are buried. Trekkers can help in a small way by taking out their batteries (and any other rubbish) and by bringing in as little as possible, especially useless packaging.

Unlike the majority of the national parks in Western countries people have always lived in the region, creating a potential conflict of interest. To minimise this, park boundaries were drawn around a number of villages; note the wiggle in the boundary around Syabru. Villages in the national park, such as Langtang village, have their household land, cropping land and kharkas registered as their own so effectively these areas aren't national park land. This was a good solution at the time but for other problems such as hunting and firewood cutting the park's omnipotent approach hasn't always been successful. In a

far-reaching move to work with the people rather than impose from the top down, a conservation area (sometimes called a buffer zone) was created in March 1996. This runs along the southern boundary of the park and is approximately five kilometres wide. It encompasses most of the villages that use land in the park but that aren't actually in it, including Syabru, Tarkeghyang and Sarmathang. In another advance of government policy around 40% of the money collected for the national park entrance fee is to be spent on buffer zone projects.

The park straddles the Himalayan range and so encompasses diverse ecosystems from rainforest to alpine. It shelters snow leopard and at least two other endangered species – musk deer and red panda – which have recently had specially protected reserves created for them.

Minimum impact trekking

Yet each man kills the thing he loves. **Oscar Wilde** *The Ballad of Reading Gaol*

Most people coming to Nepal have read stories about the mountain of rubbish at Everest Base Camp left by the conquerors or otherwise of the world's highest peak and the frightening rate of deforestation so that trekkers can have hot showers and apple pie. The media, unfortunately for Nepal, sensationalised some relatively minor issues. Visitors may be astounded not to see a continuous trail of litter to Everest Base Camp and to fly over endless forested ridges in many parts of the country.

There is no doubt, however, that tourism and especially trekking tourism has had an impact in Nepal. The ethics and issues are often debated, somewhat guiltily, around lodge potbellies or around campfires but without detailed local knowledge, answers are elusive. However, for the

---

❏ MTV and McDonald's

Most tourists are quick to cry out against development or development for development's sake but few realise just how tough life is in the hills. Ask any villager what they want and all will say health care and better education. Roads or at the least telephones and tourism (ie an income) are local priorities too. Probe deeper and the list is endless. Beyond doubt the people in the hills want a better life. The difference between the West and a typical isolated Nepali village is they don't have any choice.

This is where the hills-based development agency offices come in. Take, for example, a village that wants water taps. This is a project that, with motivation and financial organisation, they could possibly construct on their own. Their desire is merely a convenience, a 50m pipe from the nearest stream would do, even if this stream is used as a toilet. However, discussing with experts means that they might get water from a cleaner source, and more importantly learn what pollutes water; incredibly the link between faeces-contaminated water and diarrhoea is not understood in much of rural Nepal. Naturally the villagers would balk at the extra cost but this is where the agency can also help. In most cases the villagers have to supply the non-skilled labour while the technical assistance and materials are supplied free or at low cost. Most agencies train villagers in maintenance then hand the system over to them.

The vast majority of projects make a woman's life easier: water taps, treeplanting and reforestation projects. Literacy classes give women the chance to learn to write and to discuss anything from contraception to better child-rearing to setting up a business. Increasingly too, development agencies are setting up broad-based women's programmes because they are easier to work with, more motivated and are more willing to work without pay (or corruption) on a project that will obviously benefit them. The international award-winning Annapurna Conservation Area Project (ACAP) says their women's programmes have been particularly successful.

As for forcing development, it is the villagers who clamour for assistance. Essentially many agencies are facilitators more than anything else. The only unfortunate aspect is that there aren't enough development resources to go around.

People still love to argue 'But are they really happier?' They certainly don't need MTV or a McDonald's but that isn't what they are asking for. There are many convincing arguments and statistics that show villagers are better off but perhaps rather than play moral judge, leave the development decisions to them.

Langtang region the usual doom and gloom should be thrown aside. There are few experts who would say the environment and peoples of the Langtang (or the Khumbu, the Everest region, for that matter) are worse off than when Everest was first climbed in 1953.

The region has suffered relatively little deforestation and protection by the National Park should keep this to a minimum. While many lodges cook on wood, extensive forests mean abundant dead wood is available (and only dead wood can be used, according to park rules). The Kyangjin region is an area of concern but it is likely that soon it will be mandatory for lodges to use kerosene, as it is at Gosainkund. The other concern is the large number of army staff based in the park who use firewood. It is a pity that the army hasn't used its technical resources to set up mini-hydroelectric systems for itself. Instead they have tentatively agreed to use kerosene.

On the wildlife front the situation is at first less clear. Despite legal protection (at least in theory) it is hard to say whether the numbers of musk deer, Himalayan thar and danphe among others are improving. Since the army security staff have been implicated in hunting – the very people who are supposed to protect the animals – it may take some discipline before there is noticeable improvement. Certainly there has yet to be any of the almost magic regeneration of the Everest region; in the 1960s you would be lucky to see any wild animals. Now you have to be unlucky not to see even the most hunted of animals, the musk deer. However, if the Langtang was completely unprotected the situation would definitely be worse.

Less easy to quantify but just as important, the locals know they are better off; although this doesn't stop them complaining that they want more development.

Tourism and trekkers are not, however, all blameless. Litter, never a problem before packaged goods arrived in Nepal, is now an occasional eyesore, especially plastic mineral water bottles and group rubbish. Less apparent but more important are the negative effects of trekking tourism on the culture of the area. The normally cohesive community culture has not been able to prevent impressionable younger Nepalis becoming delinquent. Many mistakenly develop a Utopian image of the West and lose confidence and pride in their own culture.

Awareness of the problems is the first step, then there are a number of simple, practical measures that trekkers can and should take in order to lessen their impact on a fragile land.

Himalayan thar on a Rs 50 bank note

❏ **The Kathmandu Environmental Education Project (KEEP)**
Want to know more about how to tread gently in the Himalaya? This is the place
to find out. As well as providing environmental and cultural sensitivity information, friendly staff give basic trekking information and, during peak season,
offer occasional slide shows and lectures by trekking personalities. They also
have log books and hotel recommendations filled out by returning trekkers and
a small but interesting library of books on Nepal.
  Their office (☎ 250646, e-mail tour@keep.wlink.com.np) has moved several times. They're currently in Jyatha, sharing an office with the Himalayan
Explorers Club (HEC), only a couple of minutes' walk from central Thamel: see
the map, p81.

ENVIRONMENTAL CONCERNS

Rubbish

National parks in the West advocate the 'pack it in, pack it out' principle.
In Nepal the situation is complicated by the fact that trekkers themselves
don't carry the supplies in. However, everyone would agree that all rubbish should be properly disposed of.

The most obvious litter problems are directly related to trekking
groups. Tinned food and bottled sauces are served at every meal. The
members may be careful with their litter, putting it in the bins set up in
the camp but what happens to this rubbish? Sometimes it is burnt, the left-
overs sitting in the embers. Sometimes it is buried in the toilet, covered
by little more than an inch of dirt – inevitably to be dug up by animals. It
may be dumped at the nearest village or simply left in a hole in the snow.
The problem goes virtually unnoticed by group members because the
kitchen crew are the last to leave a camp or lunch spot. Understandably
there are very few clean campsites. Park rules specifically state that **all
rubbish generated by trekking groups must be packed out** and not
dumped in village garbage pits, which were dug for the needs of the villagers.

The problem of litter generated by individual trekkers is not so serious. Burnable litter should be left in lodge rubbish bins; non-burnables,
especially alkaline batteries, must be carried out to be disposed of in
Kathmandu.

What about the rubbish generated by lodges to supply trekkers with
dinner? There is little non-burnable litter that is not recycled, apart from
glass bottles and plastic mineral water bottles. Flour, sugar and rice come
in sacks, the cardboard from egg-boxes is reused, oil comes in tins that
are prized for roofing and no tinned food is on menus. National park staff
have dug rubbish pits at strategic sites and instructed the local people in
their use. Admittedly these pits are messy at times so do tell locals if you
come across a messy one.

❏ **A group trekkers code**
Most local trekking companies don't have a clue about environmental aware-ness, even though they profess to. This has as much to do with money as a lack of education or understanding.

Companies also have a poor record of taking care of porters; the donkeys of the industry. Trekking provides employment but sometimes the conditions are tough. Porters normally have to provide everything for themselves, includ-ing food – the company merely provides the load. This is the way it has always been and the reason that change will be difficult. Someone who earns a few pre-cious dollars a day can hardly be expected to have sunglasses or warm clothes or, when already lumbered with a 30kg load, carry another 5kg of food.

Here is a realistic code for personnel and environmental responsibility but that in part goes against the way trekking companies normally operate.

For treks that always stay in an area with lodges the trekking company should:
• supply a stove and kerosene free of charge in the National Park for porters who wish to cook their own food (note that porters often eat at the lodges);
• give porters a maximum load of 30kg.

For treks above the tree line without lodges (effectively the Kangja La crossing and camping above Kyangjin):
• provide all food including snacks for the porters;
• use kerosene for all cooking (including porters);
• provide sleeping mats for all the crew;
• carry enough pairs of sunglasses for all the crew, even if they are only to be used in snow;
• check that porters have a warm hat, gloves, blankets, socks and shoes in reasonable condition;
• carry at least one spare pair of shoes and socks;
• provide plastic bags as required by the porters;
• thoroughly burn all burnable rubbish;
• carry out all non-burnable rubbish;
• leave all campsites and lunching places spotless.

Don't use mineral water Since mineral water is sold in non-return-able, non-biodegradable plastic bottles and is now widely available in Nepal the empty bottles are a serious litter problem; so serious that min-eral water has been banned in several areas in the Annapurna region. Use iodine to purify water (see Appendix B) or ask if the lodge has some spare boiled water.

Put litter in bins There is absolutely no excuse for dropping any litter along the trails – yet many trekkers are guilty of this, even if only for the odd sweet wrapper. However, one piece of paper, multiplied several thou-sand times becomes a significant problem. Tissues, film cartons and bis-cuit wrappers are all easily stuffed into a backpack pocket for disposal in a bin or fire at a lodge. You could also help by picking up a few bits of the litter generated by other people.

Set an example The concept of litter is a relatively new one for the Nepalis. Virtually everything discarded in the past was biodegradable, so it wasn't a threat to the environment. Trekkers can help here by example.

Other pollution
Use the toilet facilities provided Most lodges have toilets which individual trekkers should use. Group trekkers should ensure that the toilets that are dug in their camps are of a sufficient depth and are properly filled in when the campsite is left. The only way to stop animals digging them up is to cover the hole with heavy rocks, something few trekking organisations do. At a few campsites there are now so many holes that finding a new space to put a toilet tent can be a problem. This is particularly acute in Kyangjin.

Dispose of toilet paper properly Nepalis use the 'water method' rather than toilet paper so all the pink streamers beside the track are generated by trekkers. Used toilet paper is easily buried under a rock, or if used for a streaming nose, carried to a lodge. When using lodge toilets if there is a bin beside, put toilet paper in that and it will be burnt later. Tampons and pads should be wrapped and put in rubbish bins.

Don't pollute water sources In the West, the provision of clean drinking water has reduced the incidence of diarrhoea-related diseases so that they are now negligible. Nepal still has a long way to go but efforts are being made to provide villages with water from uncontaminated sources. Do not defecate close to the trail or a stream. If there is no toilet ensure you are **at least 20 metres away** from any water source, burn or properly bury used toilet paper and bury your waste. Removing a large stone before squatting is the easiest method. If bathing in streams be sparing with soap or shampoo. When washing clothes toss the dirty water well away from running water (the phosphates in washing powders are actually good for gardens).

Fuel conservation
While the Langtang hasn't suffered severe deforestation, the amount of firewood used should be minimised to keep most areas on a sustainable footing. To help in a small way do not make open fires, use iodine to purify water instead of getting it boiled, order similar dishes to other trekkers and co-ordinate meal times.

In the national park, trekking companies deserve the harshest possible criticism for contravening park rules by allowing their porters to cook on open fires, although they do use kerosene for meals for the trekkers and main crew. If you're trekking with a group and see fires being lit for cooking you should complain to a company director in the strongest possible terms.

Tread lightly
Don't damage plants and stick to the trails. In the alpine areas above the tree line, plants battle to survive in a harsh environment. Being trampled on is the last straw and sliding down a slope can leave scars that never heal.

CULTURAL CONSIDERATIONS

One of the great attractions of Nepal for the first visitors was the fact that the cultures of the many different peoples living here had evolved independently of Western 'civilisation'. Day-to-day life for most people had remained virtually unchanged. Sudden outside influence has brought profound cultural change, particularly in the areas popular with tourists.

Whilst trees can be replanted in areas that have been deforested and mountains can be climbed leaving scarcely a trace of the climb, it is impossible not to leave some impression of your country and culture while visiting a foreign country and interacting with its people. The media is another major purveyor of images of India and the West, particularly through cinema and video where a fantasy world of exaggerated wealth and violence is portrayed. In Nepal, the effects of these cross-cultural exchanges may well be far more serious than environmental concerns.

There is no denying that the West is a technologically advanced society but its superiority over less 'developed' cultures does not, necessarily, extend beyond this. A visit to a country like Nepal can be a rewarding experience, especially if you have not travelled much outside the West. Many things are done differently here but this does not make the methods any less valid and in some cases they may be better. The Nepalese way of solving problems, for example, is to avoid confrontation which starkly contrasts with the head-on 'Rambo' style of the West. The incidence of murder, theft and rape (outside the family) in Nepal is negligible in comparison to most nations, although it is rising with the breakdown of community values.

> ❑ **Untying the knot**
> Divorce between Tamangs is surprisingly uncomplicated: the couple are tied together by a thread and this is cut; they also have to pay a fine which is essentially for the ceremony. They are free to remarry and there is no stigma.

Dress decently Dress standards are important despite the fact that they are overlooked by many trekkers. Whilst men may go around without a shirt in the West, this is considered indecent in Nepal. Women should not wear shorts or sleeveless tops. See p44 for further information.

Respect people's right to privacy Ask people before you take their photograph and be considerate when looking for subjects. Some older people believe that if you photograph them their life span may be reduced.

Don't flaunt your wealth By Nepali standards even the poorest foreign trekker is unimaginably wealthy. Nepalis often ask how much you earn but you should qualify your answer by giving them some examples of the cost of living in your country. Don't leave valuables lying around as this is further evidence that you have so much money you can easily afford to replace them.

Respect religious customs Pass to the left of mani-walls and chortens. Prayer wheels should be turned clockwise. Remove your boots before entering a gompa and leave a donation; there's often a box provided.

Respect traditions There are a number of other customs and traditions that you should take care to respect. Not doing so is insulting to your hosts although they will be too polite to point out your faux pas. The left hand, used for washing after defecating, is not considered clean so you should never touch anyone with it, offer them anything with it or eat with it. The head is considered the most sacred part of the body and you should never touch anyone on it. Avoid pointing the soles of your feet at a person's head. If you're sitting with your legs out-stretched and a Nepali needs to pass, he or she will dislike stepping over you. Move your legs out of the way.

Encourage pride in Nepali culture Express an interest in what people are doing and try to explain that not everything is as rosy in the West as some Nepalis might believe. In restaurants don't consistently shy away from Nepalese food. Local people are being taught by insidious example that packaged sweets, biscuits, noodles and chocolate are more desirable than local equivalents but in most cases they are actually less nutritious.

ECONOMIC IMPACT

The initial effect of independent trekkers using local lodges was a sudden increase in prices for many commodities along the major trekking routes. The villagers, naturally enough, sought the best prices for their produce and the highest bidders were the trekkers. In the short term this created a problem because villagers were more willing to sell scarce commodities to trekkers. It should, however, also be considered as a stage in the long development process: demand encourages production where previously there was no advantage in producing more. If the commodity is not available locally it must be carried in by a porter which creates work in areas where there may be few employment opportunities. Teahouse trekking particularly stimulates the local economy. Money from individual trekkers enters the local economy via the shops and lodges but it has an effect on the whole area. Porters carry in the additional goods, new buildings may need to be constructed requiring local resources and labour, staff are required at the lodges, and local producers have a new market. Collectively, these provide more jobs and lead to a higher standard of living, not just among lodge-owners. This is immediately obvious from visiting areas frequented by trekkers and comparing them with villages without this stimulus. It's often stressed that little of the money stays in the lodge-owners' pockets but people forget that a 10% profit margin is realistic, and there are many others who benefit.

The economic impact of trekking groups is somewhat different. The main beneficiaries are the government (in the form of taxes) and the trekking company directors (profits). The secondary beneficiaries are the employees who are rarely local people so their earnings do not stay in the area (but are spread to areas where trekkers don't venture). In fact, locals receive virtually nothing. Camping fees are a paltry Rs5-20 per tent and since the bulk of provisions are carried in, little food is purchased locally. Only firewood is used, and rubbish left.

Don't bargain for food and lodging These prices are fixed.

Don't give to beggars Some trekkers, embarrassed at the disparity in material wealth between their country and Nepal, have given money to beggars and sweets and pens to children. They may have thought that they were helping but the opposite is probably true. As well as fostering an unhealthy dependency attitude, begging can in some places be more profitable than earning money by portering or working in the fields. Giving sweets to children not only encourages them to see Westerners (and hence the West) as bringers of all good things but also leads to tooth decay, until recently quite rare in Nepal. On the trail you may encounter more creative forms of begging: teenagers asking for funds for their school. It's hard to judge how genuine many of the claims are but remember you don't have to give anything. You'll be shown a book with names and amounts donated; if the sums are unrealistically large, the solicitation probably isn't genuine.

❏ **Maida**

What's the pastry of your spring roll made from? Flour, of course. But which flour? Maida or rice flour.

Nepalis use maida a lot, which accounts for the light, sweeter taste of many flour-based foods. Wheat flour, however makes better pancakes; maida pancakes tend to be stodgy and don't brown so easily.

Facilities on the trail

A prison cell would have seemed overfurnished compared with that room. **Alexander Powell**, trekking in the 1920s.

LODGES

The hill peoples of Nepal have traditionally provided food and accommodation in their house for local travellers and traders. Not so long ago these teahouses were providing the same level of facilities for the first foreign trekkers: little more than dal bhaat (a rice and lentils meal eaten twice a day by the majority of Nepalese) and a hard bed. As the flow of trekkers grew it was soon realised that these foreigners were prepared to pay more for better accommodation and a choice of food. Now sheets

cover foam mattresses, toilets are standard, chimneys mean smoky lodges are rare and menus provide meals according to Western tastes. Lodges are now run as businesses, very different from the old teahouses with their hosts eager for news of the world beyond the village.

Food

A typical lodge offers a menu based on noodles, rice, flour, potatoes, eggs and the sparing use of vegetables. Meat is rarely on the menu but is sometimes available. Supplies are purchased or grown locally where possible but most things are carried in by porters. Most meal choices are carbohydrate-heavy: exactly what trekkers require.

Breakfast Offerings include muesli, eggs, a variety of porridges, pancakes and breads with jam or honey. The traditional style of Tibetan bread, *ningba*, is a flat round loaf cooked in the embers of the fire or on a hotplate. (The deep-fried style of Annapurna and Everest can be made if you ask).

Lunch The same as the dinner menu. Often the main consideration is the cooking time. Have a look in the kitchen to see what's in the pot: there may be dal bhaat cooking or potatoes already cooked. Otherwise order the quickly prepared items: soups, noodle soups, omelettes, breads and pancakes.

❏ **All-purpose tsampa**
Champa porridge (more properly *tsampa*) is found on many menus. The standard description is roasted barley flour, but what exactly is it?

After threshing, the grain is further sun-dried. Then it's mixed with hot sand in a huge frying pan over a hot fire. The barley is thrown in and soon pops – similar to popcorn – but retains its barley shape. Being light, it easily separates from the sand; at this stage it makes a delicious wholesome snack. Then it's ground, usually by special hand-turned stones one of which has a wooden handle (keen eyes will spot this 'flour mill' in many houses). The resulting flour is exceptionally light and fluffy and, because it has already been cooked, can be eaten just as it is (other flours or *pitho* must first be cooked into something, eg chapattis). Tsampa is usually made from barley (ouwa-ko tsampa), a grain similar to wheat, but it is also possible to make gau-ko tsampa (wheat), pappa-ko tsampa (buckwheat) and maakai-ko tsampa (corn). Go local and try it!

Dinner A range of soups are offered but be aware that many are made from a packet. Potato-based dishes include various fried combinations: with vegetables, egg or cheese and finger chips. Boiled potatoes are usually served with ketchup or a spicy local sauce. Similarly, rice and fried noodles come in various combinations. The tasty rosti, grated potato patted together and fried, is increasingly found on menus. Thukpa is a Tibetan noodle soup and Sherpa stew (*prakbe* in Tibetan) is a thick soup of whatever comes to hand. Desserts include delicious fried apple pie, custard (ensure they make it with milk!) and rice pudding.

Monosodium glutamate (MSG or adihamoto) and salt are used extensively for flavouring. MSG comes as small long crystals until it's crushed. Unfortunately there is no uniform name for it, indeed locals just consider it another form of salt and simply call it 'salt'. For the unaccustomed, too much MSG can give a short-lived pressure headache.

Not on the menu are some good local dishes. Easily prepared snacks are fire-roasted potatoes (they take 12-15 minutes in the hot embers), local popcorn (*maakai*) which barely pops but is nice, and *batmaas* – roasted soybeans. *(Heh) Rildoo* is a spicy main dish made from boiled potatoes that are pounded until it forms a gluey ball that is rolled and chopped into thick chunks. This is then boiled with spices and perhaps a few vegetables. *Prahbe rildoo* is the buckwheat version. (The standard buckwheat is the sour type, *tito pappa*, so buckwheat pancakes aren't what they should be). *Sukuti*, dried or semi-dried meat fried with garlic, ginger and some spices, is often tasty. In Helambu the meat may even be beef. Local chicken and goat meat tend to be tough and disappointing. In Tibetan areas there's no shame in licking a bowl clean, this is the local way.

Another, perhaps less appealing, dish is *hehgurda* – thin potato pancakes which are normally served with yoghurt, butter and chillies. They don't suit being eaten with jam, nor does the sour buckwheat bread. *Gonday* or *dirddo* is real workers food, a heavy cooked maize or millet flour dough served with a bowl of spicy vegetable soup. This is also the national food of Nepal and is considered the poor person's dal bhaat, to be eaten when rice is in short supply.

In the lower Hindu areas many simple lodges aren't set up for trekkers and lack a menu. Either order dal bhaat or lift up the pot lids and see what they have. All restaurants can cook Rara or Wai-Wai noodle soup (*chow-chow*) and omelettes.

Drinks All serve tea, coffee, hot chocolate, hot lemon and Coke. The hot drinks come in two sizes of cup and if you don't specify which they usually serve the larger. Many trekkers spend nearly half their lodge bills on hot drinks. For the economical, frequent use of a water bottle saves plenty. Tang, a packet flavouring, and fresh lemons can often be found along the way but these should only be added once the iodine has purified the water.

Bottled beer can also be found along with chang (local beer), the respected Khukri rum and the infamous raksi.

Hygiene Eating in established lodges is now as safe as eating a cooked meal on an organised group trek. The concept of washing hands, basic cleanliness and boiling water has usually been learnt from lodge management courses. The style of cooking (frying or boiling) renders much of the food safe and salads are not to be found. Hot drinks are safe but local drinks such as chang are not always hygienically prepared.

Your bill You are responsible for keeping a record of what you have consumed in the book (*copy* in Nepali) provided; usually you have to calculate your own bill. The reason for this is that some lodge owners can't read English. It always pays to be honest – locals often have phenomenal memories and experience of how big your bill should be. Also lodge owners, especially smaller ones, are perpetually struggling to get ahead and certainly don't deserve to be cheated.

Bathroom facilities

These are not so developed but a primitive hot shower or a bowl of warm water is usually available. Solar-heated showers may be introduced to the region soon.

Toilets are sometimes just a few planks over a hole in the ground to be squatted over, or at best an Asian-style squat bowl. No spotlessly-white antiseptic auto-flush toilets here, so watch your ankles. The rural Nepalese have land that needs fertilising so before foreign trekkers took to the mountains there was no need for toilets.

❏ **Lodge tips**
Some people choose a lodge simply on the cleanliness of the toilet, others on
the size of the lodge or the softness of the bed. But, materialism aside, usually
the best way is simply by the attitude and the friendliness of the lodge owners.

1. Be considerate if you smoke, the lodges are smoky enough.
2. Try to spread your business around.
3. Use iodine (or drink tea) instead of buying plastic bottles and contributing to
the garbage problem. **Devon and Paul**

There are some delightful small places to stay along the way – often much nicer
than the villages themselves. **Nicola Carney** (Ireland)

Lodgings

Most lodges in the Langtang Valley and Gosainkund have long lines of
mattresses separated by bamboo mats and a curtain for visual privacy.
There certainly isn't any noise privacy. Newer lodges now feature double
rooms and a small dormitory. Lodges in Helambu (except Tharepati) generally have double rooms. The foam mattresses, covered by a single
sheet, are of variable thickness and the pillows of variable consistency.

There is virtually no chance of getting bedbugs or fleas if you use
your own sleeping sheet and sleeping bag, especially since most lodges
wash the sheets and air the mattresses frequently. Hotel blankets and
quilts however, having often been used by porters, can contain unwanted
bed companions.

There's little privacy in some lodges but with the friendliness of the
owners and warm gear in winter they're quite satisfactory. They also
never seem to suffer the problem of being full to the extent that trekkers
are stranded without a bed; there always seems to be space somewhere.
However during October and November Kyangjin is often filled almost
to bursting.

Electricity   A few villages have rudimentary electricity but it isn't possible to charge batteries for video cameras. The only solution is a solar
charging panel.

Off the main routes

In general, wherever there is a village, accommodation can be found.
There may not be a lodge as such but people will often invite you to stay.
If this does not happen try asking around (this is not considered rude by
the Nepalis) and something will turn up. Conditions can be extremely
basic, however. In strongly Hindu areas, your presence may be considered *jutho* (polluting) so, although you may stay, you may have to eat separately and sleep on the porch.

Wilderness areas and base camps offer little shelter other than the occasional overhanging rock. You should also be aware that on detailed maps the dots marked in kharkas (high-altitude pastures) are stone buildings; these are often roofless and are occupied only in summer.

CAMPING TIPS

Choose a spot that gets early morning sun for an easier, earlier getaway. Especially on a shorter day find a place that gets late sun too. Getting the best of both worlds – a great sunset and sunrise – usually means camping on a pass or more or less atop a ridge. Carrying a water bag with at least three litres per person makes this possible.

Take plenty of stuff sacks for separating clothes, a dirty laundry sack and extra for food storage. Get into the habit of always putting things in the same place. Finally is your tent too heavy? Since it's mainly fine during the autumn season, just a tent fly or a bivvy bag might do. Hardy weight fanatics with a five-season sleeping bag could forget even these.

Meal ideas

I have survived far too many camping excursions on locally purchased muesli and milk powder for breakfast, biscuits and chocolate for lunch, and variations on noodles mixed with soups for dinner. However with a little imagination and forethought you can be spared some monotony.

Porridge is easily enlivened by the essential pinch of salt, some honey, milk powder and cinnamon (nice in coffee too), and perhaps even a dollop of jam for decoration. For crunchy more-ishness add dried fruits, granola or some muesli. Tsampa is the local equivalent of porridge. Herbal teas add variety to the morning cuppa.

For lunches, lodge-made chapattis last several days and are tasty topped by cheese or tuna mixed with cabbage, garlic and onion and spiced with masala. Papads/pappadums, the thin crispy and spicy Indian appetisers, are easily cooked in a hot pan, perhaps with a dash of oil. Prawn crackers, the Chinese snack, are also surprisingly easily prepared in very hot deep oil. Soup, perhaps with local vegetables is a warming standby.

Relatively new to the local market is excellent spicy dried buffalo meat (around US$5 a kilo). Eaten raw this is a favourite snack with Sherpas and Tibetans; it also adds considerable texture to a soupy main course. Chunks of cheese (tinned or otherwise) can also inspire the appropriate dish. Local salami is bland compared to the real stuff. A fresh cabbage or cauliflower lasts surprisingly well. Nice by themselves, both are easily mixed to add bulk. Then of course there are the old standbys, onion and garlic. Curry powder, called masala comes in many different varieties and strengths. Potatoes can usually be picked up just about anywhere and, if sliced very thinly, cook in next to no time.

SHOPS, BANKS AND POST OFFICES

Shops Most lodges also run a small shop offering bottled drinks, three or four types of biscuits, chocolate, Mars Bars and some sweets. Often tins of fruit or fish can be found along with noodles, coffee, drinking chocolate, tea, muesli, porridge, milk powder, jam, hats, gloves and cheap batteries. A few places stock film and AA alkaline batteries.

Banks There is a small bank with marginal foreign exchange facilities in Dhunche, but that is the only one in the entire trekking region. All government offices (bar checkpoints) are closed on Saturdays and the numerous public holidays. All are open on Sundays.

Post offices It is possible to post letters in Dhunche, Langtang village and Tarkeghyang. It is better to know the postage rates and have the stamps with you or simply wait until you get back to Kathmandu.

CAMPING SUPPLIES

Instant noodles and biscuits are sold by every shop in Nepal, although many small villages don't have a shop.

Basic supplies are easily found in Langtang Village, Kyangjin and Tarkeghyang. These include biscuits, Dairy Milk chocolate, Mars, Snickers, instant noodles, packet soups, cooking oil (bring a container), onions, garlic, yak cheese, coffee (tea comes in packets – tea bags are hard to find), Horlicks, drinking chocolate, sugar, tinned tuna, jam, honey, muesli, porridge, milk powder and kerosene. Prices are steep compared to Kathmandu but it does save carrying supplies up.

Better brought from Kathmandu are nuts, raisins and snacky things, pappadums, prawn crackers (sold in bluish boxes), masala (curry powder), cinnamon (*daalchini*), tomato paste (beware, it's in a tin similar to sardines), macaroni and spaghetti, tinned cheese and cheese segments, salami (from delis), dried vegetables (available in Best supermarket, Thamel), dried meat, petrol and gas cylinders. The best place to find most of this is Assan Tol, the busy local market, marked on the map on p76.

PART 5: TRAIL GUIDE AND MAPS

Using this guide

ROUTE DESCRIPTIONS

All the main routes for the Langtang region are described and each route
description is accompanied by detailed trail maps. There is no day by day
description; instead all the lodges and possible stopping places are
marked so that you can decide where to stay. To aid planning there are
sample itineraries in Appendix A.

Village names

Villages often have several names – one might be Nepali and another
Tibetan, Tamang or Yolmo. There are also older names and even a few
tourist-named places, eg Lama Hotel. This is further confused by the difficult transliteration (Langtang sounds more like Langthang or
Langdhang). I have given the common names at the first mention then
repeated the most appropriate name in the text.

Several of the local names used differ from other guide books and the
cheaper maps. Establishing the correct name for a place usually requires
checking the meaning or derivation, and finding someone who authorita-
tively knows this is often difficult. While my knowledge of Nepali and

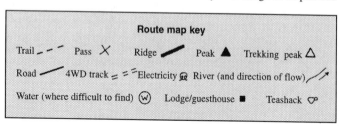

Route map key

Trail ‒ ‒ ‒   Pass ✕   Ridge ⬟   Peak ▲   Trekking peak △

Road ━━   4WD track ⹀ ⹀ ⹀ Electricity ⚡   River (and direction of flow) ⟋

Water (where difficult to find) Ⓦ   Lodge/guesthouse ■   Teashack ♉

Tibetan is limited I have been lucky to travel with good guides for most areas so I hope to have improved the accuracy. For the Kangja La crossing I was less fortunate hence the lack of depth there.

An *e* at the end of a Tibetan or Tamang name is always pronounced *é* as in *café*. So Dhunche and Langmoche are *Dhunché* and *Langmoché*. Similarly kore (a simple, small and often roofless stone shelter) is pronounced *koré*; in Nepali, kore are called *goth* (pronounced *goat* with an aspirated *t*) – a term commonly used in other guide books.

TRAIL MAPS

The main geographical features shown are major ridges, rivers and streams. Being the Himalaya, you are surrounded by huge mountains and steep gorges but the ruggedness of this terrain is not depicted. To work out which mountain you are admiring, a detailed colour topographic map is invaluable.

The trail maps in this book use a scale of approximately 1:50,000 so 20mm is 1km and 1 inch is about 0.8 miles. Features have been stylised so that roads, rivers and villages appear larger (easier to read) than on a true topographic map.

Following trails

Unlike many tracks in developed countries the trails in Nepal are unmarked. Paths lead off the main route to grazing areas, firewood-collecting areas and water sources. However the main trail is usually larger and travels in a consistent direction, so it's generally easy enough to follow. If you think you have inadvertently taken the wrong path look carefully at the size of it – on a main path you don't usually brush against branches and undergrowth. Is it still heading in the right direction? If you must climb to the village and the path has been contouring for a while, don't be afraid to turn back. Occasionally trails divide and rejoin a little while later; this has been marked on the trail maps.

The Langtang, Kangja La and Gosainkund regions are littered with stone cairns (stone men). Some mark the correct route while others merely show that it is possible to climb a point. The numerous cairns scattered around high kharkas are for locating the kore when the thick monsoon clouds limit visibility. In the route descriptions cairns are sometimes used as distinguishing features. Many of these stoutly built cairns are old, as evidenced by the amount of slow-growing moss cladding them. However occasionally they are toppled by snow, wind or animals. Frequently alpine routes are marked by small cairns; often only a few stones, one on top of the other. If you are sure that you are on the correct path, don't hesitate to rebuild these guides or add new ones. Locals take pride in the art of constructing ones that are surprisingly well balanced and in just the right spot so that they are visible from afar.

Walking times

The walking times on the trail maps give a wide spread. Walking briskly and steadily with few stops should approximate the lesser time while ambling along admiring the scenery and spotting wildlife should approximate the longer time. Times over an hour generally include a five to 10-minute break as well. The times are not meant to performance-orientate you: fast walkers, especially when heading downhill, could easily take less time than suggested. In fact, my fervent hope is that trekkers mostly ignore them; their inclusion is largely to help lunchtime and end of the day decision-making.

When taking day trips uphill you can assume that the return will take you half to two thirds of the time taken going up. Don't forget to allow time to relax and explore too. On a fine day there is no more satisfying place to bask in the sun than atop a glorious viewpoint.

Altitudes

These are given in metres on the maps and in the text the conversion to feet is also quoted. Mountain altitudes are taken from the *Helambu-Langtang* map and the two *Langthang Himal* sheets or from the most accurate source out of these areas. Village altitudes are a combination of reading the map and altimeter readings. All figures have been rounded, and are approximate anyway since there are few truly flat villages in Nepal.

Facilities

Lodges are marked as a filled-in square on village plans or directly on the route maps. All are named but a few of these will have changed by the time you read this. Drinkstops generally don't have beds but there is always a village nearby. See p111 for more details on lodges and other facilities.

While all the lodges and teahouses are listed, I haven't recommended any: lodges change, some days the cooking is better than the others, new lodges appear and old ones are taken over by new management. Basically it would be impossible to assess all of them fairly, especially since trekkers use a variety of criteria: some judge by size, some by toilets, others by a smile, still others by the food. Returning trekkers are a good source of advice, as is the log book at the HRA (see p99) which is filled with endless lodge recommendations, as well as comments and advice from trekkers who have just visited the region.

The Langtang Valley

The people of Langtang are very like the Tibetans, engagingly cheery, tough and dirty; but they have sufficient regard for appearances to wash their faces occasionally and were scrupulous to remove the lice which strayed to the outside of their garments.
Tilman, ***The Seven Mountain-Travel Books***

Since Tilman observed this in 1949 surprisingly little has changed; women still sit in the sun killing the lice in their friends' hair and it is still quite acceptable to blow one's nose on the bottom of a skirt or in a head towel. But don't let this put you off, the high country people are friendly and warm.

From the bottom of the valley the trail climbs as unfailingly up as rivers flow unerringly down. A couple of days up, the path breaks out of the magnificent forest and the Tibetan village of Langtang greets the trekker. Here the length of the silent mani walls are a mute reminder of

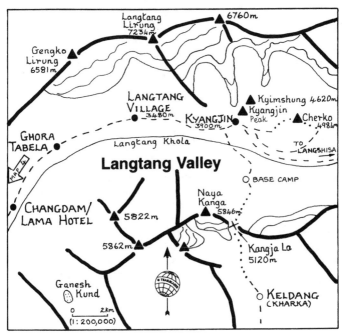

❏ **The settling of Langtang**

Many hundreds of years ago most of the high Himalayan valleys were unoccupied. The Aryan Indians farmed on or close to the plains while the Tibetan nomads wandered the high plateau tending sheep, goats and yaks. Expanding populations, trade in salt and wool and perhaps Gengis Khan's terror began migrations that discovered the beautiful high alpine valleys. Now these cultures mix in the middle hills of Nepal, accounting for the huge number of ethnic groups.

Part of Tibetan mythology is the concept of *be-yul* or sacred hidden valleys that can be revealed to gifted lamas. The Langtang is considered one of these shangri-las, so animals shouldn't be killed in it. But the discovery of the valley wasn't the result of a lama's vision; instead it was due to the adventures of a yak herder – a story undoubtedly rooted in truth.

During a big festival somewhere near or in Kyirong (Tibet) villagers were deciding whether or not to kill a bull (*lang*). The bull got wind of this and naturally enough ran away, taking with him a *brimoo* (a nak or female yak). The nomad owner gave chase, following the animals into a high valley where he lost the brimoo. He wasn't sure whether it died but he did find an auspicious footprint in a rock. This place is now called Bridim and the footprint is still embedded and worshipped.

The bull continued wandering, and the man with it. Way up another valley they came across a magnificent grazing area where the bull fattened up – Langthang or 'full bull' (some people maintain that Langdhang means 'to follow the bull'). The lush grass tempted the pair ever higher but suddenly the bull died – shisa (death), or Langshisa. The nomad spread the skin to dry on a huge rock that is still there to this day, and still bears reddish stains. This is just north of Langshisa on the main trail and is topped by prayer flags. Nowadays, together with another rock, the image of Sakyamuni, it is a place of pilgrimage during the summer.

Now empty-handed, the nomad returned to Kyirong and told of the area. At first it was used for grazing but gradually families settled there; so essentially all the people of Langtang are of pure Tibetan stock.

This tale was assembled from snippets that the locals gave. Somewhere in one of the gompas is an old text with the exact details.

how time stretches back. Harking back still further but less obvious are the many piles of moraine debris telling of the ebbs and flows of the glaciers that now lie well above.

PLANNING AND PREPARATION

A trek up the Langtang Valley fits nicely into 10 or 11 days, Kathmandu to Kathmandu. This gives some leeway and allows time for the rewarding ascent of Cherko – something which is a bit arduous for the first day in Kyangjin but perfect for the second.

The majority of independent trekkers plan to take three days walking to reach Kyangjin. Taking four gives the option of an easier first day's walking than the semi-standard first day's walk to Changdam/Lama Hotel and definitely gives better preparation for the altitude. Most trekkers don't bother to take this into account and, as a result, have to put up with, usually minor, suffering at Kyangjin. However, it would be more sensible to stay either two nights at Langtang or perhaps a night at Ghora Tabela then at Langtang before moving higher.

Once up at Kyangjin there are enough day trip options to fill anything from several days to a week. Heading back down, Syabru Bensi is two days away and Kathmandu a further day on the bus.

Although it is possible to make a quickie six-day trek, Kathmandu to Kathmandu, and even get up Kyimoshung peak, trekking at this sort of speed misses the point. See Appendix A for itinerary planners.

Winter and early spring conditions

From late December onwards, conditions are quite variable. There may be snow from Ghora Tabela up; there may be only a dusting at Pemthang Karpo through all of January. Some Kyangjin lodges try to stay open all winter and lodge owners in Langtang can confirm that they are indeed open. A particularly heavy fall may close them but more usually they are snowed in until someone makes a trail up or down again. If the winter snows have been relatively light it is usually possible to get to the top of Kyangjin Peak and the well-equipped might even make the summit of Cherko. Note that Langtang village, Kyangjin and the peaks are all on the sunny side of the valley. Be prepared for the cold – the streams at Langtang village can remain frozen all day – and for snow: sunglasses, sunscreen, good boots and waterproofing, extra socks, a ski pole, good rain jacket, thick down jacket and a good sleeping bag are essential. Budget extra for hot drinks, bring a book and have a few extra days to cover eventualities.

Monsoon conditions

Very early starts will often beat the cloud but how much clear weather you get is only a matter of luck. Cyclones, heavy rains and flooding in India is mirrored in Nepal by even more rain that sometimes lasts days. July is definitely the worst month. June and later in August have frequent fine weather windows. An umbrella is essential and be aware too that in damp mist and cloud it can be surprisingly cool. The summer days are long; a great time to catch up on reading.

It pays to plan your days and ask if lodges where you need them are open; many of the smaller lodges are closed for the monsoon and all the lodges between (Thulo) Syabru and Changdam may be closed.

Camping

Lugging tents, fuel and food from less than 2000m/6550ft (Dhunche, Bharkhu and Syabru Bensi) to Kyangjin at 3900m/12,800ft is a good job for a porter. The local going rate is US$12-18 for the trip and they pay for their food. When bargaining, remember porters are at the bottom of the heap so, if you pay higher than the going rate, the extra money will normally be used wisely.

During the autumn season there are enough, admittedly rough and small, shelters that it would be possible to survive without a tent. In the few places without rudimentary shelter the chances are that it won't rain anyway. A tent does give more flexibility and security though.

During the entire spring (to mid-June) the roofed kore above Kyangjin are full of ice and snow that absolutely can't be cleared out – bring a tent.

TO DHUNCHE, BHARKHU AND SYABRU BENSI

For many overland travellers the memories of the torturous bus journeys seem the most enduring; the bus journey to Dhunche is a one day love-hate affair which will provide plenty of memories. For the positive-inclined, especially if ensconced on the roof, the bum-numbing ride can be exhilarating. Wedged inside it can be tough, and hell if standing hunched with barely enough room for a single foot on the bucking floor.

Taming the Himalaya with a road to Somthang was a prodigious engineering feat, however nature is invariably still master. Occasionally landslides or floods close the road. About an hour before Dhunche there is a particularly unstable landslide zone which is often only passable with prayers and luck. Vehicles could not get through during the 1995 monsoon season.

Where to begin trekking

From the Dhunche road you have a choice of starting points. Years ago the bus service ended at Dhunche, the district headquarters, but now one bus continues past Bharkhu to Syabru Bensi. If you are heading up the Langtang Valley there is no need to stay in Dhunche at all; the first section of the walk is along the road to Bharkhu where the bus can drop you anyway. The lodges there are simpler but are developing. From Bharkhu a pleasant trail climbs through sparse forest then around the ridge the trail levels off and the forest thickens. A short descent leads to (Thulo) Syabru the largest village in the region and a good place for lunch if you didn't start late. A short sharp descent drops you to the valley floor to meet the trail from Syabru Bensi.

The slightly shorter and less scenic alternative is to take the bus to the end of the line, Syabru Bensi. Here at river level it is simply a case of following the Langtang Khola up the valley. Most maps don't mark this route, instead marking a higher trail via Syarpa/Sherpagaon that is also a possibility.

The difference between starting in Bharkhu and in Syabru Bensi is only a few hours' walking. The real consideration is whether you plan to finish at either place. If so, when returning the shorter route always appeals and you have a better chance of getting a decent seat in the bus at Syabru Bensi. Most people will want to visit (Thulo) Syabru at some stage but if you're heading to Gosainkund after Langtang, you must pass through it anyway.

Getting to Dhunche

By car If you fancy a quicker and more comfortable journey than by bus, get together with some other trekkers and hire a car or van (four-wheel drive in the monsoon) and driver for the journey. Prices range from US$80 upwards spread between three or four people. Either bargain with taxis hanging around Thamel, talk with your hotel or a travel agency or find a new phone directory. Ensure it is clear what happens if the vehicle breaks down.

By bus There are two buses a day to Dhunche, one of which continues to Bharkhu and then ends at Syabru Bensi. Tickets can be bought the day before from the bus station, or from some travel agents, who will add a service charge for the cost of collecting the ticket. Alternatively, arrive an hour or more before the bus departs, especially during the non-peak trekking season, and hopefully claim a seat. As you approach the central building, the ticket window is the closest to you on the right and it has a sign in English. It costs around US$1.50 to Dhunche and close to US$2 to Syabru Bensi.

The buses leave the New Bus Park at 7 and 7.45am. From Thamel to the new bus park takes 15-25 minutes and costs about US$1 by taxi. You can also catch a crowded local bus on Sora Khotay heading for Gongar Bu/Naya Bus Park. Dhunche is an optimistic eight hours away (more usually nine or 10, and 12+ in the monsoon) with Bharkhu half an hour further on, and Syabru Bensi one hour more.

Theft, once never a problem in Nepal, is now common on this bus route. This is only because passengers ride on the roof (theoretically illegal), where most of the luggage is. Instead a small backpack can sit between your legs and a larger rucksack can either go in the dusty locked boot at the rear of the bus or you can pay an extra charge to keep it beside you. Note that space inside is at a premium, just when you think the bus is filled to bursting another 10 passengers will squash in.

A pleasant alternative in good weather is to **ride on the roof**. Strategically place your rucksack on the roof (perhaps taped up in a plastic bag or at least with all the pockets empty and the zips locked), and when passengers scramble for the roof, claim this as your 'seat'. A minor disadvantage is that everybody has to cram into the already full bus to pass the checkposts so your luggage will be trampled on by a herd of elephants. While there is anyone on the roof you must be with your and your friends' rucksacks. If there is a chance of rain the baggage is covered by a tarpaulin and difficult to access – for you and thieves.

If riding the roof, wear sunglasses and sunscreen and be sure to watch ahead, especially in the first two hours. Other than April-May and October a windproof jacket is handy and in winter a fleece plus longjohns are essential too.

Kathmandu to Dhunche

Although there are rougher roads in Nepal, the uninitiated may be forgiven for not thinking so. However, the rural scenes, mountain panoramas and thrill of leaving Kathmandu for new adventures make up for the road's neglect and the overcrowded bus. Keep your trekking permit and a pen handy.

Turning right off the Ring Road, you pass through the suburb of Balaju then begin the climb out of the Kathmandu valley. The steel gates on the left mark the entrance to the walled Nagarjun Forest Reserve with its great $3/4$ day mountain bike circuit and Himalaya viewpoint.

Cresting the rim of the valley, a Matterhorn-like pyramid in the Ganesh Himal rises majestically above the middle hills. To the right of this are the Jugal Himal peaks near Gosainkund and behind are the Langtang peaks, including Langtang Lirung 7245m/23,770ft.

When Tilman passed through here there were, of course, no buses. Instead the party had to slog up the hill out of the Kathmandu Valley. They were suffering (as you might be too at this point) but he noted: 'those philosophers who assure the wretched that there is always someone worse off were quite right' (*The Seven Mountain-Travel Books*). Instead of using cows, the villagers were ploughing the fields by hand, the men bent over with their heads almost touching the ground.

About $1\frac{1}{4}$ hours from Kathmandu, just after the Kakani turn off (which leads to another Himalayan viewpoint), the bus frequently makes a toilet stop or an opportunist's photo stop. Ranipauwa is around the corner but the bus no longer stops here for dal bhaat, merely pausing to let passengers clamber onto the roof. The mountain vistas fade as the road descends, torturously winding around endless ridges to eventually cross the Tadi Khola. This drains the watershed bounded by the Gosainkund Lekh and the long ridge that the Gosainkund trek follows all the way to Shivapuri Lekh and Kathmandu.

In the hot low country close to the Trisuli is the Bidur-Nuwakot police checkpost where you have to register. A few minutes after is the lunch stop at one of the grotty Trisuli restaurants; you are now about four hours from Kathmandu and at an altitude of 550m/1800ft – 800m/2625ft lower than in Kathmandu. There is a pump station a minute north of where the bus stops for campers needing petrol. The real town of Trisuli is across the river.

Leaving Trisuli, the road passes the old hydroelectric project then climbs relentlessly for two hours or so to Kalikastan (2050m/6725ft) and another district boundary, which means registering again. Keen eyes will spot some stupas, the first signs you are entering a Buddhist area. An hour further is the Ramche Army Security checkpost. This is on the boundary of the Langtang National Park and the army base here is supposedly to protect it.

At this point you might notice the sign forbidding the honking of horns in the National Park, so as not to disturb the wildlife. However, as veterans of Asia will surely attest, an obnoxiously loud siren is more essential than tread on tires, lights or even a road to the functioning of a vehicle. Our driver's horn finger, involuntarily twitching from the torture of restraint, only lost control a couple of times. The truck driver ahead however, had no such reserves of self-control and his horn blasts echoed around the valley.

National Park Headquarters Perhaps half an hour further on, the road climbs a huge unstable hillside. Sometimes passengers must walk up while the bus valiantly struggles up. During the monsoon the bus may not be able to cross this section, which is two to three hours walk from Dhunche. At the National Park headquarters (called Brabal) you have to register and soldiers usually conduct a baggage search; your national park entrance fee receipt is also checked. If you don't have one you'll have to fork out the Rs650.

There is a small National Park information centre just above where the bus stops although it is often locked and there will be barely enough

---

❏ Ka Kha, Ga Gha and ABC

Chanting together, younger children can often be heard practising their alphabets. The Nepali alphabet features 36 letters; enough, with a couple of accents, to write every word exactly as it is said.

The English alphabet, however, is ill-equipped to show exact pronunciations of English – the spelling of 'the' bears little relation to how it is said – let alone other languages. Nepali, Tamang and Tibetan all have considerably more letters to their alphabets and subtleties unrenderable in plain English. Take Syabru: the true pronunciation is somewhere between *Shyabru* and *Syabru*. Rather than a distinct *sh* it is an aspirated *h*. The second syllable is troublesome too, being somewhere between *bru* and *pru*.

One word that should be pronounced particularly carefully, unless you want to cause no end of amusement for the locals, is the Nepali *thik-chha*, meaning *OK* (the *th* is an aspirated *t*, not *th* as in *the*). Uncomfortably similar sounding is *chik-chha*, the word for sex and a frequently used swear word.

The moral is listen carefully to the locals!

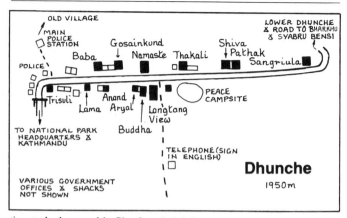

time to look around it. Sign boards briefly explain the geology, the flora and fauna and a little about the local Tamang people. If the bus tears off without you, don't worry – Dhunche is only a five-minute walk around the corner and the driver always stops for a drink there.

DHUNCHE 1950m/6400ft

A painted concrete arch heralds Dhunche. This is the sleepy district headquarters of Rasuwa. Above, spread over the hillside, are government offices and a hospital. Below is the compact old Tamang village of Dhunche that may be worth a quick wander.

In the midst of the Himalaya the views are impressive: steep hillsides surround and to the north, mystical in the haze and teasing the trekker, is a beautiful range of snow peaks in Tibet. A little to the east a couple of the Langtang ice-castles glisten and further east is a glimpse of the rugged hills around Gosainkund, often snow-covered. From the higher parts of Dhunche the Ganesh Himal comes into view.

Beginning from Bharkhu or Syabru Bensi The trekking description from Bharkhu begins on p128, and from Syabru Bensi, p133.

Lodges Although Dhunche has many hotels, most trekkers stay at the *Langtang View Hotel* where the facilities, food and management are a cut above the rest without a price penalty. In mid-1996 the Quality Tourism project and local hotel owners came to the conclusion that Rs10 was not the true cost of a bed. So now there's a more realistic minimum Rs50 charge. This also applies in Syabru Bensi.

Supplies Kerosene is readily available but petrol isn't. Standard goods

Map 1 127

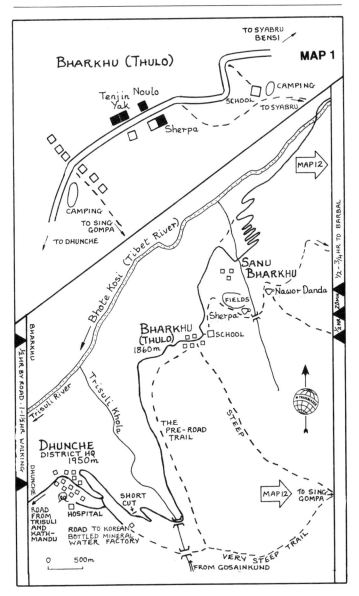

and staples can be obtained but chocolate and other luxuries sell for a higher premium than the closeness of Kathmandu would suggest.

To Kathmandu by bus The bus or buses from Syabru Bensi to Kathmandu pass through Dhunche at around 8am. A limited number of seats are available for reservation.

Planning the first day's walk

Taking three days to walk to Kyangjin means quite a tough first day to Rimche or Changdam/Lama Hotel. The walk to (Thulo) Syabru takes three to four hours not including snack and tea breaks so leave early to lunch there. The afternoon walk is 2½-3½ hours without relaxing along the way. Don't be surprised if you wake up the next morning with stiff legs.

Planning four days to Kyangjin gives more flexibility. Lunch at Barbal then staying at Langmoche is realistic. For a gentle and more cultural day consider staying in (Thulo) Syabru, although this will mean less time for acclimatisation later. The last option is just to see where you end up.

Walking to Bharkhu Simply follow the main road. There is a shortcut to a hairpin bend but it isn't obvious. The walk takes about 1-1¾ hours.

The trail to Sing Gompa Few trekkers should head in this direction because of the too rapid gain in altitude (see Appendix A). At the first hairpin in Dhunche take the side road to the new Korean mineral water factory then skirt above it. Across the khola (actually the Trisuli) the trail begins with a very steep section virtually up a rock face.

DHUNCHE AND BHARKHU [MAP 1, p127]
BHARKHU

While Dhunche is a town and Syabru Bensi aspiring to be one, Bharkhu is most definitely a modest village. It is set amid terraced fields and, once the dust from the bus subsides, is pleasant enough. The kids are playful and the atmosphere relaxed. One of the joys of no electricity is watching the fire-flies dance in the early autumn or late spring.

Lodges There's little to distinguish between the handful of lodges. Village-style popcorn goes down well with an end-of-the-bus-journey beer.

Planning the first day from Bharkhu

If you're aiming to get to Kyangjin in three days you'll have quite a tough

---

(**Opposite**) The locals are always well dressed in Tarkeghyang (see p196).

day to Changdam, even though you have just saved at least an hour's walking by finishing the bus ride here. Lunch is best taken at (Thulo) Syabru. In the afternoon have plenty of snacks to boost your energy for the last uphill stretch. With time to spare it doesn't matter where you end up.

To Sing Gompa The locals tout that the trail from Bharkhu to Sing Gompa is more gentle than the Dhunche trail but there is no getting away from the fact that the altitude difference is 1500m/4900ft. This trail is unmarked on all maps and is difficult to follow.

To (Thulo) Syabru
The trail begins from the small primary school at the northern end of the village. It immediately begins climbing and traversing across steep, sometimes rough country. It is a delightful trail surrounded by beauty – exactly what trekking is about – and in the morning it is pleasantly shaded. Views open out to include parts of the Ganesh Himal and round a ridge, the Langtang Himal. The tall straight pine trees with thin high branches and sparse needles are chir pines, more commonly seen in West Nepal. The other type of pine, lean with a rough grey bark, is *salla* or the blue pine. In the spring its petal-less flowers dust the trail with pollen. Note that Syabru is often called Thulo Syabru to avoid confusion with Syabru Bensi.

To Sing Gompa From the Nawor Danda teashop (a possible lunch spot), a little-used and easily lost track climbs to a grazing area on the ridge, the real Nawor Danda, then meets the main (Thulo) Syabru to Sing Gompa trail, joining it 15 minutes from the teashops on the ridge at 3200m/10,500ft.

Barbal 2300m/7545ft Maple trees and an apple orchard herald the teashops of Barbal. The map is on p138. With 450 vertical metres already under your belt you have completed the bulk of the climb to (Thulo) Syabru. On the north-west valley wall the Chilime hydropower project and the continuation of the amazing road to Somthang can be seen.

The thickening forest is alive with the singing and squawking of birds. In particular, watch for green parrots and listen for woodpeckers. On the forest floor, cattle and plump pheasants rustle the fallen leaves. The wild animals hiding in the undergrowth include the small *mirka* or barking deer which, with luck you might see, and a few others which are better avoided; pigs or perhaps even a bear rooting around. Brown monkeys often cavort Tarzan-style in the tree tops.

(Opposite) Top: Looking east from high in Helambu the hills seem to stretch forever. **Bottom:** In winter through spring snow lies around Gosainkund (see p171).

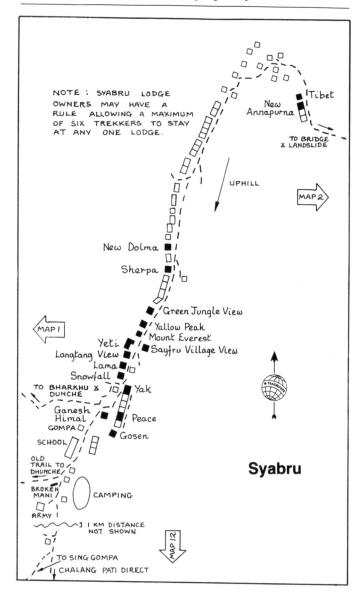

NOTE : SYABRU LODGE
OWNERS MAY HAVE A
RULE ALLOWING A MAXIMUM
OF SIX TREKKERS TO STAY
AT ANY ONE LODGE.

Tibet
New
Annapurna

TO BRIDGE
& LANDSLIDE

UPHILL

MAP 2

New Dolma

Sherpa

MAP 1

Green Jungle View

Yellow Peak
Mount Everest
Sayfru Village View

Yeti
Langtang View
Lama
Snowfall

TO BHARKHU &
DUNCHE

Yak

Ganesh
Himal
GOMPA

Peace

SCHOOL

Gosen

Syabru

OLD
TRAIL TO
DHUNCHE

BROKEN
MANI

CAMPING

ARMY

1 KM DISTANCE
NOT SHOWN

MAP 12

TO SING GOMPA
CHALANG PATI DIRECT

This first day of walking features a surprising amount of variation in the vegetation. Even in a few minutes there can be changes: in the moister shaded areas the forest turns mainly sub-tropical with the first bamboo making an appearance but on the more exposed and dry slopes fir and pine predominate.

After passing slightly above the gompa of Barbal, (Thulo) Syabru soon comes into view as a line of steel roofs and a few fields. Now you are looking directly up part of the Langtang Valley and can begin to appreciate how steep and rugged the valley walls are. Just visible behind (Thulo) Syabru you can make out the landslide (see map p139). From that a long tall ridge rises all the way to the mountains above and where the trail to Gosainkund is. This is the best overall view of the trail up the Langtang you get.

SYABRU 2200m/7220ft

The line of houses sits atop a prominent ridge. Some are made of stone with shingle roofs and a pleasing number of traditional windows, while others show the rub of tourism with their painted concrete-plastered walls and shiny steel roofs. Each has its own sunny flat work area. Here grain is threshed, bamboo mats are woven and women oil their babies. Tables and chairs await the trekker and lodge owners eager for business don't give up until you are seated somewhere.

The people are industrious in other ways too, seldom being still. During planting time the fields are ploughed by men driving an ox team while the women scatter the seeds and cover them before the birds can get them. These fields need occasional weeding but the busiest and happiest time is at harvest when there is an abundance of food. After the back-breaking work of cutting and drying, each grain is threshed in a different way. Millet is pounded using a long stick with a hinged end section that, with some skill, can be landed flat (this is the crop often laid out on rural roads for buses to drive over in order to save threshing). Wheat is first shaken out then ox and cows are driven around in a circle to trample out the rest. The straw is stacked for winter feed.

At other times of the year the cattle need taking out to graze. When crops are in fields they are herded to high pastures a day or two away from the village. Their milk is either turned into butter or sometimes cheese, or it is carried to the various cheese factories where it's sold. Even the women sitting around the village chatting with friends keep busy; they spin wool, knit or pick the lice from each others' hair and they always have a breast ready for the young ones. It is a great place to watch the local world go by. There are also good mountain views if you venture behind the houses to look west. By the time you read this the village should also have electricity.

❑ **So close, yet so far – Tibet**
Half a day up the main valley and across the border is the large Tibetan village of Kyirong (Kyirong Qu), where many of Langtang's more recent immigrants hail from. This is one of the lowest points in Tibet and in geography resembles the Langtang region more than Tibet. In fact until 1788 it was nominally part of Nepal, then the Nepalese invaded parts of Tibet proper. The Tibetans asked the Chinese for help and, in 1791, 70,000 soldiers invaded the valley, fighting their way to Betrawati. This was alarmingly close to Kathmandu for it was from Nuwakot, less than a day's walk south, that Prithvi Nayaran had invaded the valley of Kathmandu, so the Nepalese hurriedly called on the British. They were equally alarmed that 70,000 soldiers could fight their way through the Himalaya (the Russians were swallowing up the Central Asian Khanates and had their sights set on India, inspiring an espionage jousting match called the Great Game to find out what exactly lay between the countries and who the rulers would align themselves with), but interests in Canton (Hong Kong) prevented them from sending over a force. So the Nepalese sued for peace. In return they gave up Kyirong and the high section of the valley that the Arniko (Kathmandu-Lhasa) Highway now follows. In a strange twist the Nepalese blamed the Tibetans who were forced to pay tribute to Kathmandu (which they did only once) while the Nepalese paid tribute once every five years to Beijing, which they did, apparently until 1908.

Kyirong is accessible by jeep track from the Tibetan section of the Kathmandu-Lhasa Friendship highway. For information on trekking here consult Viktor Chan's incredible *Tibet Handbook*, published by Moon Publications.

The village is called Syabru and only occasionally Thulo Syabru but, for some reason known only to locals, if you say Syabru the villagers are immediately confused; is the trekker speaking about Syabru or Syabru Bensi – calling it Thulo (big) Syabru solves this.

Lodges The majority of lodges are clustered at the top end of town where the line of houses on the ridge degenerates into several ragged lines. More are scattered before and after the village. Shops sell Coke, cheeseballs, chocolate and other trekkers' delights. In early 1996, as part of a local initiative to share tourism wealth, lodge owners decided to limit the number of trekkers staying in any one lodge to six, so don't be surprised if you are told the lodge is full. Will this system last? Who knows!

To the landslide
After descending through the fields of (Thulo) Syabru and some cool forest a strong steel bridge spans a bubbly steep khola. A while later are a couple of drinkstops strategically placed for trekkers who have struggled up the half-hour hill (see map p138/166). At the bottom of this the trail merges with the direct trail from Syabru Bensi to cross the landslide. The trail map and description continues on p138.

❏ **Roughing it under the stars**
There is nothing more glorious than sleeping out under the stars. For a single roofless night you don't need a tent, expensive bivvy bag, stove or even a foam pad – just do it!

First, make sure the weather is fine. Next find a spot which gets the early sun and has a view as well as water nearby. If you don't have a sleeping mat, insulate where you are going to sleep with clothes – perhaps even with your empty rucksack. Noodles (two packets?) can be eaten dry (Wai-Wai are the tastiest) with the flavour sachet sprinkled through. Top your water bottle up before nodding off; crunchy noodles make you thirsty. The decadent might bring a can of beer from Kathmandu for this purpose. Of course you deserve chocolate for dessert. Fruit, vegetables or biscuits do for breakfast. Your sleeping bag might be damp with dew by the morning, an excuse to bask in the sun longer...

Finally don't expect a lot of sleep; I was so excited and the stars were so bright that morning came all too soon.

Jen and Andy (Australia)

To Gosainkund See the section beginning p167.

STARTING FROM SYABRU BENSI

Leaving Bharkhu by bus, the endless zigzag descent may trouble the discerning trekker who, of course, will realise that some of the hard-won height is being lost. A few minutes after the Bailey bridge (perhaps even a new bridge) across the Bhote Kosi you can at last remove your battered self from the bus and relax.

SYABRU BENSI 1450m/4757ft

With the arrival of a road and more recently the bus service a new, not particularly attractive, roadhead settlement has sprung up. Aiming the development of tourism facilities in the right direction is a Non-government organisation (NGO) called Quality Tourism. Its successes include the establishment of kitchen gardens and proper toilets.

Above the village is a medium-sized hydro-electricity project (still under construction in March 1997). This scheme will take water from the Chilime stream and pipe it through the mountain to here. The electricity will then be fed into the national grid. Nepal has huge hydroelectric potential but the lackadaisical Nepal Electricity Authority (NEA) has, until recently, only reacted to shortages rather than planned for the future. Nepal and India have finally reached a sensible pricing agreement for cross-border selling; India suffers a chronic power shortage and has spiralling demand.

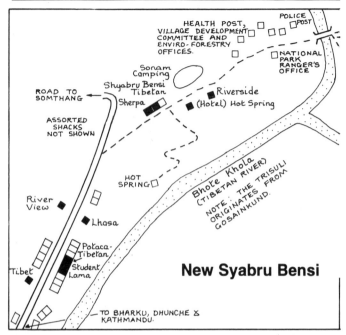

Lodges In contrast to long-developed Dhunche, the lodges lining the road are of recent creation, the first one opening its doors in 1989. All are pleasant enough to stay in, with mattresses thick enough for bruised bodies but for the intrepid who also perhaps have a torch handy, the village map shows more lodges only a few minutes down. If the mention of hot springs bring thoughts of ecstasy, be warned that the water supply is erratic and unreliable in temperature. Sometimes the small concrete pools are bliss, but mostly they disappoint. (There are better pools in the Chilime valley).

Police For a change, Syabru Bensi's police post doesn't want to record your bureaucratic vitals; they merely watch that you aren't heading towards Tibet. From here the border is less than a day's walk away and, in contrast to much of the border which follows mountain ranges, it simply involves a hop across the river near Rasuwa (which the district is named after). Unfortunately the crossing isn't legally open for tourists which, looking back from Laurebina at the incredible mountains, will sadden the avid explorer.

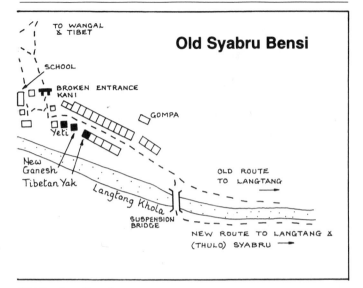

Old Syabru Bensi

After crossing the Bhote Khola a *kani*, a Buddhist devil-cleansing entrance gate, ushers the trekker in. The gompa is sometimes open in the morning and evening and can be opened at other times for tourists. Mime, or ask nearby locals, for the door to be unlocked. As with all gompas you should leave a donation, Rs20 or more, and bear in mind that renovation costs run into tens of thousands of rupees.

Lodges There are a few houses masquerading as lodges; however, facilities are basic. Waking up in the oldest and more cultural part of the village doesn't usually disappoint, especially since the winter sun strikes here first.

Planning the first day

Taking the direct valley route it is 3-4$\frac{1}{2}$ hours actual walking time (perhaps six hours with stops) to Changdam/Lama Hotel. So, once drink breaks, lunch and wildlife spotting time are added, this is a pleasant full day's trekking. It is a gentle but steady uphill walk the whole way so stopping at Rimche often suits tired legs. The fit may want to continue beyond Changdam to the couple of lodges an hour above.

Options for the following day are either take it easy and stay at Ghora Tabela (then Langtang village, then Kyangjin), or push straight on to Langtang village for a three-day trek to Kyangjin and feel the altitude.

❏ **The Great Traders**
The border peoples of Tibet and Nepal have been traders for at least the last 1500 years. This pattern was severely disrupted by China's *Great Leap Forward*, the cultural revolution, but recent inter-government discussion has resulted in a relaxation of restrictions. One of the most visible ancient patterns restored is trade in sheep. As part of Nepal's major festival, Dasain, most Hindus make an animal sacrifice to celebrate the triumph of good over evil. The sacrificial blood runs freely and not just in the temples. It is also used to bless the front wheel of most motorbikes, cars and trucks and even every one of Royal Nepal's planes. Many of the sheep and goats required come from Tibet, having been driven over trading passes a few weeks before the late September or October festival. Originating from Kyirong, huge flocks of sheep stream along the road to Trisuli and beyond.

TO LANDSLIDE
The valley trail
Most maps only show the rather daunting trail that heads from Wangal up to Khangchema/Kangjung and across to Syarpa/Sherpagaon before descending to Rimche and Changdam. Now there are two new trails from Syabru Bensi that follow the river to Landslide. The north bank trail was built in 1991 by Syabru Bensi village volunteers who, when the bus service finished at their door, could see gold in the dust from trekkers' boots. Given the Nepalese ability to walk on anything but water, it is a modest trail with a few short steep stone stairs but can be trekked quite easily. Recently the south bank trail (which begins at the suspension bridge a minute out of old Syabru Bensi) has been upgraded, making this the new main trail.

Once on the south bank the trail flirts with the damp bamboo jungle until Dhomen (1620m/5315ft) where rising smoke signals the teashop, and closer, rising mist reveals a powerful waterfall. With flowers and a kitchen garden, this is a pleasant place for elevenses. Leaving Dhomen, the trail meets the main trail from (Thulo) Syabru to cross the landslide.

The trail description continues on p138.

Via (Thulo) Syabru
After crossing the suspension bridge at the end of old Syabru Bensi, a good trail climbs 750m/2460ft to (Thulo) Syabru and then drops 550m/1800ft to Landslide – which explains why trekkers rarely use this route. The trail climbs through dense bamboo and pine where monkeys frequently frolic. Just before arriving at (Thulo) Syabru the trail opens into a huge field and splits up in view of the village. Follow any of the main paths.

The Bharkhu-(Thulo) Syabru-Landslide alternative is longer than this route but involves considerably less sweat.

THE SHERPAGAON/SYARPA ALTERNATIVE

This involves a stiff climb of more than 600m/2000ft then a bitty traverse to Sherpagaon where there are a couple of lodges. So, rather than the steady gentle climb of the new valley route, the ascent is packed into a steep few hours. The climb aside, the magnificent panorama and the wonderful camping spots mean this trail still deserves consideration – which is why groups favour this route. Other groups haven't yet realised there is a new trail! It is longer than the direct valley route and also involves more up and down.

Independent trekkers have made Rimche in a day, but even the fit have arrived exhausted, and this virtually defeats the purpose of taking this scenic route. It is still a hard first day to Sherpagaon but other than taking a short day only to Bhanjyanggaon or Khangchema, there is little alternative unless you have enough equipment to camp or bivvy out.

There are two possible routes to Sherpagaon. The direct trail from Syabru Bensi to Bhanjyanggaon is unmarked on all maps but is easy enough to find and follow. The longer route, that locals may recommend, begins by heading north after crossing the bridge that divides new and old Syabru Bensi. At Wangal the trail climbs steeply to Khangchema (usually pronounced Kangjung or Kamjung) where there are a few simple lodges, and, close by, a Tibetan refugee settlement. The trail, now heading south, continues climbing and many confusing grazing trails lead off it. Around the ridge the trail is clearer and the views are stunning.

Note that the word *gaon*, which means village in Nepali, is really pronounced *gau,* with a nasalised end to it.

Bhanjyanggaon A cup of tea and biscuits are easy enough to find although there are no real lodges. Numerous grazing trails lead off the main path so don't be afraid to ask locals for directions.

Sherpagaon Syarpa is the historic name of the village but now it's usually called Sherpagaon. A couple of houses have signboards purporting to be lodges and other villagers offer cups of tea. Way above is the Pangsang Kharka. Further east this ridge turns mountainous, forming the Langtang peaks. The track joins the main Langtang trail at Rimche, p140.

❑ **Naming children**

Children are usually named three days after the birth when the mother and child are ritually washed. The naming ceremony is usually performed by a lama and this is the day when lady luck is said to come and write the destiny of the child.

The first feeding of solid food is celebrated and a decorative spoon is used, sometimes made from a bird's beak so as to give a sweet voice.

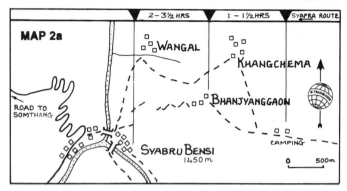

SYABRU BENSI AND LANDSLIDE   [MAPS 2&3]

LANDSLIDE TO LANGTANG

The trails from (Thulo) Syabru and Syabru Bensi join at the western edge of the landslide. The junction is small and unless looking for it, easy to miss. Continuing movement of the 1985 landslide may also change the geography.

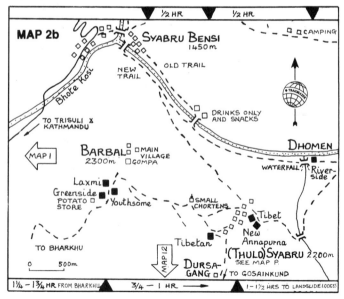

The two sides of the valley are strikingly different here. The sunny north side is steep and dry; cacti grow and the hillsides of golden grass are too steep to be grazed. In contrast the south side is moist, shady forest.

Landslide/Pahero 1650m/5413ft The simple teahouses of Landslide are a safe ¼hour from the actual landslide.

To Langmoche From the teahouses the trail broadens into an old and well-used path. Gnarled roots form natural steps and fallen leaves carpet the trail. The canopy shades the forest floor leaving much of it open, a sure sign of a mature forest. Several troupes of Langur monkeys live among these huge trees. A startled rustle in the branches might alert you as they flee. Careful eyes will usually spot them. With their handsome grey coats, white-framed fine black faces with fearful eyes and their long tails, they are easy to differentiate from the other species found in Nepal.

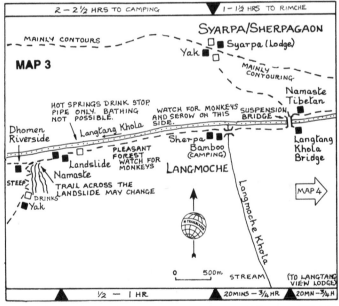

The brown monkey prefers more open terrain, especially steep hillsides like the opposite side of the valley from here, where they can often be spotted. With a thinner coat they also prefer warmer sunnier climates. While Langurs are generally shy of people, brown monkeys aren't always. They will boldly snatch food or pick the pockets of the unwary, especially children. They have even been known to attack a lone villager in the forest. Also they occasionally imitate people and learn to throw stones so beware of accidentally teaching them!

Both species have an unfortunate liking for crops such as potatoes and especially bananas (strange, that!) and suntala (Nepalese mandarin orange), which earns them the wrath of villagers. As a result monkeys and villagers have a mutual fear and hatred of each other.

Villagers will attack troublesome troupes of monkeys but not the *eklai dehduwa*, the lone male out to form a new troupe. He is considered special, a form of Hanuman, the monkey god.

Langmoche Khola/Bamboo 1980m/6500ft

For a long time the only lodge here was Bamboo, hence the name. Now that there are more, perhaps it should be called Langmoche (pronounced Langmoché), the name of the khola and the old local name.

The valley walls pitilessly tighten above you and the violent boulder-choked khola steepens to a death-to-kayakers grade. In the dappled shade the less optimistic could call the barely sunned gorge forbidding or gloomy, but with good hosts, warm fires and copious food it takes on a different perspective. In the hot season, when trekkers are sweltering in the strong sun elsewhere, this shaded gorge is particularly pleasant.

The suspension bridge 2100m/6890ft Here, by a couple of lodges, the trail crosses to the northern side of the effervescent Langtang Khola, remaining on this side all the way to Kyangjin.

The Schneider map and copies of it mark a trail heading from the bridge up the south valley wall to Chadang and Gosainkund. There was a trail once but it no longer exists and the steepness of the cliffs reveals why; several ill-informed trekkers have died descending it.

On the next section of trail beware of the stinging nettles that line the path. Locals occasionally cut these down, not so much for the benefit of the passers-by but to make soup with. If boiled for at least 10 minutes the leaves are softened and the sting neutralised. Smaller lodges occasionally use nettles to bulk out vegetable dishes. If you wish to try it, ask for *sisnoo*. Stinging nettles can also be used to make a fabric called *allo*, the latest trend, together with hemp clothing, in Kathmandu.

RIMCHE & CHANGDAM TO GHORA TABELA   [MAP 4]

Rimche/Rimiche 2300m/7550ft

Nestled in the cool forest is *Hotel Langtang View*, the first of the lodges preceding Changdam (Lama Hotel). *Hotel Ganesh View* is next. Neither are accurately named but at least by this stage there are occasional views. Close by is the third of the trio, the warmly named *Hotel Evening View*. All three are pleasant and are good alternatives to the lodges at Changdam. Sometimes rich curd can be found here. Between Hotel

Map 4 141

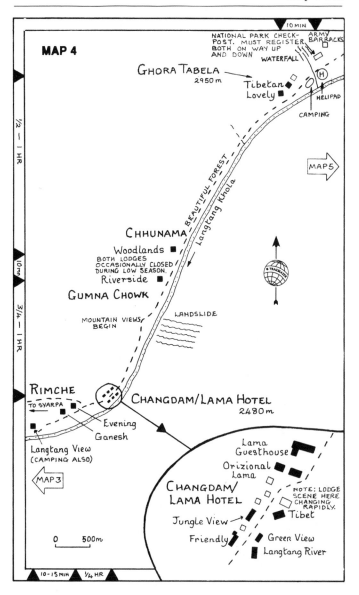

MAP 4

10 MIN

NATIONAL PARK CHECK-
POST. MUST REGISTER
BOTH ON WAY UP
AND DOWN

ARMY
BARRACKS

WATERFALL

GHORA TABELA
2950 m

Tibetan ◆
Lovely ■

(H)

HELIPAD

CAMPING

MAP 5

BEAUTIFUL FOREST

Langtang Khola

CHHUNAMA

Woodlands ■
BOTH LODGES
OCCASIONALLY CLOSED
DURING LOW SEASON.
Riverside ■

GUMNA CHOWK

MOUNTAIN VIEWS
BEGIN

LANDSLIDE

½ – 1 HR

10 mn

¾ – 1 HR

RIMCHE
TO SYARPA ■ ← ■

Evening
Ganesh

■ Langtang View
(CAMPING ALSO)

MAP 3

CHANGDAM/LAMA HOTEL
2480 m

Lama
Guesthouse

Orizional
Lama

CHANGDAM/
LAMA HOTEL

NOTE: LODGE
SCENE HERE
CHANGING
RAPIDLY.

■ Tibet

Jungle View ■

Friendly ■

■ Green View

■ Langtang River

0   500m

10 – 15 MIN   ¼ HR

Langtang View and Hotel Ganesh View the trail climbs into sunnier regions, a blessing in the cold and a minor curse in the heat.

Changdam/Lama Hotel 2480m/8136ft

Once this was a single hotel (hence the tourist name), but now Changdam is a compact lodge-village. Many trekkers and most groups stay here so it gets busy. Crowds can easily be avoided by staying at one of the three lodges at Rimche. The latest addition to the lodge scene is the New Lama Guesthouse at the top of town. Grander than the rest, this lodge has started a spate of building as other lodges try to compete on the basis of looks, rather than service. Since all lodges charge a nominal sum for a bed, the food in the larger lodges tends to be more expensive; this is something trekkers on a tight budget should note for here, Langtang and Kyangjin. The New Lama Guesthouse is owned by a corrupt Langtang businessman (see p146).

To Ghora Tabela There are a couple of lodges en route. These are always open in the peak season, otherwise somewhat randomly.

Some sections of the forest are particularly beautiful – 'big scraggly fuzzy trees', says Mary (USA).

Ghora Tabela/Qurpu-nesa/Tara 2950m/9678ft

The valley begins opening out close to Ghora Tabela and once at the lodges you suddenly feel as if you have finally got somewhere. Looking back, your eyes tell you what your legs have known for several days – you have gained considerable height. Now the altitude is close to 3000m. A feature of most treks in Nepal is the higher you climb up a valley the bigger and more disdainful the mountains above seem to get – this is particularly true here.

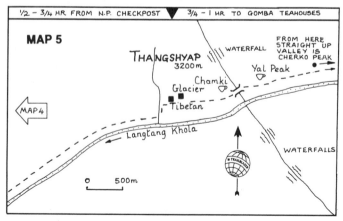

When the inveterate trekker Hugh Swift first visited here at the end of the 1960s it was inhabited by Tibetan Khampas and everyone – trekkers and Khampas alike – slept in the gompa. Now there are a couple of nondescript lodges.

For an insignificant-looking place it has many names. Ghora Tabela in Nepali means horse grazing area which the extensive pastures suit perfectly; horses are less protected against the cold than yaks and so need lower altitude grazing areas. Qurpu-nesa is the Tibetan name and relates to where the man of the Langtang story (see 'The settling of Langtang', p120) rested (*nesa*); *Qurpu,* or variations of this, is the name for the many small trees loaded with yellow berries (in season). In Nepali these berries are called *rhuiss*. They are sour but edible and are used in *achhaar* and in medicines. Monkeys and bears eat them too. The red berries of the similar-looking tree, however, are poisonous.

The last name, *Tara,* means stars in Nepali and perhaps relates to this being the first place you can easily see them on the way up. Strangely no village name refers to the other striking feature around here – the incredible waterfalls.

National Park Checkpost 3040m/9975ft
Here your trekking permit details are noted and your National Park entrance fee receipt is checked by the friendly staff. Around 40 army security personnel and a couple of National Park staff are based here.

Now in open country this is where, in winter, you might meet snow. At this point is it usually short-lived; the amount of traffic to Langtang village means it is often just a muddy path.

THANGSHYAP TO LANGTANG   [MAPS 5&6]

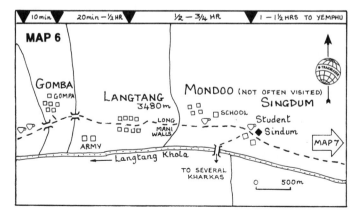

Thangshyap 3200m/10,500ft

Fields begin here, all belonging to Langtang village. There are a couple of simple but pleasant lodges and some random drinkstops further up.

Langtang Gompa

First, two teahouses vie for your attention, then – around the corner and just far enough up the hill to discourage casual visitors – is the Langtang Gompa. The weary can save the hill for the rest day in Langtang village. The gompa is occasionally open in the morning or evening but isn't normally unlocked just for tourists to look around. The smaller temple beside it is often open though.

One of the lama's jobs is to pray for rain when the crops are planted, and if the rain comes at an inappropriate time, to ask for it to be stopped. I remarked that his prayers seemed to be working but the villagers said that there are usually light afternoon showers in May and what was needed was some real rain, so his job is more difficult than at first imagined. And rain at the right time is critical. The 3500m altitude means the frost-free growing season is short, leaving the villagers very dependent on the success of the one crop a year. At this altitude what they can grow is also limited to a few vegetables including mulla (giant radish), potatoes, garlic and onion. The cereals grown are buckwheat, barley and sometimes wheat. Corn, millet and rice don't grow. Now at least tourism offers a monetary buffer against crop failure. Previously people would either starve or have to temporarily move from the area.

Any lama worth his butter in Langtang or Helambu can mystically drill holes in rock and around this gompa you can find several of these mysterious holes. Another feature of the rocks around here are garnets.

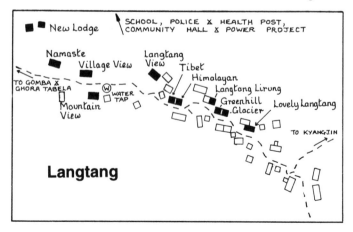

The better quality ones are rough red crystals but most look more like crystals of rust in the hard white quartz rock. A gem-quality vein has yet to be found.

Towering above to the north (left) are a couple of peaks, both of which locals call Langtang Lirung. This is the sacred peak for the area so the lama makes special prayers for those who attempt to climb it – not just to wish them luck but to protect the area in case the spirits become angry with the climbers.

LANGTANG 3480m/11,417ft

Close to the village, water-powered manis greet the trekker and perhaps some lodge-owners or their children keen for your business. In contrast to the lodge settlements between (Thulo) Syabru and here, Langtang is a proper village. The houses have shingle roofs instead of Tibetan flat roofs. Walls are a mixture of local stone, the gaps often filled with dung, and a few are graced by traditional latticed windows.

You are now more than a thousand metres higher than Changdam and will probably be feeling the extra altitude; a rest day is recommended although rarely taken. Drinking plenty of fluids also helps.

The valley is still steep-sided, with little opportunity for exploring except to a couple of kharkas on the opposite side. Only a few mountain tips can be seen from the village but 10 minutes or so up the path to Kyangjin the views open out. Sunsets there can be spectacular, with Kangchenpo/Fluted Peak turning pink or occasionally crimson.

The Hydro-electric scheme and the nearby community building are part of a small Japanese development project. During 1997 the hydro system should generate around 2kw then, once it is running smoothly, it has the potential to produce around 8kw (which is roughly the peak use of a single house in the west with the hot water heater, stove and other gadgets running). The lights often burn late at the community hall when adult education classes are held. These are well attended, especially by the women of the village.

Lodges Most of the lodges have double rooms and a separate dining room with a stove for warmth. Despite long exposure to trekkers, for many of the Langtang people speaking Nepali is difficult enough, let alone English.

❏ Langtang cookies
Sue nudged me, 'Take a look at that!' – she had noticed a local eating what looked like the strongest hash cookie I had ever seen. In fact it looked as if it was entirely hash, never mind the cookie. Alas it turned out to be *alum*, dried vegetables that are crushed and moulded into a snack-sized biscuit.

❏ Power people

The long-time chairman of the Village Development Committee (VDC) is known as an astute businessman. Despite his modest salary and the demands of his job he and his family now own a string of lodges in the Langtang valley: Namaste in Dhunche; Lama Guesthouse in Changdam; one of the Ghora Tabela lodges; Village View in Langtang village; Yala Peak and Himalayan in Kyangjin. Not only that, the only working water tap in the village (in 1996) just happened to be beside his house and lodge.

In the last election he won by the narrow margin of six votes, and this – according to the opposition – was despite the fact that other candidates were banned from the village for the three days before the election by the police in his pocket. Apparently he bought everyone in the village raksi and gave cash handouts.

A good VDC committee can catalyse considerable development but here blatant self-interest has ruled. As part of the *Aphno gaon, aphno bounaaunu* or 'you make your village' decentralisation policy, VDCs are given funds to spend as they like. The Langtang villages' share of the Rs800,000 for 1995-6 was languishing in the bank, despite the fact the school had lost its roof and had been unusable for half a year in 1996. He stood for election again in 1997.

Police and Health post Between the main village and the hydro scheme, by the school, is a combined police post and health post. You are supposed to register with the policeman here but, being off the main trail, many people don't. The health post is similarly relaxed. As is semi-typical around Nepal the health assistant (the person in charge) spends most of his/her time in Kathmandu. Why? Well, here it's too cold in winter (October to May) and during the monsoon it rains a lot, and of course Kathmandu is the best place to sell the medicine which is supposed to be given out free. Then if you don't have supplies, what is the use of being here?

For a developing country Nepal has a surprisingly good health system – that is on paper. Each district headquarters should have a hospital and each Village Development Committee (VDC) area should have a sub-healthpost run by several health assistants while areas with large concentrations of people have a full health post staffed by a doctor, several nurses and health assistants. The realities are unfortunately different. The most effective way to run health posts for the benefit of the community, not just the salaried workers' pocket, is to use local staff – as most development agencies have realised. Someone from the village has a much greater sense of responsibility to their community and, as often as not, actually wants to live there. This accounts for the success of health posts set up by Hillary's Himalayan Trust in the Khumbu, and Ghandruk's in the Annapurna region which was set up with the help of the Annapurna Conservation Area Project (ACAP). Similarly schools produce better

❏ **Ultimate water-ice**

The north-facing slopes of the Langtang Valley boast some outstanding water-ice climbing routes, incredible frozen waterfalls and ice-choked mixed route gullies. There must be at least 15 climbs of grade three up to the limit. If this valley was in the US the concentration of routes would make it big time famous.

Across from Shingdum we climbed a steep six-pitch gully route that we named 'O2 and you'. The ice was azure blue and a perfect consistency for screws. The altitude certainly got the lungs pumping and the view of Langtang Lirung was exhilarating.

There are many more classics awaiting a first ascent. Scout anything east of Ghora Tabela. The best period is January through February and instinct says that heavier winter snows might produce the best conditions. Best of all, most of the routes could be climbed in a day from lodges in the valley. Go for it!
Shane Capron (with Paul Lachapelle) (USA)

results using local teachers, and police are less troublesome if a few locals are in the force too. Unfortunately the standard Nepali system has yet to take these factors into account and worse still it discourages development agencies' attempts to improve health posts and schools.

Around Langtang village

If you take a rest day or half a rest day don't feel guilty if you didn't even make it out of the village. There is comparatively little to see and nothing that shouldn't be missed. If you skipped the gompa on the way in visiting it is an obvious choice, although it may not be open.

Simply watching village life can be rewarding. In the morning, children who don't attend school herd the sheep and cattle out with excessive vigour, each of them proudly displaying their bag with lunch in it and the accompanying level of responsibility.

The village of **Mondoo**, just off the trail to Kyangjin, is one that sees few trekkers. The long mani wall on the trail to Kyangjin is also worth looking at unencumbered. During May the surrounding fields are ploughed and sown. September into early October is harvest time. The trail up to the glacier that lies hidden to the north above Langtang village unfortunately requires a rope and prickle-proof trousers for any worthwhile views. The energetic could scramble up through the kharkas of **Palbu**, across from Shingdum – the views get better and better.

If you aren't planning to stay any higher it is quite possible to visit Kyangjin and Kyangjin Peak, even Kyimoshung Peak, in a day from Langtang.

Heading down, if you are cutting it fine, it's just possible to reach Syabru Bensi in a long tough day from Langtang village.

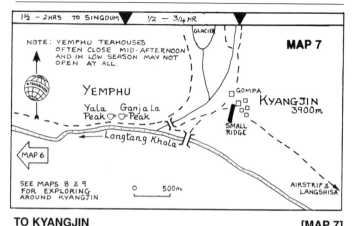

TO KYANGJIN [MAP 7]

This is a half-day walk with a hill at the beginning and end just so that it isn't too easy. Visiting Mondoo village is an option if you want to extend your day.

Yemphu A few women either come up from Langtang or down from Kyangjin to open the teahouses here, so if you're passing by late in the afternoon don't count on them being open. While here I watched crows waiting to steal chocolate bars – the reason why many shops have wire netting doors. However, the mesh you see over lodge windows is to stop the weight of winter snow smashing the window panes.

Directly across the valley adventurous climbers may want to check out a possible route up Naya Kanga that isn't mentioned in Bill O'Connor's *Trekking Peaks of Nepal*. The first part, climbing out of the valley floor, may be difficult though.

Out of Yemphu the trail heads for the bridge across the stream from the Langtang Lirung Glacier then climbs among moraine to the still-hidden lodges of Kyangjin.

KYANGJIN 3900m/12,800ft

Cresting a minor ridge, a surprising array of lodges greets the trekker. Prices vary considerably but all owners complain about how far they are from Kathmandu, quite a misconception if compared with many other areas of Nepal.

According to knowledgeable locals, Kyangjin is erroneously called Kyangjin Gompa by cheaper maps and other guide books. The gompa's name is Gyaltshan while the area is called Kyangjin or Kyangjin Kharka, as on the Austrian Alpine Club map.

Some people who have taken three days to get here from the road suffer minor altitude problems at first. If you find yourself troubled, take it easy and drink plenty of fluids; Diamox may also help. Although not common, it's possible to suffer serious problems at this altitude. A Nepali porter died of AMS here in autumn 1996. Altitude sickness is covered in detail in Appendix B.

A new army post has been constructed just below Kyangjin as part of the musk deer reserve project. The opposite side of the valley is perfect musk deer country but they have suffered at the hands of hunters who lay sprung leg wires to trap them. The musk pod of a mature male fetches up to US$500, which is why hunting is difficult to control. Recently, Chinese have began farming musk deer and have discovered a way of extracting the musk without killing the animal; this may eventually have an impact on illegally hunted pods. (The ideal solution might be to set up a similar farm here too). Musk is often used in perfumes, a market that is growing rapidly. It is a shame that musk deer have been hunted so ruthlessly. Normally they are quiet animals who, if left alone, are at ease with humans. In the Khumbu it is now possible to approach within 10 metres of deer before they get nervous; when they are threatened by other wild animals they often seek refuge in a village where they know predators won't risk venturing.

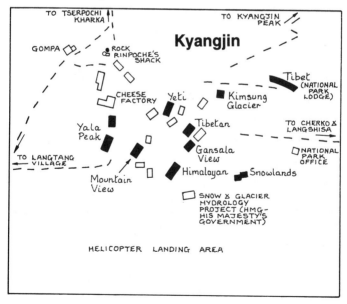

❏ **Yaks and naks**
Around Kyangjin you are bound to see yaks (males), and brimoos/naks (females). There are also crossbreeds which are often mistaken for the real thing but, with experience, telling them apart is easy. Mature yaks and naks have a distinctive double curve in their symmetric horns; up, out and back. The cross-breeds have only a single curve with the horns pointing up and out, often lop-sided. Additionally real yaks are heavier in build and have longer shaggier hair, the better to withstand the brisk winter. Zopkio, the male cross between a Tibetan bull and a brimoo, are used for ploughing. The female cross, a chauri, chaunri or dimo is valued for producing twice as much milk as a nak. The Tibetan word for good is *yakpo* and *yakpodoo*, a measure of how important the yak is to Tibetans.

Cheese factory Kyangjin boasts Nepal's first cheese factory. It was set up with Swiss technical assistance in 1965 and is still government run. During the production season, June to November, villagers bring full aluminium milk urns from the kharkas nearby. Milk is brought to the boil to pasteurise it, then it is turned into a rich cheese using traditional swiss methods. The modest factory turns out around 6500kg of yak (really *brimoo* or *nak* cheese in a season. The cheese rounds are carried to the road where they go to Kathmandu; some are exported to India. Strong yak cheese is available during the season for just under US$4 per kg. The cheese factory is also a good place to breakfast on delicious curd. This comes either mixed with thick honey or honey and muesli. Out of season they often still have curd; it's partially made from milk powder but it's still good.

Gyaltshan Gompa This is open only during festivals, the key being held by the Langtang lama. Nearby is a large rock and the retreat of a Tibetan Rinpoche. He hates visitors and has a dog whose barking made me want to keep my distance.

Heading down The description begins p162.

DAY TRIPS FROM KYANGJIN [MAPS 8&9, p152-3]
Kyangjin and Kyimoshung peaks
Climbing these twin peaks (Kyangjin is 4350m/14,271ft and Kyimoshung 4620m/15,157ft) is a must for even the shortest of visits to Kyangjin. The prayer flags on the rocky peak directly above Kyangjin are only 1-1½ hours up and the as yet unseen but higher peak behind is a further ½-¾ hour up. From the top, the face of Langtang Lirung is formidable. Note that the walls of the mountain are so steep that the snow avalanches off to form the glacier below rather than collecting up the sides of the bowl. To the south-east, Cherko (Tsergo Ri) squats just left of

the savagely beautiful 6387m/20,955ft Kangchenpo or Fluted Peak.

Past the saddle to the east is a slightly higher point, 4670m/15,321ft high. The first summit is easily reached but is exposed and airy. Somehow it is less satisfying than Kyimoshung since the jagged ridge continues to get higher.

Locals were surprisingly vague about the real name for Kyangjin Peak; Phrana Chombo/Phrana Chenpo which means 'big black rock', was one suggestion. Others called the higher point Phushung (which means 'deep, windy valley'). Still others said these places didn't really have a name, and indeed Schneider left them unnamed on the first Helambu-Langtang map.

Going down There are several choices:
• go back the way you came;
• from the saddle east of Kyimoshung drop down the valley to the south;
• from the saddle drop down around the back. At the beginning there are a couple of good trails but on the valley floor they peter out. The options are wading through the scrub, staying mainly on the south side of the main khola, or picking up small trails on the north side of the khola. Allow one to two hours to return to Kyangjin.

Tserpochi Kharka
This small kharka north of Kyangjin is an hour or so away. It is a good place to eye-ball Langtang Lirung's awesome face and to check out the rough Lirung Glacier close up. The scary Kyimoshung icefall is at a neck-cricking angle above. Ever wondered how big a hole a 50-tonne boulder would make if it fell out of the sky. Well, even if you haven't, you can see the result of a 200m or so fall; a few of the larger boulders landed here during the spring of 1996. It is possible to follow the ablation valley up further but beware of rock fall from the huge 1500m rock face above.

Tshona Kharka tarns and forest
From the edge of Kyangjin you can see tarns (small lakes) on the main valley floor. These are only half an hour's walk from Kyangjin. Wandering around them is pleasant and relaxing. In late spring the forest floor above is littered with wildflowers.

Cherko (Tsergo Ri) 4984m/16,351ft
Situated like an island of enlightenment among a sea of ice and mountains, this is the most rewarding day trip out of Kyangjin. It is also the most strenuous and is better attempted after being at Kyangjin for a couple of nights. Take windproof clothing, sunscreen, plenty of water, some snacks and something for lunch.

There are several routes up. The quickest and most brutal is via Tarche Pesa and the west spur. Leaving Kyangjin, take the upper trail a

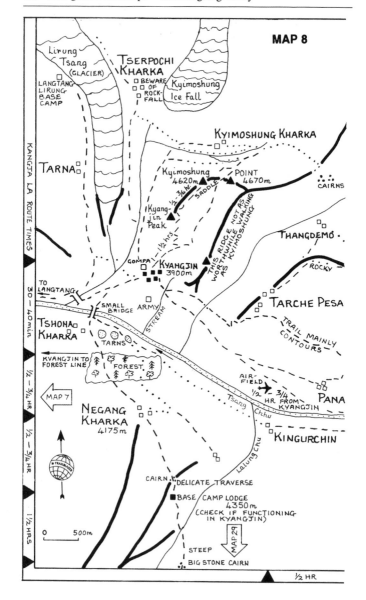

MAP 8

Lirung Tsang (GLACIER)

TSERPOCHI KHARKA

BEWARE OF ROCK-FALL

Kyimoshung Ice Fall

LANGTANG LIRUNG BASE CAMP

KANGJA LA ROUTE TIMES

KYIMOSHUNG KHARKA

TARNA

Kyimoshung 4620m

POINT 4670m

CAIRNS

SADDLE

¾ hr

Kyang-jin Peak

THANGDEMO

½ hrs

THIS RIDGE NOT AS WORTHWHILE WALKING AS KYIMOSHUNG

GOMPA

KYANGJIN 3900m

ROCKY

TO LANGTANG

30 – 40 min

SMALL BRIDGE

ARMY

STREAM

TARCHE PESA

TSHOHA KHARKA

TARNS

TRAIL MAINLY CONTOURS

½ – ¾ HR

KYANGJIN TO FOREST LINE

FOREST

AIR-FIELD

½

¾ HR FROM KYANGJIN

PANA

MAP 7

½ – ¾ HR

Tsang Chu

NEGANG KHARKA 4175m

KINGURCHIN

½ – ¾ HR

N TRAILBLAZER

Lalung Chu

0   500m

CAIRN

DELICATE TRAVERSE

½ HRS

BASE CAMP LODGE 4350m (CHECK IF FUNCTIONING IN KYANGJIN)

MAP 29

STEEP

BIG STONE CAIRN

½ HR

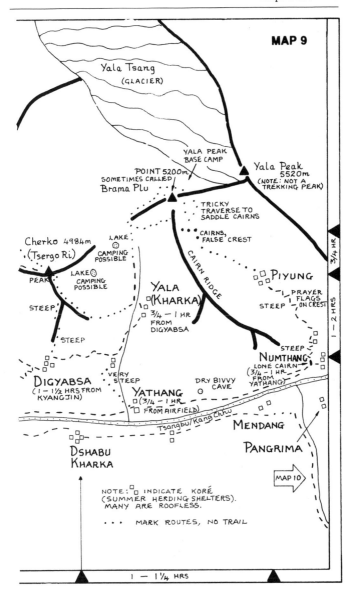

MAP 9

Yala Tsang
(GLACIER)

YALA PEAK
BASE CAMP

POINT 5200m
SOMETIMES CALLED
Brama Plu

▲ Yala Peak
5520m
(NOTE: NOT A
TREKKING PEAK)

TRICKY
TRAVERSE TO
SADDLE CAIRNS

CAIRNS,
FALSE CREST

Cherko 4984m
(Tsergo Ri)

LAKE
CAMPING
POSSIBLE

LAKE
CAMPING
POSSIBLE

PEAK

STEEP

STEEP

YALA
(KHARKA)
3/4 - 1 HR
FROM
DIGYABSA

CAIRN RIDGE

PIYUNG

PRAYER
FLAGS
ON CREST

STEEP

3/4 HR

1 - 2 HRS

DIGYABSA
(1 - 1½ HRS FROM
KYANGJIN)

VERY
STEEP

YATHANG
(3/4 - 1 HR
FROM AIRFIELD)

DRY BIVVY
CAVE

STEEP

Numthang
LONE CAIRN
(3/4 - 1 HR
FROM
YATHANG)

MENDANG

Tsangbu/Kang Chhu

PANGRIMA

DSHABU
KHARKA

MAP 10

NOTE: ☐ INDICATE KORÉ
(SUMMER HERDING SHELTERS).
MANY ARE ROOFLESS.

• • • MARK ROUTES, NO TRAIL

1 - 1¼ HRS

few minutes out (this is usually marked). Over the khola the trail begins climbing. Simply continue up that ridge. Pass mainly above the first set of kore and climb to the next set. From here, Cherko is straight up on the right and the route heads to the ridge where there is a vague track that clambers up among boulders. The summit is a tough three to four hours from Kyangjin. Mountain machines could make it in two hours.

An alternative route traverses from just below the first set of huts. The clear trail roughly traverses to the stacked kore of Digyabsa. Climb up beside these. The quick way to the summit is simply to head up the ridge from here then join the main, more gentle ridge to the summit.

Otherwise continue contouring and climbing. Passing above a few more kore, the path crosses the stream and climbs to the kore of Yala and several more choices. The most direct way is to recross the stream and climb and skirt around on the vague tracks until you find yourself on a ridge that leads to the summit, $^3/_4$-$1^1/_4$ hours up. Alternatively, continue up until the soft summit appears to the east and make your way over the bitty terrain.

The summit This has got to be one of the best trekkers viewpoints on planet earth or at least planet Langtang. From the prayer flags you can see Kyangjin and, further down the valley, a couple of the villages near Langtang, but not Langtang village itself. You look down on Kyangjin Peak and Kyimoshung while Langtang Lirung rears above them. To the north-east is the wide stepped Yala Glacier and at the right end of this is Yala Peak. More or less below this, but part of the closer ridge system, is the cairn-topped point (5200m/17,060ft). This is a jagged ridge but nevertheless has been traversed by master cairn-builders.

Across the main valley is the complex terrain around the trekking peak Naya Kanga and the Kangja La. With the aid of a map you might be able to pick out the rough route. If the rocky ridge across the stream from the base camp lodge is snow-covered then the pass is a no-go. Look also for the large cairn at the top of this minor ridge. You may be able to cross the pass if there is light snow only above this higher point.

Heading down The options are similar to those on the way up. For Yala follow the gentle ridge down heading in the same direction if the trail peters out. Yala is $^1/_2$-$^3/_4$ hour down.

Taking the steep, partly scree descent to Digyabsa loses altitude rapidly.

Yala The lowest kore is a one-roomed lodge that is open only during peak season. Until it is expanded it can sleep only three or four people. For security take a sleeping mat and check the situation with people returning from there. There are enough tent spots for a group to camp here.

Camping near Cherko The large semi-flat area to the east of the summit has several small lakes which provide the water needed for camping. Comfortable flat spots for tents are harder to come by.

LANGSHISA AND PANGRIMA   [MAP 10, p157]

To Langshisa

This popular day trip will only partially satisfy a craving to find out how far the valley extends. Although the trail mainly follows the valley floor there are good mountain views, especially after the small climb over the moraine of the Phrul Rangtshan Glacier. Yaks and sometimes horses graze along here, except during winter.

It is a long day trip and many people choose to stop at the moraine rather than Langshisa. The views are worth the walk but if tossing up between Langshisa and Cherko (Tsergo Ri), the Cherko climb definitely wins.

The Airstrip Once used for six-seater Pilatus Porter charters, the airstrip now sees little use. Instead helicopters prefer to land directly at Kyangjin.

Yathang This is where the Yala Chu falls into the valley. About 20 minutes past it you can see a bivvy cave full of sheep shit. When Tilman was walking up to Langshisa in 1949 he noted:

In the course of the conversation these herdsmen confirmed the existence, or rather the recent presence of, the Abominable Snowman in the Langtang, pointing out to us a cave which had been his favourite haunt. Six years previously these beasts (whose existence is surely no longer a matter of conjecture) had been constant visitors but had apparently migrated elsewhere. The small kind, the size of a child, they called 'chumi', while the big fellow went by the name of 'yilmu'. Since sceptics like to affirm that the tracks made by these creatures are in reality bear tracks, it is worth mentioning that the herdsmen were able to show us some fresh bear tracks. Tilman, *The Seven Mountain-Travel Books*

It might have been this very cave.

Numthang Unmarked on any map, this set of roofed kore are just past the distinctive lone cairn. During October and November, drinks and snacks are sold from one of the small buildings. If you wish to stay the night it would pay to bring a sleeping mat. It is quite possible that in a few years a slightly more substantial lodge may be built but, if so, it will still only be a peak season affair.

The trail moves further away from the main river past Numthang. Further up a glacier moraine pushes across the valley. There are cairns on top but don't head for these; instead stay low and cross the stream. This washed the trail out a while ago so follow a small trail that climbs to the old main path. Climbing further around, the valley opens out and the single roofed kore of Langshisa comes into view.

Langshisa

There's not much to do at Langshisa other than admire the view and wonder where all the valleys end. The massive, heavily glaciated peak is Dome Blanc and the peak with the long scree slopes running half way up it is Langshisa Ri.

In spring 1997 there was no lodge. During the peak season drinks and snacks are sometimes available here: ask at Kyangjin.

A few minutes further up the valley is a large rock close to the river, which is usually topped by prayer flags. This is the rock where the Langtang bull's skin was stretched out; locals point out the blood marks that still remain though sometimes they say this is part of the skin which has now fused with the rock (see 'The settling of Langtang', p120).

CAMPING ABOVE KYANGJIN

There are lots of choices and probably the most difficult decision is where to go first. A good map aids the process of identifying peaks and features. Note the security warning on p72.

During May naks and year-old calves are moved up to Kyangjin and further up the valley. Meanwhile the yaks and the zopkio plough the fields and planting begins. This massive job is finished in late May so from the beginning of June all yaks, naks and crossbreeds are banned from the cropping areas. First the animals are taken to Kyangjin and up the valley. Then as the grass at lower altitudes is consumed family members move the animals to the high kharkas off the main valley. The naks are milked to produce cheese, butter and delicious curd. By October the crops have been harvested and the animals slowly return to the village areas.

Yala Peak 5520m/17,060ft

On a satisfaction level the ascent of Yala Peak is hard to beat, especially for the non-mountaineer. Walking on a glacier is fascinating, provided you know you are safe.

This is true alpine territory so take a guide who knows the mountain unless you are a mountaineer. Several locals at Kyangjin purport to be guides; they are hardly skilled mountaineers but they do have what it takes for Yala, providing the conditions are good. The standard plan is to camp a night at Yala Peak Base Camp then go for the summit early the next morning and return to Kyangjin. The guides provide tents and meals and lead the way on the glacier. You need a ski pole or even better, an ice axe; crampons are useful too. The guides have a limited supply of equipment but it is better not to count on this. Whether crampons are needed

Map 10 157

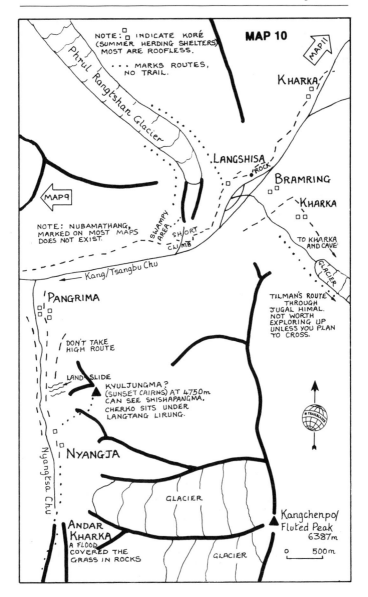

MAP 10

NOTE: ☐ INDICATE KORÉ
(SUMMER HERDING SHELTERS)
MOST ARE ROOFLESS.

· · · · MARKS ROUTES,
NO TRAIL.

Phrul Rangtshan Glacier

KHARKA

LANGSHISA
ROCK

BRAMRING

KHARKA

NOTE: NUBAMATHANG,
MARKED ON MOST MAPS
DOES NOT EXIST.

SWAMPY AREA

SHORT CLIMB

TO KHARKA
AND CAVE

GLACIER

Kang/Tsangbu Chu

TILMAN'S ROUTE
THROUGH
JUGAL HIMAL.
NOT WORTH
EXPLORING UP
UNLESS YOU PLAN
TO CROSS.

PANGRIMA

DON'T TAKE
HIGH ROUTE

LAND SLIDE

KYULJUNGMA?
(SUNSET CAIRNS) AT 4750m
CAN SEE SHISHAPANGMA.
CHERKO SITS UNDER
LANGTANG LIRUNG.

Nyangtsa Chu

NYANGJA

GLACIER

ANDAR
KHARKA
A FLOOD
COVERED THE
GRASS IN ROCKS

Kangchenpo/
Fluted Peak
6387m

GLACIER

0   500m

on the mountain depends entirely on the condition of the snow. Hard snow or ice is particularly hazardous without crampons since one person slipping can yank everyone else on the rope with them before there's even time to blink.

Ask around at Kyangjin if you are interested. Rates will require negotiation and check the equipment before putting any money down.

Pangrima and the valley to the south

Getting here means crossing the Tsangbu Chu. It may be possible to cross near the airstrip in low flows but it is much safer to use the bridge immediately below Kyangjin. Finding a convenient water supply for camping between the Lalung Chu and the Nyangtsa Chu is difficult. Approaching from Langshisa, begin scouting the river from west of the small climb. It is only possible, and still difficult, to cross in low flows. Consult locals and read the warning on p72.

Nyangtsa Kharka 4450m/14,600ft There are few flat spots here; camping inside a roofless kore may be the best idea. There aren't any better spots further up either, so this is as good a base as any.

Sunset cairns 4750m/15,585ft This viewpoint is more difficult to reach than a glance would suggest but the rewards are better than expected too. On the first ridge from Nyangtsa Kharka the stream and slip area become visible. Depending on conditions, these can be crossed directly, or by climbing higher or lower. Atop the next ridge the view dramatically opens out and includes the pale granite wall of Shishapangma.

Exploring up the valley Further up are rewarding views of Kangchenpo (Fluted peak) and enough rubble to make you wonder where it all comes from. High on a moraine (5050m/16,568ft) looking at the wizened glacier, you can see mountains in Tibet, including Shishapangma.

Mountaineers could explore the possibility of crossing either the glacier just south of Ponggen Dokpu or the three-way glacier system west of Tenbathang Drosakhang down to Monsa, thereby crossing the main range.

Bramring and above

Getting here means crossing the Tsangbu Chu. There's no bridge and this can be a difficult, dangerous river to cross. Head a little way up from Langshisa to above where the stream from the south-east enters and carefully choose your crossing point. If the flow looks high, cross where the river is braided, undoing your pack's waistband and holding each other's shoulders for support. Using a ski pole or stick is much safer if crossing alone. Note that knee-deep fast flowing water is little trouble with a stick but even a small section approaching hip depth is extremely dangerous. Don't under-estimate river crossings.

The high kharka and cave From the small multi-level kharka pick up a vague track that soon moves close into the mountain wall above an ever narrowing ablation valley. About $3/_4$-1 hour up at 4500m/14,764ft is a small kharka with one roofless kore and a cave that could hold four people. It is snow-proof but perhaps not so dry in rain. A mouse-hare made a meal out of my *Chums* sunglasses retainers here.

Continuing up the valley, about half an hour later a huge debris fan chugs into the valley from Langshisa Ri. Overlooking the glacier on the crest of the moraine at 4620m/15,157ft is a cairn perched perilously close to the edge. It isn't possible to trek much further along.

Looking across the glacier and to the messy ablation valley on the other side, you have to admire Tilman and a few other crazies who have used this route to Panch Pokhari.

It is possible to climb up the debris fan behind but be warned: it gets progressively steeper and there is avalanche danger, although by staying on grass and mossy (ie undisturbed) boulders this is minimised. Acclimatised mountaineers may want to camp at the top of the fan, 3-4$^1/_2$ hours up.

Piyung (Pijung)
From Numthang (unmarked on other maps) an obvious trail climbs to some prayer flags at the crest of the steep grassy slopes. Begin from the lone cairn and pick up one of many minor trails heading up. They soon consolidate to pass a few roofless and usually waterless kore. The prayer-flagged crest is false but it isn't too much further up to Piyung. This place could be called cairn kore or cairn city; the whole area is littered with them, even the ridges that form the bowl. Most of the kore are roofed but out of the monsoon the only water supply is a thin stream fed by melting snow from the basin above. No snow means no water.

PEMTHANG KARPO   [MAP 11, p160]

Pemthang Karpo 4600m/15,091ft
There are other potential camping spots near the Langtang Glacier but this is the best, being a pleasant place and well positioned for exploring.

It is possible to reach here in a long day from Kyangjin but note the altitude difference. From Langshisa the flat valley and the easy walking soon end. Climbing among the grassy moraines there are several small trails all heading to the same place, the small grass plain above. The area isn't quite flat but there are a few spots for small tents. A boulder offers some wind protection for cooking but isn't a rain-proof bivvy.

North-west Ablation Valley and Drag Ri This is an area worthy of exploration. I was hampered by unusually heavy spring snow so the description isn't complete. Just beyond the first swath of scree entering

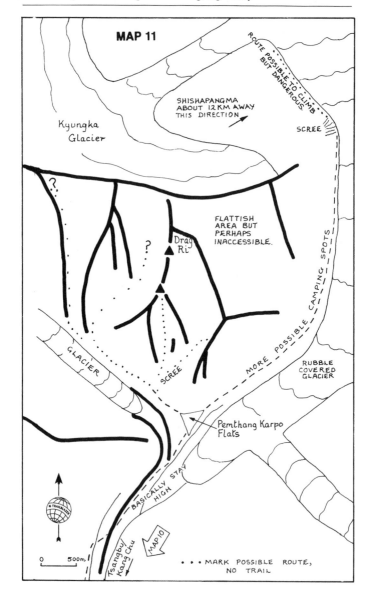

MAP 11

ROUTE POSSIBLE TO CLIMB BUT DANGEROUS.

SHISHAPANGMA ABOUT 12 KM AWAY THIS DIRECTION

SCREE

Kyungka Glacier

?

FLATTISH AREA BUT PERHAPS INACCESSIBLE.

?

Drag Ri

MORE POSSIBLE CAMPING SPOTS

GLACIER

SCREE

RUBBLE COVERED GLACIER

Pemthang Karpo Flats

BASICALLY STAY HIGH

TRAILBLAZER

0   500m

Tsangbu Kang Chu

MAP 10

• • • MARK POSSIBLE ROUTE, NO TRAIL

Map 11 161

from the right (north) are some grassier slopes with a faint trail. Heading up, the grazing runs out but it is possible, though quite steep, to reach a rounded summit for spectacular views. Apparently the point labelled Drag Ri on the Austrian Alpine Club map can be best climbed from around the back, the west face. It may also be possible to climb up a ridge further up the valley.

The Langtang Glacier
Continuing up the ablation valley from Pemthang Karpo there are a few more possible camping spots. On the opposite side of the Langtang Glacier, unseen behind the staggering Pemthang wall, is Shishapangma and Tibet.

The valley draws you ever up but mountaineers aside, there is no hope of reaching the end of it. A steep scree slope indecisively stops the trekker just at a point where the map indicates you might be able to see up the whole valley. If you've got the climbing ability of a Himalayan Thar it is possible to go around half an hour further up the valley on tricky steep ground to a few daringly placed cairns at 4950m/16,240ft, but this definitely isn't worth the risk especially since the view, maddeningly, doesn't get a lot better.

Sitting among the fragrant dwarf rhododendron on the edge of the moraine, there's a constant clatter of rocks on the glacier below showing that its tortured surface is indeed moving. Occasional avalanches rake the faces above, further polishing them. Looking around steep valley walls, it is easy to figure how the Langtang Glacier carved the valley out. In many ways the terrain is similar to that found lower down the valley and several ice-ages ago the glaciers did indeed reach where Langtang village now is, and beyond.

Back to camp An alternative trail follows the moraine edge for part of the way and this may be the easier route in spring snow. On you way look up and admire the black pyramid above.

Tilman's Col and Hagen's Col Both of these intriguing points are marked on the Austrian Alpine Club map. The views must be stupendous but a glance at the terrain reveals that both people were true mountaineers rather than trekkers. Toni Hagen, a Swiss geologist, walked the length of Nepal in the 1950s, mapping the geology and exploring the country. In 1936 Tilman climbed India's Nanda Devi to make that the highest peak climbed at the time. He also climbed on Everest in the 1930s.

On his 1949 Langtang trip Tilman was accompanied by Tensing Norgay. Together they in fact climbed three cols around the head of the Langtang glacier. They also explored the flat glacier immediately west of Langshisa Ri and crossed under Dorje Lakpa to reach Panch Pokhari.

Later, in 1953, Tensing Norgay (Sherpa) was the first person, together with Sir Edmund Hillary to climb Everest.

HEADING DOWN

It always seems shorter walking a trail a second time. To Syabru Bensi, Bharkhu or Dhunche from Kyangjin takes most people two to three days. Providing you didn't start in Syabru Bensi, finishing there perhaps makes the most sense. It is the quickest route down and means no hill climbing. However, if you haven't already been to (Thulo) Syabru spending a night (usually the second going down), and a relaxing morning there before the afternoon walk to Bharkhu or Dhunche is also a good plan.

For the Mercury-footed, Langtang Village to Syabru Bensi is a long day, making it 1½ days out, but for mere mortals aiming for Changdam then Syabru Bensi makes more sense. Note that in Syabru Bensi, seats on the bus can be reserved the day before. The Dhunche ticket office also has a small allocation of seats for the bus from Syabru Bensi. Bharkhu has no such system.

To Gosainkund

The trail choices begin at (Thulo) Syabru, a convenient two days down from Kyangjin. Speedsters may reach (Thulo) Syabru earlier in which case there are several alternatives. The Gosainkund section begins on p165.

Quick reference times:

Walking times only.

  2-3 hours Kyangjin to Langtang village
  ¾-1 hour (sign out at National Park post) to Ghora Tabela
  1-1¾ hours to Changdam
  1-1¾ hours to Langmoche Khola
  ½-¾ hour to Landslide
  1½-2 hours to Syabru Bensi, 1-1½ hours from Landslide to (Thulo) Syabru

At the far side of the landslide the trail divides, almost imperceptibly, into two. The upper path to (Thulo) Syabru, which is momentarily level before climbing steeply up the half-hour hill. There is 550m/1800ft of ascent to (Thulo) Syabru in total. The lower path leads to Riverside where, if you took the wrong trail, the lodge owner can point out his steep shortcut to the main trail up to Syabru Bensi.

Gosainkund

PLANNING AND PREPARATION

It wasn't until 1991 that the trek across Gosainkund became a reliable teahouse trek and still, whether trekking with a group or using lodges, it is better attempted only in the peak seasons.

Lodge shops are expensive once above villages; chocolate lovers may want to stock up from Kathmandu or (Thulo) Syabru.

Proper pronunciation of Gosainkund requires care; the *n* of Gosain is really a nasalised *i*, a lot more subtle than the hard *n* that the English spelling suggests. It is also often called Gosainkund*a*.

Monsoon conditions Conditions are not pleasant and the route has little to recommend it. During the monsoon the lodges open only for the annual August Janai Purnima pilgrimage and then are filled to bursting with pilgrims.

Winter conditions The first real snowfall, usually around Christmas, closes the Gosainkund and Laurebina lodges and the route up. Around this time it is hard to reliably find out whether the lodges are still operating. If it is before Christmas and it hasn't yet snowed heavily then it is safe to assume the route is still possible. The lodge owners at Laurebina always know if a Gosainkund lodge is open. Villagers in (Thulo) Syabru and elsewhere don't know reliably. The Jugal Himal and Gosainkund, being the first high range to the north, get a lot of snow – more than many other trekking areas of Nepal.

Spring conditions The Gosainkund lodges try to reopen early in March; once the sun has taken a heavy toll on the winter snow. Fine weather for a week to ten days clears most of the exposed snow. Shaded snow is more durable but it softens considerably and it only takes a few people to make a trail through it for the route to be called open. From March to mid-May occasional afternoon snowfalls can still be expected but the few centimetres of snow rarely cause problems; it just looks pretty. However, a heavy dump can block the route to all but the most determined, sometimes for a week or more. Luckily this happens infrequently. By mid-April the route is reliable, although not the weather.

When trekking during spring, right up to June, you must be prepared for walking in snow. This means good boots, spare socks, sunglasses, a ski pole or stick, gaiters and some cord to wrap around the front of your boot for grip on ice. Conditions are quite variable – at times you'll wonder what all the fuss is about then you'll come across slippery trails that take twice as long as expected.

Kathmandu to Gosainkund

The first section of this trek, Kathmandu to Tharepati or Melamchi Pul to Tharepati, is covered in the Helambu section beginning p182. In contrast to the Helambu Circuit, planning a day by day itinerary isn't necessary; seeing where you end up is enough. The only proviso is if you haven't recently been to altitude you must take acclimatisation into account. The minimum is to spend three nights between Tharepati and Ayethang, the last lodge before the pass. Even this acclimatisation programme will mean headaches and some discomfort for a few trekkers when staying at Gosainkund.

Gosainkund to Kathmandu without Langtang

Similar to the above, sensible acclimatisation is the main concern. Beginning from Dhunche, this means spending a night each at Sing Gompa, Chalang Pati and Laurebina Yak before staying in Gosainkund. Similarly this is not a perfect programme, but is the minimum recommended.

It is also possible to begin from Syabru Bensi and take the little-used trail (by trekkers, that is) to (Thulo) Syabru, covered on p129.

Langtang-(Thulo) Syabru-Gosainkund-Kathmandu

You are already acclimatised from the Langtang Valley and so don't need to plan this in. Even if you experienced minor problems at Kyangjin you are unlikely to suffer at all at Gosainkund.

There's a choice of two routes to Chalang Pati from (Thulo) Syabru (see Map 2b); via Sing Gompa is the more scenic and more commonly taken. Once over Gosainkund the trail joins the Helambu Circuit at Tharepati.

From Tharepati there are several route options for returning to Kathmandu: the most direct and logical is to continue following the long ridge that Tharepati sits on all the way to Chisopani and Sundarijal, or from Chisopani head to Sankhu. The alternative route via Melamchi is a similar time and distance but involves a concentrated descent to Melamchi and the Melamchi Khola then a 650m/2100ft ascent to Tarkeghyang. The rice-planting season around the end of March/early April is a particularly beautiful time to trek the lower country from Timbu down (providing the road and bus service hasn't reached there yet).

The probable road-building may shorten either or both options, however this barely changes the basis for decision-making. The walking distances are roughly the same to Sundarijal or Melamchi Pul but the bus from Melamchi Pul adds half a day. If that road is extended to Timbu that would even up the time taken. The real differences are that the Sundarijal route has less interesting villages meaning it is easier to rush while the route via Tarkeghyang to Sarmathang or Timbu/Melamchi Pul demands a slower pace to fully appreciate the region.

The trail description details the walk from (Thulo) Syabru over Gosainkund to Tharepati. Dhunche to (Thulo) Syabru and Bharkhu to (Thulo) Syabru are covered in the Langtang section. See p162 for Kyangjin to (Thulo) Syabru.

SYABRU TO GOSAINKUND DIRECT

There are several trails, none of which are major. Look as you leave (Thulo) Syabru. Up near the skyline are some *darche* – prayerflag poles, the route to Dursa Gang. Slightly left (west) and lower, are a few houses. Head for these. Continue up through fields and scattered houses. Keep heading up and around the valley and check with locals that you are on the correct path.

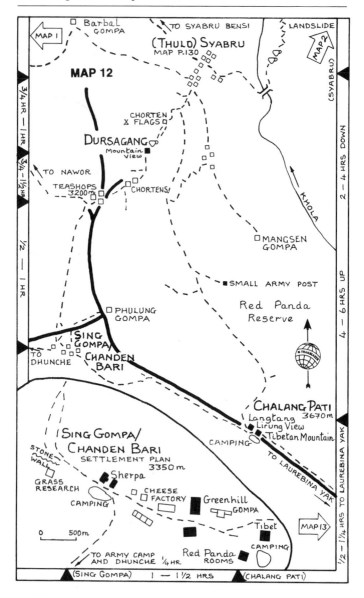

MAP 1

TO SYABRU BENSI

LANDSLIDE

MAP 2

Barbal
GOMPA

(THULD) SYABRU
MAP P.130

MAP 12

CHORTEN
X FLAGS

DURSAGANG
Mountain
View

TO NAWOR
TEASHOPS
3200m
CHORTENS

(SYABRU)

2 – 4 HRS DOWN

KHOLA

MANGSEN
GOMPA

SMALL ARMY POST

PHULUNG
GOMPA

Red Panda
Reserve

SING
GOMPA/
CHANDEN
BARI

TO
DHUNCHE

CHALANG PATI 3670m
Langtang
Lirung View
Tibetan Mountain
CAMPING

TO LAUREBINA YAK

SING GOMPA/
CHANDEN BARI
SETTLEMENT PLAN
3350m

STONE
WALL

GRASS
RESEARCH

CAMPING

Sherpa

CHEESE
FACTORY

Greenhill
GOMPA

Tibet

MAP 13

CAMPING

0   500m

Red Panda
ROOMS

TO ARMY CAMP
AND DHUNCHE   ¼ HR

4 – 6 HRS UP

½ – 1¼ HRS TO LAUREBINA YAK

(SING GOMPA)   1 – 1½ HRS   (CHALANG PATI)

¾ HR – 1 HR   ¾ – 1½ HR   ½ – 1 HR

Map 12 167

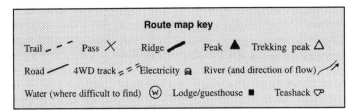

Route map key

Trail `- -` Pass ✕ Ridge Peak ▲ Trekking peak △

Road 4WD track Electricity River (and direction of flow)

Water (where difficult to find) (W) Lodge/guesthouse ■ Teashack

(THULO) SYABRU TO SING GOMPA   [MAP 12]
SYABRU TO GOSAINKUND VIA SING GOMPA

While in (Thulo) Syabru take a careful look up at the hillside. Dursa Gang is straight up, following the ridge that extends up from (Thulo) Syabru. 'What ridge?' you might wonder, especially when you're only 15 minutes up and are vaguely lost; it is admittedly only a minor feature of a uniform hillside. Also look for some prayer flag poles (*darche*) which are on the route and perhaps half an hour up.

Dursa Gang 2700m/8858ft The couple of houses and the orchard here have the distinction of not being shown on any trekking map. The panorama is more distinguished and the 1995-built lodge is pleasant enough. (Thulo) Syabru hoteliers might say this lodge is closed to tempt you to stay with them, especially if you are having lunch and are about to press on. It is always open.

Continuing up, the trail soon enters the forest. Churned patches of the forest floor are made by wild pigs rooting with their snouts for edible roots. They make a lot of noise so you'll hear them if they are nearby. Pigs also like munching crops. Previously this would earn them death but now they are protected under national park rules. Gradually the trail

---

❏ **Pikas**

The furry balls with mickey-mouse ears darting among the alpine grass and rocks are pikas, a Himalayan mouse-hare. Winnie the Pooh-like, they live in holes that certainly don't seem large enough; one can imagine that if they eat too much, rather than being unable to get out, they might not be able to get back into their homes.

While sitting by a potbelly stove in Laurebina the lodge manager and I watched a pika scurry over to my boot then after a quick sniff, hurry under the glowing fire. And there in the shadows he stayed warming himself. Full of glowing thoughts about the Buddhist doctrine of not killing, I was amused to spot a small mouse furtively scurrying around. Thwack! And there, squashed bloody under a hunk of wood, it died. Seeing my startled look, the manager explained that pikas eat only grass whereas, the small mouse is fond of rice. Later in the conversation he explained he was Christian.

climbs out of the forest and rejoins the crest of the ridge at a modest collection of teashops.

Danda teashops 3200m/10,500ft During the main seasons it is possible to stay here but they are often closed in winter. The outdoor benches take in a beautiful panorama. Looking north, there's a tempting array of snowy peaks and wooded valleys. Unfortunately these are in Tibet. Tilman, in the days before the Chinese invasion, was caught in the process of sneaking across north of Rasuwa:

(There was nothing) 'to denote that one had crossed a frontier. And this absence of any hint of might, majesty, dominion or power, is in accord with the Tibetan genius which up to recent years has managed to maintain its privacy behind quite imaginary barriers. Of course, should one happen to intrude, sooner rather than later one is seen off, not by an armed guard but by some stout (affable) official in a Homburg hat and dark spectacles'. *The Seven Mountain-Travel Books*

(And he was).

It is also possible to see Laurebina; follow the forested saddle to the south-east where the forest runs out. Just above, but difficult to see, are the lodges of Laurebina. Good eyes may pick some of the trail to Gosainkund and the concrete mandir further up.

The trail now crosses to the Ganesh Himal side of the ridge for a pleasant traverse that dances in and out of the forest. Just when you think you should be getting there the trail divides. Either branch will do because they meet again. Around the corner, along a stone wall (there is no need to pass through this to the buildings), is the unusual settlement of Sing Gompa.

Sing Gompa/Chandan Bari 3350m/11,000ft
This is really just a few cheese factory buildings, some lodges and a gompa. Sing is the Tibetan name of the trees around here, most of which burnt in a forest fire about 20 years ago. Chandan is the Nepali name for the same trees and *bari* is a cropping field. The cheese factory is another

---

❏ **Who says Nepal is deforested?**
Around Sing Gompa a re-forestation scheme is being planned. The Lodge Management Committee of Gosainkund approached the National Park to assist with some conservation work for the hill around Sing Gompa. The idea is that a small nursery will be set up so that locals can continue annual planting around Sing Gompa.

Many visitors to Nepal believe that Nepal is deforested to the extent that there are only a few trees left. This simply isn't true, and while there are some problems, there is an increasing general awareness of them. In fact Nepal apparently has one of the best re-forestation programmes in the developing world. As many people will attest, there is a truly surprising amount of conservation work happening in Nepal.   **Shane Capron and Sue Behrenfeld** (USA)

of the government's Dairy Development Corporation factories. Cheese is available but the scales are notoriously wrong: 'Beware of the crooked cheese vendor with an attitude' warns Adam Wise. This is one of the few areas where trekkers come into direct contact with corruption. Note that the staff are rotated every few years so this might change. The lodges also sell cheese and often have delicious curd. The local equivalent of muesli and curd is tsampa (light and fluffy roasted barley flour) and curd. A little sugar enlivens it for those with a sweet-tooth.

Lodges During 1996 and 1997 there was a flurry of lodge-building here to cope with increasing trekker traffic. The new *Sherpa* and *Tibet* lodges compete with the enduring *Red Panda* (previously named Evergreen) and the newly rebuilt *Greenhill*. All have big, well set up cooking stoves in the kitchens and warming potbellies in the dining rooms.

Phulung Gompa This old gompa sits on the ridge well above Sing Gompa. Although rundown, it is still used for special ceremonies. Being atop a hill, there are stunning views including Langtang Lirung.

To Dhunche or Bharkhu The Dhunche trail is steep! The average gradient for the second half of the 1500m/5000ft descent is around 45°, and feels like much more.

Just below the army base, perhaps $\frac{1}{4}$ hour down, the trail divides – take the left fork for Dhunche and right for Bharkhu. This may be signposted. Dhunche or Bharkhu are anywhere from 2-3$\frac{1}{2}$ hours down, depending on your downhill ability.

To Chalang Pati The trail gently climbs to the ridge where it becomes a pleasant ridge walk. Note the striking differences between the sides of the ridge. The sheltered side holds water better hence the real trees, while on the dry sunny side juniper scrub thrives. The wind sometimes howls through the bend in the trees - you might also experience this at Larebina Yak.

Chalang Pati 3670m/12,040ft The direct trail from (Thulo) Syabru joins the ridge here. To the north and a little below is the newly set up Red Panda Reserve and an army post to guard it. Climbing the small hill nearby gives the most extensive views.

If heading in the opposite direction the Sing Gompa trail is wide and flat.

LAUREBINA TO GOSAINKUND [MAP 13, p170]

Laurebina Yak 3925m/12,877ft

Starkly placed along the ridge, the lodges bask in the sun. At other times this exposure means they are cold and draughty. Most hotels advertise

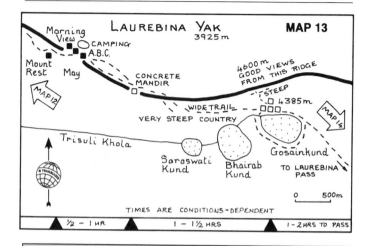

LAUREBINA YAK 3925m

MAP 13

Morning View

CAMPING

A.B.C.

Mount Rest

May

MAP 12

CONCRETE MANDIR

4600m GOOD VIEWS FROM THIS RIDGE

STEEP

4385m

MAP 14

WIDE TRAIL

VERY STEEP COUNTRY

Trisuli Khola

Saraswati Kund

Bhairab Kund

Gosainkund

TO LAUREBINA PASS

0   500m

TIMES ARE CONDITIONS-DEPENDENT

½ – 1 HR   1 – 1½ HRS   1 – 2 HRS TO PASS

☐ **Janai Purnima**

On the day of the August full moon all Hindus take a ritual cleansing bath and the twice-born Brahman and Chhetri castes change their *Janai*, the sacred thread worn across one shoulder and under one arm. The holiest places to do this are Gosainkund and the Khumbeswar Mahadev in Patan, which is said to be linked with Gosainkund. On this day Shiva is said to revisit the lake.

A priest blesses the pile of new Janai then men line up to receive a new one. In addition they are given a smaller version, the yellow *rakshya bandhan* (or *dorro*) for their wrist (which should be worn until the Laxmi Puja in October) and a rice tika on their forehead. In exchange the priest receives a donation. In the countryside villagers give uncooked rice, dal, salt, besaar (turmeric) and ghee served on a leaf or they provide a meal for him in the house. As the new thread is received the old one is removed and the priest indicates the direction in which the old one must be disposed of. Since this is still sacred it is either tied to a cow's tail or if there are no willing cows around, thrown in a holy river or failing that, draped over the holy toolasee plant beside the house.

The other circumstance in which the Janai must be changed is less of a celebration. If a Brahman touches a woman who is having her period or has just given birth (ie spilt blood) then the man must undergo a ritual wash and change the thread; this is why, in some areas, women sleep in a separate house or, more usually, in the cowshed during this time.

The Buddhists celebrate this day as the day that Buddha received enlightenment. It's a day and night of singing and dancing with some trying to drink themselves to enlightenment. The Newars, who are essentially mixed Hindus and Buddhists, spend this day eating a special nine bean soup (Kwati) and other delicacies.

Janai Purnima is also the day that farming communities honour the common frog because it is believed that the frog brings the monsoon.

free hot showers to tempt you to stay but since all water is heated over wood fires it isn't ecologically sound to take up the offer. They all also advertise that extra blankets are available, testimony to how cold it can get; in December it is freezing. However once the fire is stoked (more wood), the dining rooms are cosy enough.

Quick eyes may catch a glimpse of a weasel or the fur-ball mouse-hares.

Out of the main trekking season the lodge owners here can tell you reliably whether a lodge at Gosainkund is open or not.

Heading down Dhunche, (Thulo) Syabru and most of the trail to Sing Gompa is visible from here but the settlement itself is just out of view. Sing Gompa is 1-1¾ hours down.

Heading up The wide trail roughly follows the ridge on the sheltered side to the concrete mandir. A little above this the trail contours to the sunny side and you catch a glimpse of the first lake. There are several trails. It is imperative to take the widest one. Take particular care in snow, this is steep country. The track passes well above the first lake (Saraswati) and continues to traverse and climb above the second lake (Bhairab). The third large lake is Gosainkund. Note that there is some confusion as to which is Saraswati and which is Bhairab Kund.

Gosainkund 4385m/14,346ft

A small mandir with Shiva's symbol, the phallic lingam, inside sits beside the revered Gosainkund (*kund* means lake). There is also a collection of stone shacks purporting to be lodges.

There are many other lakes in the region and Shiva devotees occasionally attempt to visit them all. Legend has it that there are 108 lakes

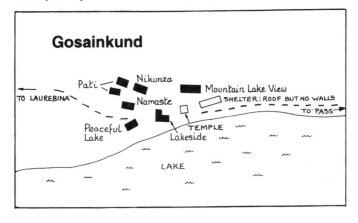

❏ **Monsoon madness**
The Janai Purnima Mela (gathering) in August was a blast. It was cold, wet and non-stop. The shivering Hindu pilgrims, the singing Jankris and the dancing Buddhists all looked surreal amid the thick monsoon cloud. The nine or so foreigners were outnumbered around a thousand to one by the Nepalese who made us welcome (but bring a waterproof tent). The festivities may be to celebrate higher beings but 9,000 people make one hell of a mess, which, admirably, the local conservation committee cleaned up, using VDC (Village Development Committee) funds. There is another mela sometime in late spring too.

Shane Capron (USA)

---

but devout pilgrims have only counted around 58. Others say there are 54 and there's a duplicate of each in the spirit world.

The lakes begin icing up in December and are frozen over during January and February, and sometimes into March. During this time the wo-wo-wobble of the lakes talking to each other is haunting.

More views The view from the top of the ridge behind the lodges is well worth the effort, especially if you missed it at Laurebina Yak. To the west the closer range is the Ganesh Himal while further in the distance is the bulky Manaslu Himal. On a particularly clear day you can even see the Annapurna-Lamjung range and the famed fishtail mountain, Machhapuchhare. There is a vague track up until the going gets steep. Don't attempt this if the grass is wet or covered in snow.

▲ **Gosainkund to Laurebina in reverse** Normally the route is straightforward. However, if conditions are more challenging it can be difficult to find even the beginning of the trail. It briefly climbs out of Gosainkund parallel to the lake exit, then it traverses almost level on a 1½ metre wide path for perhaps ½ -¾ hour. Don't descend to any lakes. Once the rocky ridge to your right fades, descend on the actual ridge crest and you can't miss the lodges at Laurebina.

GOSAINKUND OVER LAUREBINA LA [MAP 14

To Laurebina La
This is a staggeringly beautiful route on a fine day. Many people begin before sunrise but if the weather is stable this isn't necessary. However, the pass should only be crossed when there is good visibility and, especially in spring, this is more likely to occur early in the day. If there is thick cloud about and you are without a good guide wait for clear weather. Don't do a James Scott (see p174).

On the way up look out for Himalayan thar, pikas and perhaps even the larger martens.

Map 14 173

Crossing in winter The trail can get dangerously icy after some snow and some freeze-thaw patterns. In December 1995 a trekker slipped on hard snow and died in sight of Gosainkund. A stick (or ice axe) is essential and crampons, even the small instep versions, are handy – although most people make do without them. On moderately slippery snow the porter's trick of tightly winding string around your boots at the ball of your foot can significantly improve grip. In these conditions sometimes lodge owners will suggest leaving early while the ice is still very cold. The temperature difference between your boots and the snow can often give good grip. At other times they may suggest waiting until the surface layer has softened slightly.

In deep soft snow be sure to stay on the trail or, if you are making a fresh trail, follow the correct route. There is little (but not zero) avalanche danger on the standard route between Gosainkund and the pass. Also beware of frostbite.

Laurebina La 4600m/15,100ft
The pass is marked by lots of cairns and a couple of shelters that sell tea and biscuits in the October-November season. Otherwise they are roofless.

The view is worth the effort. To the south-east most of the trail to Tharepati can be seen and stretching into the distance is the ridge to

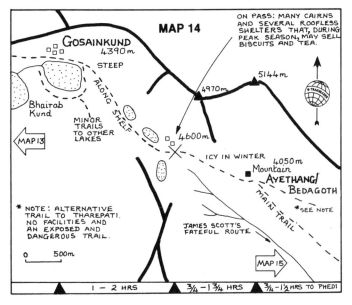

❏ **James Scott**

Australian medical student James Scott made world headlines when he was found alive 43 days after becoming lost in a snow storm while crossing the Laurebina La.

He, and a Canadian trekking companion called Mark whom he had met in Kathmandu, set off from Phedi (the Tharepati side of the pass) just before Christmas 1992, heading for Gosainkund. The weather didn't look encouraging so it was now or never. By the time they reached the top of the pass it was snowing; 10 minutes down they began to get worried. After a debate Mark decided to keep going while James elected to turn back. Ironically Mark made it to Gosainkund in time to catch the last lodge owner heading down to Laurebina while James got lost. With fresh snow falling and covering the trail, he lost his way before even making it over the pass. In the heat (or cold) of the moment he decided to follow a river down rather than hunt above it for the trail, a big mistake given the steepness of the terrain, something he was soon to learn. The terrain beside the river was difficult however somehow he managed to descend. Eventually he found an overhanging rock where he could shelter. The next morning the snow was still falling. By the time it stopped James was weak and still had no idea of where he was. He opted to wait, perhaps for rescue, or at least until conditions improved. They didn't, and severely weakened by lack of food (he had a famous single chocolate bar), the deep snow trapped him.

It took a while before anyone realised that he was missing and when rescue efforts finally began they were hampered by lack of information and deep snow. It wasn't until Mark (who was in Thailand, unaware of James's plight) was contacted that the rescuers began aerial searches of the right area. After a ground search and many helicopter flights, his family and the search team were ready to give up. Then on the last planned flight he was spotted. Almost unbelievably, he was still alive. He was a few hours walk from the village of Talu. He had lost around a third of his body weight and has suffered permanent eye damage from lack of vitamins.

Chisopani and Sundarijal. Walking sticks litter the pass area, especially at the beginning of the season. These have been left by pilgrims, just as Shiva was believed to have done.

Descending to Tharepati Continue in the same direction. A little way down, the trail stays on the left side of the valley, avoiding the valley bottom. This section can be icy. At Ayethang, the first lodge, the trail divides into two. In fact, it isn't much of a choice; the high trail is very exposed and in sections so narrow that loaded porters can't take it. Virtually everybody takes the lower trail. From here to Tharepati are well-spaced lodges. From Phedi, at a similar altitude to Tharepati, the trail begins a rollercoaster trip that can be tricky in snow.

In 1992 in a horrific crash a Thai airbus flew into the hillside a little below Phedi. Ask locals the way down if you would like to see just how many pieces the plane broke into.

Map 15 175

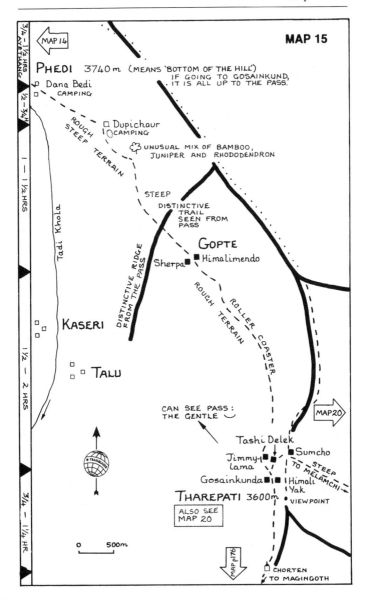

MAP 15

← MAP 14

PHEDI 3740 m (MEANS 'BOTTOM OF THE HILL')
IF GOING TO GOSAINKUND,
IT IS ALL UP TO THE PASS.

Dana Bedi
CAMPING

ROUGH STEEP TERRAIN

Dupichaur
CAMPING

UNUSUAL MIX OF BAMBOO,
JUNIPER AND RHODODENDRON

STEEP

DISTINCTIVE
TRAIL
SEEN FROM
PASS

GOPTE
Sherpa ■ ■ Himalimendo

DISTINCTIVE RIDGE FROM THE PASS

ROUGH TERRAIN

ROLLER COASTER

Tadi Khola

KASERI

TALU

CAN SEE PASS:
THE GENTLE ⌣

MAP 20

Tashi Delek
Jimmy-lama ■ ■ ■ Sumcho
STEEP TO MELAMCHI
Gosainkunda ■ ■ Himali Yak
• VIEWPOINT

THAREPATI 3600m

ALSO SEE
MAP 20

N TRAILBLAZER

0   500m

MAP p176

CHORTEN
TO MAGINGOTH

¾ – 1½ HRS AVE THANG
½ – ¾ H
1 – 1½ HRS
1½ – 2 HRS
¾ – 1¼ HR

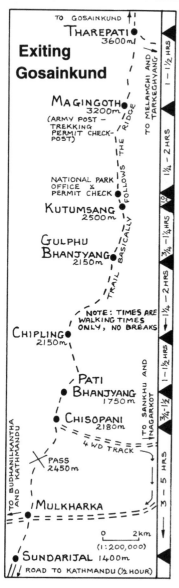

Descending to Gosainkund from the pass In cloud or difficult conditions take careful note of the positions of the lakes on the map en route to Gosainkund. The trail is almost level for the first section past the two lakes and only then does it get steeper. The altitude difference between the pass and Gosainkund is only 200 vertical metres.

TO THAREPATI
[MAP 15, p175]

Tharepati 3600m/11,800ft

The trail joins the Helambu Circuit trek here. The Sundarijal and Melamchi Pul route descriptions both begin from Tharepati, p190. Tharepati to Sundarijal is described backwards, ie in the Sundarijal to Tharepati direction. Gosainkund to Sundarijal takes quicker trekkers three days, four days is more normal but, if you're fit and flying, getting out in two very long days is just possible.

The Helambu Circuit

This is primarily a cultural trek so perhaps some history is in order. Locals say the name Helambu is derived from *Heh* – potato, and *La-phug* – radish, the land of potatoes and radishes, which it is. But ask the locals what they call themselves and the answer might be *Sherpa*, which isn't strictly correct. It takes some understanding of the history to know why. The Tamangs migrated from Tibet many hundreds of years ago, some to the region of Helambu, as they call it; the two long ridges of the trek and the valley in between. Then during the 1600s and onwards Tibetans from Kyirong, especially lamas coming to visit a cave used by Milarepa near Tarkeghyang, began staying there. They called the area *Yolmu* or *Yermu*. Being mainly lamas they positioned themselves as the highest class, ie above Tamangs, which is still readily apparent today. Appropriately enough their caste and language is commonly called *Lama* by Nepalis. Among themselves they are the *Yolmo* or *Yolmo-wa* but when tourists began arriving and the fame of the Sherpas had spread they adopted the more beneficial name.

To complete the picture, the people of Dhunche and Syabru consider themselves Tamang while the people of Langtang village defy easy classification. These high country people all originate from Tibet and so perhaps could all be Tibetans in general terms.

PLANNING AND PREPARATION

At a less than leisurely pace the Helambu Circuit could be completed in as little as four and a half days, Kathmandu to Kathmandu. However to walk this quickly is completely missing the point; it is a trek to be savoured.

The circuit can be walked in either direction. Most trekkers begin from Sundarijal but walking in the opposite direction gives slightly better acclimatisation for staying at Tharepati, 3600m/11,800ft. During the winter, beginning from Melamchi Pul allows the option of a shorter, smaller circuit (Melamchi Pul, Timbu, Tarkeghyang, Sarmathang, Melamchi Pul) if snow at Tharepati is a problem.

To get the most from the Helambu trek means planning where to stay rather than the more carefree idea of seeing where you end up. Here are some guidelines for overnight stopping points. Note that between Tarkeghyang and Melamchi Pul there are two alternatives: the lower river route via Timbu and the slightly more popular higher route via

Sarmathang. The tables don't include any rest days although you might want to have one or more. Groups with tents, a kitchen and porters must trek at the group pace.

Clockwise

Route Pace	via Timbu Leisurely (group)	via Timbu Medium	via Sarmathang Leisurely	via Sarmathang Winter (group)
Night	Kathmandu	Kathmandu	Kathmandu	Kathmandu
1	Chisopani	Chisopani	Chisopani	Chisopani
2	Gulphu	Kutumsang	Gulphu	Gulphu
3	Magin	Tharepati	Magin	Magin
4	Tharepati	Melamchi	Tharepati	Melamchi
5	Melamchi	Tarkeghyang	Melamchi	Tarkeghyang
6	Tarkeghyang	Timbu/ Kiul Tar	Tarkeghyang	Sarmathang
7	Kiul Tar	Melamchi Pul	Sarmathang	Melamchi Pul
8	Two Rivers	Kathmandu	Melamchi Pul	Kathmandu
9	Kathmandu		Kathmandu	

Anti-clockwise

Route Pace	via Timbu Medium	via Sarmathang Medium	via Sarmathang Leisurely (group)	Winter loop Leisurely
Night	Kathmandu	Kathmandu	Kathmandu	Kathmandu
1	Two Rivers	Pokhari/Kakani	Dubachaur	Pokhari/ Kakani
2	Timbu	Sarmathang	Sarmathang	Sarmathang
3	Tarkeghyang	Tarkeghyang	Tarkeghyang	Tarkeghyang
4	Melamchi	Melamchi	Tarkeghyang	Timbu
5	Tharepati	Tharepati	Melamchi	Two Rivers
6	Kutumsang	Kutumsang	Tharepati	Kathmandu
7	Chisopani	Chisopani	Kutumsang	
8	Kathmandu	Kathmandu	Chisopani	
9			Kathmandu	

For a more adventurous beginning than the standard Sundarijal start, consider walking (or mountain-biking) from Sankhu or Nagarkot. From Sankhu the most straightforward trail is a four-wheel drive track that torturously winds its way over the rim of the valley then trek cross-country to the entrance of the Shivapuri Integrated Watershed. Just above here there's a dirt road to Chisopani. The more worthwhile option is to visit the temple of Vajra Yogini then trek some minor trails to the entrance of the reserve. This takes some route-finding skills and an adventurous spirit since there is no easy-to-follow main trail. Kathmandu to Chisopani is also a longish day, especially if you aren't very fit.

Beginning from Nagarkot sounds like killing two birds with one stone or, in this case, seeing a Himalayan sunrise then going trekking without

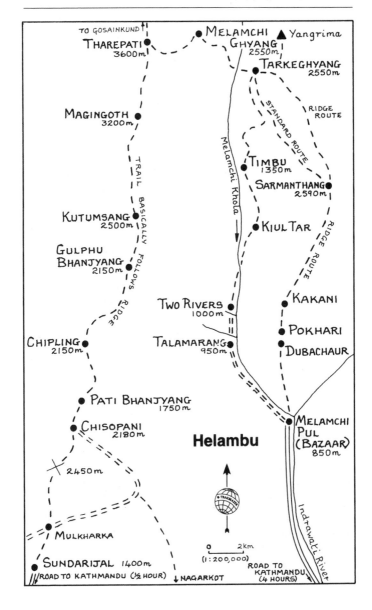

TO GOSAINKUND

THAREPATI
3600m

MELAMCHI
GHYANG
2550m

▲ Yangrima

TARKEGHYANG
2550m

MAGINGOTH
3200m

RIDGE
ROUTE

STANDARD ROUTE

TRAIL

Melamchi Khola

TIMBU
1350m

SARMANTHANG
2590m

BASICALLY FOLLOWS RIDGE

KUTUMSANG
2500m

GULPHU
BHANJYANG
2150m

KIUL TAR

RIDGE ROUTE

TWO RIVERS
1000m

KAKANI

CHIPLING
2150m

TALAMARANG
950m

POKHARI

DUBACHAUR

PATI BHANJYANG
1750m

CHISOPANI
2180m

Helambu

2450m

MELAMCHI
PUL
(BAZAAR)
850m

Indrawati River

0   2km
(1:200,000)

MULKHARKA

SUNDARIJAL 1400m
ROAD TO KATHMANDU (½ HOUR)   ↓ NAGARKOT

ROAD TO
KATHMANDU
(4 HOURS)

the usual bus ride in between. However, the views are arguably better from Chisopani, so unless you want several sunrises (and sunsets), trekking the shortest route is probably better. The one minor advantage, if you take the bus up, is that Nagarkot is already on top of the valley rim. The trade-off is the extra horizontal distance and the minor hills en route, however these probably involve comparable effort to the slog up from Sudarijal. Unless you are very fit, Nagarkot to Chisopani isn't possible in one day and there aren't any tourist lodges to stay in en route. Route descriptions of these options begin on p210.

Mountain-biking to Chisopani

Beginning from Kakani, Budhanilkantha, Sundarijal, Sankhu or Nagarkot it is possible to mountain-bike to Chisopani. There is, of course, the minor problem of what to do with the bike for the rest of the trek. This is where a mountain bike company comes in handy; see Dawn 'til Dusk in the Kathmandu Guest House compound or Himalayan Mountain Bikes in the compound beside. They can also arrange to have your rucksack carried to Chisopani. The cost should be approximately US$25-40 per day.

❑ The Melamchi drinking water project

Kathmandu has several drinking water problems. The first is the water deficiency: Kathmandu receives around 60 million litres a day in the dry season while demand is around 130 million litres a day. In addition it was estimated that as much as 50% of the water was lost from the system before reaching a tap. The second is the quality of the water: only part of the city supply is chlorinated and much of this is negated by the broken pipes that mean sewerage and drinking water can get mixed, with unhealthy consequences. Beginning in 1995, water pipes throughout the city have been dug up and replaced in an effort to begin solving these problems.

Bridging the water deficit is more difficult. After many project feasibility studies the one that came out on top was the Melamchi diversion scheme. This will take up to 170 million litres a day from the Melamchi Khola, ensuring the city has enough water to match its growth for at least a couple of decades.

Because Kathmandu is surrounded by hills, the project will use a 27km tunnel and this will incorporate a 15MW hydro-electric scheme at Mahankal to help Kathmandu's electricity supply too. The US$60 million project is scheduled for completion around 2001.

According to studies (probably undertaken by the World Bank) the scheme has been found to be technically and financially feasible, socially desirable and environmentally acceptable. As with all large projects there is a trade-off between development – in this case to provide the most basic of human needs: clean drinking water – and damage to the environment, which appears minimal, especially given the benefits. Apparently surplus water might occasionally be used to flush the holy but disgustingly dirty Bagmati River (see *White Water Nepal* for Jerry Moffat's amusing account of the dangers of kayaking it).

The dirt roads are relatively safe and the riding is easy; only a handful of vehicles a day use the road. There is, however, a ½km section between Sankhu or Nagarkot and the Shivapuri Integrated Watershed Reserve which is unrideable, so you have to carry your bike. Beginning from Nagarkot or Kakani saves some hill ascent, unless of course you were keen enough to cycle up there. Talk with the companies to work out which is the best option for you.

The Pati Bhanjyang road

In 1995 the four-wheel drive track around the Shivapuri Reserve was extended from Chisopani to Pati Bhanjyang to enable the drilling of a test tunnel for the Melamchi drinking water project. It has since been neglected and in 1996 this road was too rough for taxis. It may yet be tidied up enough to be useable. It is doubtful if there will be enough business to start a bus service but it does have the potential at some point in the future to change the starting point of the trek.

The Timbu road

A major part of the Melamchi drinking water scheme is a road part way up the Melamchi Khola, probably to Timbu. This will increase the trekking options in Helambu. While the road is being constructed the dynamics will constantly change. Upgrading the existing road to the Ghyalthum Khola should happen quickly but pushing further up will take longer. The last point to note is that the road may only be open to construction vehicles.

Gazing into a crystal ball these are possible changes (see the map of Helambu, p179):

Helambu Circuit The full circuit via Sarmathang will still be an attractive and worthwhile trek. Taking the lower Timbu route from Tarkeghyang will make the trek a day shorter but cuts out the most beautiful section – the walk along the valley.

Mini Helambu Circuit This is a new trek, Timbu to Timbu. The best direction would be to Tarkeghyang, then Melamchi and Tharepati. From Tharepati there are several options. From Mere Danda a ridge leads down to Gohare and Mahankal by-the-river; descending via Kutumsang is also possible.

Gosainkund Possibly the greatest impact will be on trekkers heading south from Gosainkund. It will be marginally quicker and perhaps more enjoyable to drop from Tharepati to Melamchi and Tarkeghyang then Timbu rather than the Sundarijal ending. Beginning the Gosainkund trek this way will mean staying in Tarkeghyang and Melamchi to acclimatise and from there still taking it slowly.

THE FIRST DAY'S TREK

Over the first few days of a march (trek) it is wise to draw a veil... you wonder if man really was intended to walk, whether motoring after all is not his natural mode of progression, and whether the call of the open road is as insistent as you yourself thought or as the poets of that school sing. Tilman, *The Seven Mountain-Travel Books*

Whether you begin from Sundarijal, Sankhu or Melamchi Pul for Sarmathang, Tilman's quote is particularly apt, at least for the first day and that first hill. All are not just any hill but are particularly tough ones on what is supposed to be a gentle trek.

It pays to be organised before taking the first step. A hat, sunscreen and full water bottle are essential. If you are trekking with a group realise that on leaving Kathmandu you may not have access to the bags carried by the porters until arriving at camp. Be sure to have your trekking permit and a pen handy for the various checkposts along the way.

Sundarijal start An early start will beat the heat but is not easy to achieve. If you don't think you can make it to Sundarijal before 8am forget rushing around and take a more leisurely start. By catching a taxi in Kathmandu at 8.30am and sightseeing along the way, providing you're on the trail by 11am or so you will still make Chisopani, even at a snail's pace. Fast walkers might note that the cumulative walking time to Chisopani is around three hours so reaching Pati Bhanjyang is comfortable and walking further, possible.

Most trekkers spend their first night at Chisopani to catch the wonderful Himalayan panorama the next morning. Despite walking closer to the mountain ranges over the next few days this is the best overall view, the only reason Chisopani exists and the only reason to visit. For the first time Himalayan trekker it is a pleasant enough place but with a few days' experience you realise it is more Kathmandu than rural Nepal. Getting to Sundarijal begins on p183.

Melamchi Pul start Leaving Kathmandu early, you could have a late lunch at Melamchi Pul and hit the trail. On the Sarmathang route, groups tend to camp at Dubachaur while individual trekkers will make it to the simple Pokhari or Kakani lodges (two to four hours up).

Taking the Kiul/Timbu route, assuming the bus service ends at Melamchi Pul, the ideal place to stay is ***Two Rivers Lodge***, 2½-3½ hours away. Late starters could stay at Talamarang. From either place Tarkeghyang is a long, hot-hill day away. Unless staying at Two Rivers Lodge the accommodation for the first night will be basic; you can look forward to much better.

TO MELAMCHI PUL

By bus There are no direct buses so first take one of the frequent buses from the Ratna Park (old) bus station (see Kathmandu map, p76) to Banepa. From the far end of Banepa, buses or more usually old Mercedes trucks, leave roughly every half hour for Melamchi Pul. Groups normally travel by private bus.

By taxi This is not a common destination so pricing it will be difficult. Taking a metered taxi at double the meter is a good option. This should come in at just under US$100.

The road journey and route description (in reverse) begins on p205.

TO SUNDARIJAI

On the edge of the Kathmandu Valley flats, Sundarijal is ³/₄-1¹/₂ hour's drive from Thamel.

By bus From the Ratna Park bus station, run-down No 2 Mercedes vans leave every hour or so for the 1-1¹/₂ hour journey. Alternatively take a taxi to Baudha or the road junction a kilometre past then wait for the crowded bus. Sundarijal is at the end of the road.

By taxi If you want to take a taxi it's probably best to use a metered one. However, since the driver is unlikely to have passengers for the return journey it's worth bargaining for up to twice the meter fare, which will come to US$8-16. This is still likely to be cheaper than an unmetered taxi.

The journey
The route passes the huge stupa of Baudha (see p91) giving you a chance to see it if you haven't already, and the pleasant Gokarna Mahadev (temple) which is also well worth a visit.

Gokarna Mahadev/Gokarneswar Graciously old but still very much alive, this pagoda temple is situated by the Holy Bagmati river; it used to be a cremation site. The complex is in excellent condition thanks to a UNESCO-sponsored preservation project.

SUNDARIJAL [MAP 16, 185]

TREKKING TO THAREPATI

Sundarijal 1400m/4600ft
Beautiful water is the translation but the stream no longer tinkles down, instead it is piped to Kathmandu as part of the city water supply. The Himalayan Rescue Dog Squad used to be based in Sundarijal but moved to Melamchi Pul in March 1996.

Sundarijal is principally a drinks and snack stop. For the trekker about to take the first steps, be prepared; this is a brutal hill. Even in mid-winter it is hot work, and at any other time the sun can be blistering. Comfort can be taken from the number of shady teahouses and the fact that it shouldn't be this hot again. Since you are gaining, or less euphemistically, slogging up 1000m/3280ft, it gets noticeably cooler the higher you go. The other reward is a glance backwards; you gain height surprisingly rapidly and the view expands satisfyingly. You also quickly leave behind the trappings of Kathmandu to enter rural Nepal although concrete buildings haunt you to at least Chisopani. This is the longest and toughest hill on the Helambu trek.

A few minutes along the trail is a police post that checks you have a trekking permit and beside them is a similar office to check your National Park entrance fee receipt; you can pay the fee here. Further up the Shivapuri Integrated Watershed and Wildlife Reserve office charges you Rs250 for entry.

Kids pester for pens and sweets knowing that most trekkers on the first day of their first trek are naive. Don't give them – see p109. Mulkharka is the last spread out village and the last place for snacks or an early lunch. At the army camp just above the trail you enter the wilderness area of the Shivapuri Integrated Watershed Reserve. When this was created the higher villages were moved out hence the odd building in ruins.

The crest of the pass might revive hill-fatigued spirits. Creased hills fold into the distance, layered by endless terraces with pockets of forest and scattered villages, typical middle-hills rural Nepal. The snow peaks of the Jugal and Ganesh Himals jut above the horizon.

Any churned patches of dirt on the forest floor around here are the work of pigs rooting around. They use their acute sense of smell to locate bulbs and roots underground then dig these up exclusively with their snout. Don't sleep outside around here; the pigs have been known to attack, but you'll have no problems in a tent.

Chisopani 2180m/7150ft

There is only one reason to stay here and that is for the morning and, if you are lucky, evening view of the Himalaya. The panorama spreads from the mountains south of Everest to the Manaslu range.

The place itself isn't particularly pretty: a handful of concrete buildings and a few shacks. Try to avoid staying at BK's restaurant and

---

❏ **The picnic**
Kathmandu families often take a picnic by the water reservoir on Saturdays and festival days. Beside sweating trekkers and groaning porters, women in elegant surawals or saris with high heels wobble under umbrellas. The men, in suits, carry the supplies and kids skip around whining for coke. Most proudly show their city heritage by being completely unprepared for the rude steps and the rigorous walk. Driving to Chisopani for lunch is fashionable among the well-wheeled.

Map 16 185

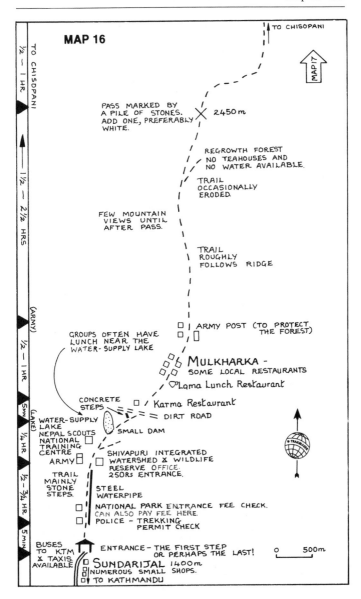

MAP 16

TO CHISOPANI

MAP17

TO CHISOPANI
½ — 1 HR.
1½ — 2½ HRS
(ARMY) ½ — 1 HR.
(LAKE) 5mm ¼ HR.
½ — ¾ HR.
5 MIN

PASS MARKED BY
A PILE OF STONES.
ADD ONE, PREFERABLY
WHITE.
✕ 2450 m

REGROWTH FOREST
NO TEAHOUSES AND
NO WATER AVAILABLE.

TRAIL
OCCASIONALLY
ERODED.

FEW MOUNTAIN
VIEWS UNTIL
AFTER PASS.

TRAIL
ROUGHLY
FOLLOWS RIDGE

ARMY POST (TO PROTECT
THE FOREST)

GROUPS OFTEN HAVE
LUNCH NEAR THE
WATER-SUPPLY LAKE

MULKHARKA -
SOME LOCAL RESTAURANTS
♡ Lama Lunch Restaurant

CONCRETE
STEPS
Karma Restaurant
= DIRT ROAD

WATER-SUPPLY
LAKE
NEPAL SCOUTS
NATIONAL
TRAINING
CENTRE
SMALL DAM

ARMY
SHIVAPURI INTEGRATED
WATERSHED & WILDLIFE
RESERVE OFFICE.
250Rs ENTRANCE.

TRAIL
MAINLY
STONE
STEPS.
STEEL
WATERPIPE

NATIONAL PARK ENTRANCE FEE CHECK.
CAN ALSO PAY FEE HERE.
POLICE - TREKKING
PERMIT CHECK

BUSES
TO KTM
& TAXIS
AVAILABLE
ENTRANCE - THE FIRST STEP
OR PERHAPS THE LAST!
0   500m

SUNDARIJAL 1400 m
NUMEROUS SMALL SHOPS.
TO KATHMANDU

□ **Chautara**

'The coolies' joy and the traveller's bane. In this pleasant land where all loads are carried upon men's backs, where the tracks are rough and steep and the days hot, various pious and public-spirited men – of whom in my opinion there have been too many – perpetuate their names by planting two fast-growing shady trees and training around them a rectangular or sometimes circular stone dias with a lower parapet as a seat – the perfect height for resting a load'. Tilman, *The Seven Mountain-Travel Books*

It is around this area that you may first come to appreciate chautaras, particularly if you're lugging a heavy rucksack.

Himalayan Lodge – the owner can get abusive and troublesome, especially after a few drinks.

Leaving Chisopani, Pati Bhanjyang remains well-hidden until you are about to trip over it. The original trail leads roughly down the ridge crest, often worn several metres into the red soil. The newer road also leads, more circuitously, to Pati Bhanjyang.

CHISOPANI, PATI BHANJYANG & CHIPLING   [MAP 17]

Pati Bhanjyang 1750m/5750ft
Pati means a simple shelter for passers by. From that the village has developed into a clutch of lodges and shops. Unlike Chisopani, it is a village of character. The buildings are more traditional in style, made of wood and mud although many have steel roofs. Chickens listlessly pick at the dirt and children play in it. Babies suckle and locals chuckle. It is a good place to sit over a cup of tea and watch the world go by.

There are several offices here, all part of the ambitious Melamchi project. A little below the village is the site of a 400m/1300ft access tunnel. This test tunnel has been financed by the United Nations Development Programme (UNDP) and is under the management of the United Mission to Nepal (UMN), originally a Christian NGO which has turned into a skilled project management service, still based on Christian principles.

Chipling 2150m/7050ft
The trail climbs out of Hindu country into Buddhist Tamang and Tibetan country. Heavier rounded features showing the Tamang's ancient Tibetan heritage replace the fine Brahman features. Gone too are the favoured reds, the Brahman caste colour and the colour of marriage. The tight bright short *blouse* (bodice) of the Hindu women gives way to the duller but necessarily warmer full *cholo* (long-sleeved blouse with a tie at the shoulder) and perhaps a cardigan. Although the Tamangs still favour the *lungi*, the wraparound skirt common to Hindu women as well, the difference is that when Hindu women dress up their first choice is the sari while

Map 17 187

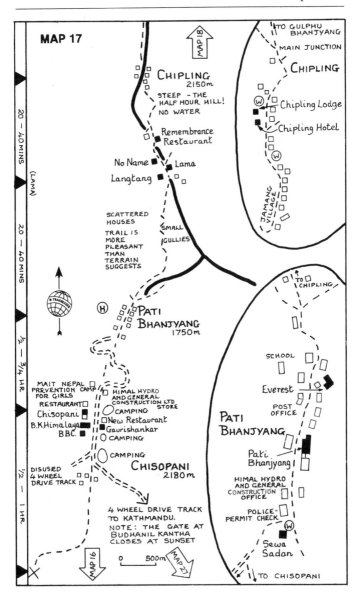

MAP 17

TO MAP 18

TO GULPHU BHANJYANG

MAIN JUNCTION

CHIPLING
2150m

CHIPLING

STEEP – THE
HALF HOUR HILL!
NO WATER

(W) Chipling Lodge

Chipling Hotel

Remembrance
Restaurant

(W)

No Name   Lama

Langtang

JAMANG VILLAGE

SCATTERED
HOUSES

SMALL
GULLIES

TRAIL IS
MORE
PLEASANT
THAN
TERRAIN
SUGGESTS

TO
CHIPLING

(Lama)

20 – 40 MINS

20 – 40 MINS

½ – ¾ HR

½ – 1 HR

(H) PATI
BHANJYANG
1750m

SCHOOL

Everest

POST
OFFICE

MAIT NEPAL
PREVENTION CAMP
FOR GIRLS
RESTAURANT

HIMAL HYDRO
AND GENERAL
CONSTRUCTION LTD
STORE

Chisopani

CAMPING

B.K.Himalaya
BBC.

New Restaurant

Gaurishankar

CAMPING

PATI
BHANJYANG

Pati
Bhanjyang

CAMPING

DISUSED
4 WHEEL
DRIVE TRACK

CHISOPANI
2180m

HIMAL HYDRO
AND GENERAL
CONSTRUCTION
OFFICE

POLICE –
PERMIT CHECK

4 WHEEL DRIVE TRACK
TO KATHMANDU.
NOTE: THE GATE AT
BUDHANIL KANTHA
CLOSES AT SUNSET

(W)

Sewa
Sadan

TO MAP 16

0   500m

TO MAP 27

TO CHISOPANI

Tamangs, who place less emphasis on appearance, choose the *phorier*, something similar to the *lungi* but with special folds at the top. The *partooka*, a folded scarf around the waist, is the place where money is often kept and it can be worn with all of these. The tillary, the multi-strand necklace featuring a chunk of tooled gold that is the proud symbol of high caste Hindu marriage is replaced by heavy gold earrings and the occasional turquoise or red coral although neither denote marriage; even though marriage is celebrated in the Tibetan-based cultures, it isn't constantly displayed. The differences between the men are clearer in the farming cultures below Tarkeghyang and Sarmathang than here.

The Hindus' first language of Nepali that in the past was a great advantage in winning government jobs has been replaced by the locals' first language of *lama barsa*, which is essentially Tibetan. However, one of the government's ongoing policies to unify the vast variety of ethnic groups in the country is to conduct all classes in Nepali, except compulsory English, so now the vast majority of Nepalis, no matter what their cultural background or first language is, can speak the language of their country.

The simple restaurants and lodges of Chipling begin in a small saddle and are spread over half an hour of hill-climbing.

KUTUMSANG AND GUL BHANJYANG   [MAP 18]
Gulphu Bhanjyang 2150m/7050ft
Gulphu means where cattle are sheltered. The village was started by two Gurung brothers from the Ganesh area sometime in the 1940s and now it is an unusual mixture of Gurungs (who are normally found only in the around Pokhara) and Tamangs. It is a bazaar village with shops, simple restaurants and a couple of offices lining the main paved trail. Groups normally camp in the school grounds.

Kutumsang 2500m/8200ft
Slung in a saddle, this trekkers settlement has well-stocked shops and a variety of lodges. The real village is perhaps half an hour off the ridge. In winter if there have been heavy snowfalls it may be better to head directly to Melamchi and bypass Tharepati.

Between Gulphu and Kutumsang is another cultural shift, from Tamang dominated areas to Yolmo or Tibetan domination. The Tamangs moved from Tibet hundreds of years before the Yolmo, in migrations that are still not well understood. The Yolmo consider themselves of higher and purer Tibetan stock, most coming from the lama or priest class from around Kyirong. This is shown among the women by dressing more traditionally and keeping their houses tidier. The Yolmo men, although they usually dress in a more fashionable Nepali style, take care to always look presentable. Being of a lama background there is more emphasis on reli-

Map 18 189

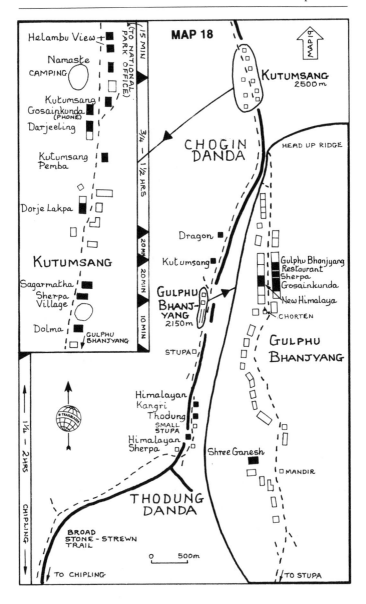

MAP 18

Helambu View
Namaste
CAMPING
Kutumsang
Gosainkunda (PHONE)
Darjeeling
Kutumsang
Pemba
Dorje Lakpa
KUTUMSANG
Sagarmatha
Sherpa
Village
Dolma
GULPHU
BHANJYANG

(TO NATIONAL PARK OFFICE)
/15 MIN
3/4
1/2 HRS
20 MIN
20 MIN
10 MIN

KUTUMSANG
2500m

CHOGIN
DANDA

HEAD UP RIDGE

Dragon

Kutumsang

GULPHU
BHANJ-
YANG
2150m

Gulphu Bhanjyang
Restaurant
Sherpa
Gosainkunda
New Himalaya
CHORTEN

GULPHU
BHANJYANG

STUPA

Himalayan
Kangri
Thodung
SMALL
STUPA
Himalayan
Sherpa

Shree Ganesh

MANDIR

THODUNG
DANDA

TO TRAILHEAD

1 1/4 — 2 HRS
CHIPLING

BROAD
STONE-STREWN
TRAIL

0   500m

TO CHIPLING

TO STUPA

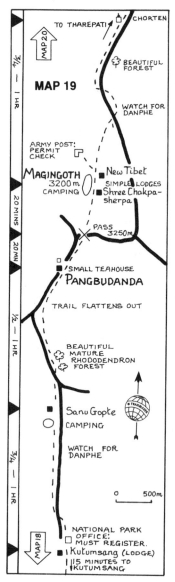

gion, as evidenced by the gompas or *ghyangs* central to villages further around the Helambu Circuit. Prayer beads are common and the older men often spin a hand-held prayer wheel. Their purer form of Tibetan language is also quite different from the corrupted Tamang (and Solu-Khumbu Sherpa) version.

There is little or no water to be found between Kutumsang and Magin Goth. In the forested sections along here look out for the male Danphe pheasant, the richly coloured national bird of Nepal. It has iridescent midnight blue body plumage and green colouring around its neck. Its head sports a small royal plume and the tail is bronze and white in flight. It clucks calls of alarm when startled and glides down skimming the treetops, being too plump to actually fly up far. In the evenings they nest near the top of open trees. The female is a tardier speckled brown.

Magingoth 3200m/10,500ft

Magingoth, pronounced Magingoat-h, is still very much in the development phase. The army camp inspired the first lodge-shop, mainly to sell alcohol. Now there are two simple lodges. Teahouse trekkers occasionally stay here but mostly it is used by porters from organised trekking groups. See **MAP 19**, opposite.

THAREPATI 3600m/11,800ft

This kharka (grazing area), originally used only during the warmer

Map 19 191

months, has sprouted lodges, some of which are open virtually year round. The lodges, similar to the ones at Gosainkund, date from 1990, the year it became possible to teahouse trek the Helambu Circuit and Gosainkund route. Previously trekkers either went in a group or carried tents.

Laurebina pass is the gentle U-pass, smiling at you slightly left (west) of the main ridge. With binoculars you can even pick out trekkers there. The trail stays entirely on the west face of the ridge beginning by gently dropping out of Tharepati.

▲ **For the opposite direction** Looking south from the Gosainkunda and Himali Yak lodges is a distinct trail climbing to a small pass, visible in the middle distance. This is the main trail just south of Magingoth.

To Gosainkund The trail description and maps continue on p176.

To Melamchi The trail drops steeply and enters beautiful mixed forest almost immediately. After descending a minor ridge the track enters what looks like a minor stream bed. There is a kharka to the south but don't head to this. Instead the trail comes to a confluence of a couple of streams and across this the path is clear enough. The track soon heads north, the descent becoming more of a traverse, and rounds several ridges.

THAREPATI, MELAMCHI & TARKEGHYANG [MAP 20/21, p194]

Melamchi 2550m/8366ft
The real name of this village is Melamchighyang or Melamchimghyang, not Melamchigoan. The 110 or so houses are loosely scattered around the gompa on a plain with good cropping land. Despite their apparent absence, the villagers have many cows and crossbreeds; most are kept at high kharkas in the summer and in simple jungle camps for the rest of the year.

Many of the lodges are traditional houses with a few extra rooms. Similar to some of the Tarkeghyang and Sarmathang lodges, the dining room may have an elegant set of dark shelves neatly filled with stunning polished brass and copper pots. They are arranged decoratively but each has a use and after the initial surprise you may be able to find order in the array. The largest store water and may be used for cooking for festivals and weddings. Smaller pots are used for cooking and storage. The most recent addition may be a matched set of pressure-cookers. The shelves or cupboards hide jars of herbs and spices and perhaps a mortar and pestle for preparing them fresh. Other cupboards are actually bins for storing the staples: rice, dal, wheat flour, tsampa, potatoes and cooking oil. Housewives proudly, often obsessively, keep this room spotless, forever sweeping imaginary specks of dust.

❏ **The price of education in Melamchi**
In Melamchi, an old man told a story that illustrated the feudal ways of Nepal prior to the opening up that began in the 1950s. Chandra Samsher, prime minister in the 1920s, visited the region. He was shocked to see a villager writing. Saying that farmers had no need to write, he had the man's fingers cut off. The Ranas preferred their population uneducated so that they would cause less trouble and to this end, until the 1950s, Nepal had only a single school for the Rana children.

The layout of the L-shaped room is always the same. In the outer corner of the 'L' is the fireplace. This is usually a small squat steel stove with an effective chimney (unusual in rural Nepal other than in trekkers lodges). This is the woman's domain and all the kitchen necessities are handy. In the outer smaller section of the 'L' is the spiritual area. Beside a Buddha statue will usually be a photo of a high Lama, often the Dalai Lama. A traditional prayer book will be hidden somewhere. It is the man's job to read this but all the people in the household prostrate in front of the image of Buddha and maintain the butter candles and the seven bowls of water which symbolise purity – an offering of the most abundant resource, because, of course, Buddhism is all about giving up thirst for material goods. On the inner wall of the 'L' is the other status symbol of the man of the house, his travel trunks. Many of the male villagers here work or trade in India, scorning work in Kathmandu as not well paid, although that isn't exactly the truth. This is why trekking guides from Helambu are almost impossible to come by.

In traditional Sherpa and Tibetan culture the most respected guest (or the man of the house when there are no guests) is always offered the warmest place to the right of the fire. Lamas, however, should be offered a place closest to the spiritual area. So, since many locals are essentially trained lamas, the ordering of who sits where gets complicated. With many guests, the ordering is a polite but visible mark of social standing and it often takes a considerable time to sort out as etiquette demands a humble approach. Seating is also a problem at ceremonies held in gompas.

As a tourist-guest simply sit where your host suggests. During gompa ceremonies this will be closest to the door, ie furthest away from the altar. During festivals all the food and drink is provided free. Take your fill if you can stomach the offerings because satisfying the guests is a matter of village pride; it's also a reason for giving generous donations to the gompa on other occasions.

(Opposite) Top: Pemthang Karpo (see p159) is surrounded by mountains and glaciers. **Bottom:** A Tarkeghyang herding family share their hearth with the baby yaks.

❏ **Fashion**
The men, here and in Tarkeghyang, mainly wear a traditional form of Nepali dress, not Tibetan dress. Why? The answer is fashion! The narrow trousers/pants are called *surawal*, the front-crossed shirt *daura* (the names also used by the female equivalents) and the waistcoat, an *ascot* (you can guess the origin of the word). The black hat is the conservative Nepali government style. The men look sober and official in the mainly dark blue or grey colours (see photo opposite p128). Some wear a cummerbund while others proudly wear a thick leather belt with an embossed silver buckle – their old army belt.

If there's a pile of shoes outside a house or gompa you should take yours off too, and certainly never step on carpets without removing them.

Staying at Melamchi may also be your first chance to try *tzarjah* or Tibetan tea. Locals start the day with this and early in the morning you may hear it being prepared. First the water in a special teapot is brought to the boil, then the tea is added. Often this is tea dust but on special occasions leaves may be broken off a brick of old Tibetan tea. This is then poured into a tea-churn, the long wooden cylinder. Salt and butter (of variable rancidity) are added and mixed with a long handle, producing a distinctive sloshing sound. Once thoroughly mixed it's poured back into the teapot and brought to the boil again. Tibetan tea is normally served in ornamental wooden bowls or china bowls and a prayer is said before drinking it. Etiquette says that after a few sips the bowl should be refilled. After a polite length of time the guest may finish the bowl signifying they have had enough. Among the locals it is quite a game involving lots of protestations to make sure that the bowl can never be emptied. Similar to chang drinking, the host would be a poor one if the guest wasn't completely full and, in the case of chang, could leave still walking in a straight line.

A traditional snack that often accompanies *tzarjah* is *polda* – tea and tsampa mixed. This can be made with salt tea, as it usually is in the morning, or with sweet tea (it also goes well with coffee). There's a certain skill in mixing it to edible proportions and then eating it without choking, especially if the mixture is too thick. The next trick is licking the bowl without pie-on-the-face consequences. If you have rapidly acquired these skills the last trick is to eat it without mixing; watch how the locals deftly toss a few fingers-full down. To save trekkers potential mixing and eating embarrassment *polda* is often served as the smooth tsampa porridge on the menu. A pinch of salt, as with all porridges, is the ingredient needed for perfection. Another morning ritual, often completed before the trekker has realised it is another day, is burning incense. Embers from the

---

(Opposite) Langtang Lirung (7234m, see p151) dwarfs the popular Cherko (Tsergo Ri) viewpoint. Some spring snow lingers.

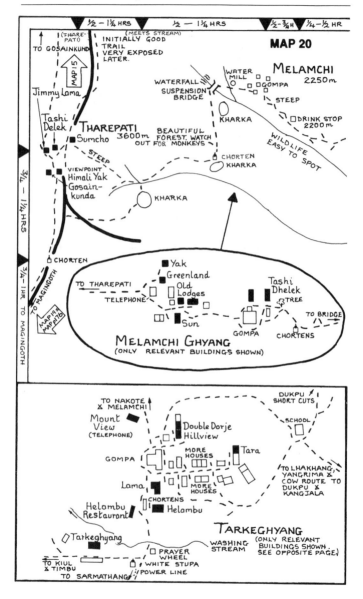

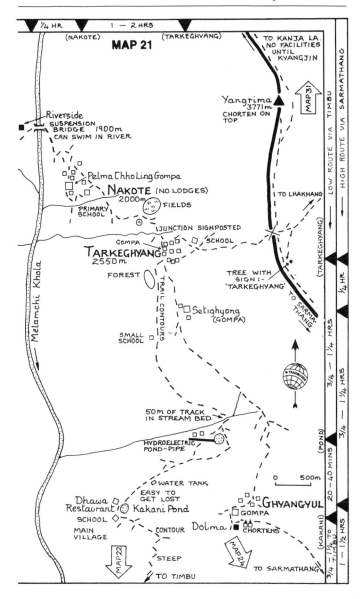

MAP 21

¼ HR   1 – 2 HRS
(NAKOTE)   (TARKEGHYANG)

TO KANJA LA.
NO FACILITIES
UNTIL
KYANGJIN

Yangrima
3771m
CHORTEN ON
TOP

MAP 31

Riverside
SUSPENSION
BRIDGE   1900m
CAN SWIM IN RIVER

Pelma Chho Ling Gompa
NAKOTE (NO LODGES)
2000m   FIELDS

PRIMARY
SCHOOL

TO LHAKHANG

JUNCTION SIGNPOSTED

GOMPA   SCHOOL

TARKEGHYANG
2550 m

FOREST

TREE WITH
SIGN :-
'TARKEGHYANG'

TO SARMA-
THANG

Setighyong
(GOMPA)

SMALL
SCHOOL

LOW ROUTE VIA TIMBU

HIGH ROUTE VIA SARMATHANG

(TARKEGHYANG)

Melamchi Khola

TRAIL CONTOURS

⊕ TRAILBLAZER

50m OF TRACK
IN STREAM BED

HYDROELECTRIC
POND-PIPE

0   500m

WATER TANK

EASY TO
GET LOST

Dhawa
Restaurant   Kakani Pond

SCHOOL

MAIN
VILLAGE

CONTOUR   Dolma

GHYANGYUL

GOMPA

CHORTENS

MAP 22

STEEP

TO TIMBU

MAP 24

TO SARMATHANG

¼ HR.   ¾ – 1¼ HRS   ¾ – 1¼ HRS   20 – 40 MINS   ¾ – 1¼ TO TIMBU   1 – 1½ HRS

(POND)   (KAKANI)

fire are put in a squat brass jar with chains to hang it by, then juniper is added. The smoking pot is then waved around the house and especially the openings in it, to protect against an invasion of evil spirits.

Electricity comes from the old Nepal Electricity Authority hydro station between Tarkeghyang and Timbu. As with the majority of state-run projects it could do with revitalising – as you might notice. The telephone system began in February 1996. The villagers paid for the system themselves using money accrued in the village street development committee, which you will probably be asked to contribute to. A solar system supplies power.

The ghyang (gompa) is old but underwent extensive renovations, including the repainting of the murals, in 1991. Most foreigners prefer old things, the older the better, but the locals take quite a different view. They renovate with pride to show that the village has money. Skilled mural painters command Rs250 to Rs500 a day, making any work expensive and prestigious.

▲ Melamchi to Tharepati (ie the opposite direction)

Beware! Once well out of Melamchi it is easy to take the wrong trail, especially at the confluence of the streams. The wrong route brings you up on top of the ridge somewhere between Kutumsang and Tharepati, rather than walking straight into Tharepati. If in doubt take the right-hand path that heads directly up to the top of the ridge.

Tarkeghyang 2550m/8366ft   [see MAP 20, p194]

Several hundred years ago a terrible plague struck Kathmandu. Many people died while high priests unsuccessfully prayed to end the horror. Eventually the king called for a high Lama from Kyirong who lived in a Yolmo village. After several days of praying, the plague slowed then stopped. In return the King offered whatever the Lama wanted. He asked for 100 of the finest horses. Once back in his village he changed his mind and returned to Kathmandu and the King. Instead he asked for land. The King gratefully granted the ghyang (gompa), and therefore the village, all the land to the north up to the mountains as well as some land to the south. This is the origin of the village's name because *Ta* or *Tar* in Tibetan means horse and *Khye* means 100; it also explains why the village is comparatively wealthy and why, between here and Keldang, you will only meet shepherds and herders from Tarkeghyang. Although these families

---

❏ **Tumna**
Around you are likely to see the Tibetan instrument, the four-stringed tumna for sale. You may even hear it being played - the Yolmo are the only culture who use them. Unlike the Nepali *saarangee* (violin) which is available in Kathmandu, the tumna is plucked and strummed and the same few cords are used for different songs.

are from a lower caste than the people who live permanently in the village, their way of life is looked upon rather romantically by many of the high status villagers. In a strange circle of support it is the villagers who buy most of the butter and cheese produced by the herders.

It also explains why the village is a charming warren of narrow alleys and densely packed houses. The land to the south is leased to farmers who pay rent in the form of part of the crop so the Tarkeghyang people don't need to farm land themselves, hence the lack of cropping land here. This leaves the male population with enough time on their hands to study Buddhism – the highest, most noble vocation – so most males are non-practising lamas.

Animals can't be killed here so trekking groups are requested either not to kill meat here or to kill it well south of the village. The gompa can be opened for tourists but donations are expected.

Around Tarkeghyang
Being roughly the half way point around the Helambu Circuit some people plan a rest day here. Aside from enjoying the village and washing clothes, day trip options are visiting Lhakhang or the holy peak of Yangrima.

Lhakhang means the inner room of a gompa and it is a reference to the sacred status of the area. A newish gompa and a scattering of shacks for monks are set among massive fir trees and millions of prayer flags. The area is increasingly used as a Buddhist retreat and the Rinpoche occasionally arrives by helicopter. The gompa is worth visiting but the forest is more impressive.

Following the ridge down from the saddle is a direct trail to Sarmathang. It is also possible to trek east of Lhakhang then down to Melamchi Pul in three days through an area similar to Helambu except that few trekkers venture this way. Further east are the holy lakes of Panch Pokhari and a route to the Arniko Highway, the Kathmandu to Lhasa road. This is often called the Jugal Himal trek.

Yangrima 3771m/12,372ft This is the best view point of the area. In addition to the entire Jugal range to the north, snow peaks form the east and west skylines. The 1200m/4000ft climb takes three to five hours, so pack a hill-climbing attitude, lunch and plenty of water. The descent is considerably quicker. On the Buddha's birthday the people from the surrounding areas meet at the top of Yangrima for a picnic and blessings, then retire to Tarkeghyang for more evening celebrations.

Leaving Tarkeghyang
The description of the standard trail to Sarmathang begins on p200. For Timbu and Kiul see below. For Dhukpu and the Kangja La the description (in reverse) begins on p221.

TO MELAMCHI PUL VIA TIMBU AND KIUL

The trail roughly contours as it leave Tarkeghyang then it descends to the hydro-electric project. By the time you have contoured to the pond at Kakani the trail has lost 500m/1650ft in altitude. The 700m/2300ft more of descent to Timbu is more concentrated and you can't help thinking that it must be horrible to climb.

MELAMCHI KHOLA   [MAP 22]

Timbu 1350m/4430ft

The descent brings you to the same altitude as Kathmandu and changes all round. In the warmth it is hard to remember the cooler climate above. The Yolmo culture is replaced by a mix of Tamang and Hindu and lots of school children. The locals have an idle curiosity, a strange indifference to everything and everyone and say some odd things, but a smile often turns the curious stare into a smile returned – from the same sex anyway.

Lodges A few shops purport to be lodges; as in much of rural Nepal, some are restaurants only, the finer points of the English language being lost. Others do have a few dusty beds somewhere. Trekking in the low country can be ridiculously cheap, sometimes less than US$2 a day but it is a case of you pay for what you get. Menus don't exist so the choice is narrowed to dal bhaat, omelettes and noodle soups. If there are lots of pots around, take a look under the lids. If Nepali chiya, sweet milk tea, doesn't appeal soft drinks may be down to bearable prices (the empties are recycled).

To Kiultar The altitude is now below even that of Kathmandu. Take care in the heat to drink plenty and wear a hat if sunny. Swimming in the river becomes pleasant although the water's temperature still hints at its glacial origins. You are now back amongst fine-featured women and lean sun-parched men with beanpole legs. Shorts are typically accompanied by shirts, waistcoats and the *Palpa topi*, the multi-coloured Nepali hat. When off to visit relatives everyone dresses up – the women in their finest sari, the men in a suit jacket, skinny white *surawal* trousers/pants and shoes.

The ochre-coloured, thatched houses are surrounded by terraces which, because it is now too warm for frosts, can be cropped year round – as long as they are irrigated. The first rice-planting season is late March/early April – the rice plants are plucked in clumps from the small bright green fields (*biew*) that look more like a dense mat of grass. These are transplanted less densely by hard-working teams in water-logged paddies. Good irrigation is essential. For less well-irrigated fields the main rice-planting season is in July, once the fields have been inundated

Map 22 199

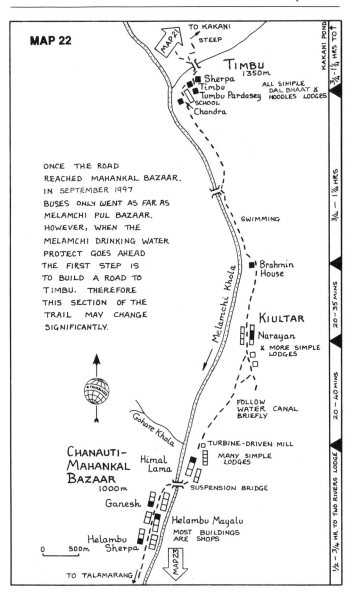

MAP 22

TO KAKANI

STEEP

MAP 21

TIMBU 1350m

Sherpa
Timbu
Tumbu Pardasey
SCHOOL
Chandra

ALL SIMPLE
DAL BHAAT &
NOODLES LODGES

KAKANI POND

3/4 - 1 1/4 HRS TO ↑

ONCE THE ROAD
REACHED MAHANKAL BAZAAR.
IN SEPTEMBER 1997
BUSES ONLY WENT AS FAR AS
MELAMCHI PUL BAZAAR.
HOWEVER, WHEN THE
MELAMCHI DRINKING WATER
PROJECT GOES AHEAD
THE FIRST STEP IS
TO BUILD A ROAD TO
TIMBU. THEREFORE
THIS SECTION OF THE
TRAIL MAY CHANGE
SIGNIFICANTLY.

3/4 - 1 1/4 HRS

SWIMMING

Melamchi Khola

Brahmin
House

20 - 35 MINS

KIULTAR

Narayan
X MORE SIMPLE
LODGES

TRAILBLAZER

FOLLOW
WATER CANAL
BRIEFLY

20 - 40 MINS

Gohare Khola

TURBINE-DRIVEN MILL

MANY SIMPLE
LODGES

CHANAUTI-
MAHANKAL
BAZAAR
1000m

Himal
Lama

SUSPENSION BRIDGE

Ganesh

Helambu Mayalu
MOST BUILDINGS
ARE SHOPS

1/2 - 3/4 HR TO TWO RIVERS LODGE

Helambu
Sherpa

0   500m

MAP 23

TO TALAMARANG

by the monsoon. Prayers are made to the snake-god *Nag-deota* and a priest chooses an auspicious date for the planting to begin. Fields are usually weeded twice before being dried out. The crop is cut and left to dry in the sun for three to four days, a period when rain is a disaster. Then the cut plants are clumped together for a further two weeks to loosen the rice seeds from the husk. A brisk shake removes most of the rice. The rest is released by cattle trampling round in a circle. The nutritious straw is fed to the cows over several months.

Kiultar and Chanauti-Mahankal Bazaar
Tar means flat, which is virtually what the bottom of this valley is. Villages become more frequent and one gets the feeling that the road can't be far away (and indeed may have reached here by the time you read this). Both places have curious locals, simple lodges and many places to eat.

If you fancy a little more luxury, further down the valley is the delightful **Two Rivers Lodge**. A generous-hearted chain-smoking Frenchman set up a dispensary (health clinic) and school, then a lodge to help support them.

The lodge has double rooms (Rs70 per person) with attached showers and toilets and is well-run. Undoubtedly more useful to the area though, is the dispensary. This is one of the few health clinics in Nepal where the qualified staff actually work (hard) full-time and have fully-stocked cabinets of medicine to dispense. Its quality and reliability mean there is a constant queue of people waiting to be attended and it's a crying shame that all healthposts in Nepal don't function even half as well as this, although on paper they are supposed to. The running costs are high though, more than US$15,000 worth of medicine are dispensed each year. From here to Melamchi Pul the trail is an easy walk on a real road. Melamchi Pul and getting to Kathmandu is covered from p205.

KAKANI AND MELAMCHI PUL BAZAAR [MAP 23]

TO MELAMCHI PUL VIA SARMATHANG

Setighyang A little way out of Tarkeghyang, just above the trail, is the 1996-97 rebuilt Gyalchaling Sang Photang (gompa). It is possible to stay with the family here. The trail continues, entering forest. The locals call this trail flat and by Nepalese standards it is, but there are still plenty of minor ups and downs.

Ghyang-yul The trail enters from the top of the village where locals may offer tea. Make your way down to pass around the back of the gompa then perhaps 15 metres down cross to the visible Dolma lodge. The trail initially contours across a steep hillside. After rounding another ridge Sarmathang is visible, recognisable by the skyline gompa in a saddle.

Map 23 201

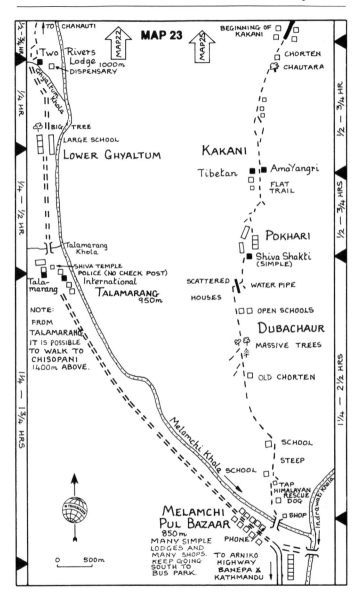

TO CHANAUTI

MAP 23

MAP22

MAP23

BEGINNING OF KAKANI

Two Rivers Lodge 1000m
DISPENSARY

Ghyalteum Khola

CHORTEN

CHAUTARA

BIG TREE

LARGE SCHOOL

LOWER GHYALTUM

KAKANI

Tibetan

AmaYangri

FLAT TRAIL

Talamarang Khola

POKHARI

Shiva Shakti (SIMPLE)

SHIVA TEMPLE
POLICE (NO CHECK POST)
International
TALAMARANG 950m

Tala-marang

SCATTERED

HOUSES

WATER PIPE

OPEN SCHOOLS

DUBACHAUR

NOTE:
FROM TALAMARANG
IT IS POSSIBLE
TO WALK TO
CHISOPANI
1400m ABOVE.

MASSIVE TREES

OLD CHORTEN

Melamchi Khola

Indrawati Khola

SCHOOL

STEEP

SCHOOL

TAP
HIMALAYAN
RESCUE
DOG

SHOP

MELAMCHI
PUL BAZAAR
850m
MANY SIMPLE
LODGES AND
MANY SHOPS.
KEEP GOING
SOUTH TO
BUS PARK.

PHONE

TO ARNIKO
HIGHWAY
BANEPA &
KATHMANDU

TRAILBLAZER

0   500m

½ – ¾ HR
¼ HR
¼ – ½ HR
¼ HR
¼ – 1¾ HRS
¾ HR
½ – ¾ HRS
½ – ¾ HRS
1¼ – 2½ HRS

Chimighyang The trail divides close to this village and either will get you to Sarmathang. It is possible to stay in Chimi but they aren't used to foreigners.

SARMATHANG   [MAP 24]

Sarmathang 2590m/8500ft
Sheltered in the lee of the main ridge Sarmathang is a pleasant Yolmo village and a usual overnighting point for trekkers. Amid the tidy gardens and orchards are clumps of houses, a couple of gompas and even a rather austere retreat for monks recruited from Kathmandu. A variety of vegetables are grown, something that the government is trying to encourage in the rest of the country in a drive towards better nutrition. The locals of this area are infamous with the lower dwelling Hindus for occasionally eating cow meat. They also cremate their dead at the viewpoint above the village – another practice which is strange to Hindus who prefer the bank of a river especially one which eventually flows into the holy Ganges.

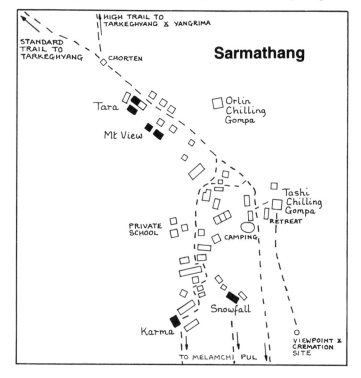

Map 24 203

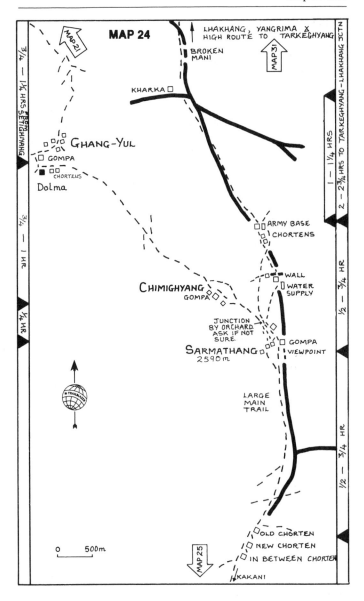

MAP 24

MAP 21

LHAKHANG, YANGRIMA &
HIGH ROUTE TO TARKEGHYANG

MAP 31

BROKEN
MANI

KHARKA

GHANG-YUL

GOMPA

CHORTENS

Dolma

¾ — 1¼ HRS FROM SETIGHYANG

1 — 1¼ HRS TO TARKEGHYANG — LHAKHANG JCTN

2 — 2¾ HRS TO TARKEGHYANG — LHAKHANG JCTN

ARMY BASE
CHORTENS

WALL

WATER
SUPPLY

CHIMIGHYANG
GOMPA

JUNCTION
BY ORCHARD
ASK IF NOT
SURE.

SARMATHANG
2590 m

GOMPA
VIEWPOINT

¾ — 1 HR

¼ HR

½ — ¾ HR

LARGE
MAIN
TRAIL

● TRAILBLAZER

½ — ¾ HR

0   500m

MAP 25

OLD CHORTEN

NEW CHORTEN

IN BETWEEN CHORTEN

KAKANI

Lodges Each cluster of houses has a lodge or two. Many feature a traditional dining room, see the description on Melamchighyang p192.

Ridge route to Lhakhang, Yangrima and Tarkeghyang Initial route-finding for this alternative route to Tarkeghyang isn't easy but once up on the main ridge the trail is clear.

❏ **Ashes to Ashes**

Tamangs and Yolmo-wa prefer to cremate their dead but the ceremony involves several rituals – the dead person's body is placed in a pot in a curled sitting position. Food and other useful items (for their new life) are placed around it then the family guards it until the lama decides on an auspicious time for it to be removed from the house. With solemn ceremony the body is burnt on top of a hill. The family is considered ritually polluted for a further three days (or sometimes seven) so they don't eat salt or oil; a purification rite is required before they can rejoin normal village life. After 49 days, but sometimes as long as six months or a year, they host a huge, expensive two-day feast with dancing. This lets the soul ascend to heaven. Sometimes a mani is constructed somewhere.

To Melamchi Pul

Locals who leave early can easily get to Kathmandu in a day, as can individual trekkers. Groups normally take the day at a more leisurely pace and camp on the bank of the Melamchi Khola and leave the next morning. Note that today involves 1750 vertical metres of descent.

The descent is more than just a change in altitude, the Tibetan culture gives way to Hindu farmers and buffalo. Although there are lodges along this stretch few are used to putting up trekkers so ordering dal bhaat or whatever they actually have is generally the best idea.

KAKANI RIDGE   [MAP 25]

Melamchi Pul Bazaar 850m/2775ft

A rather ugly type of development usually accompanies roadheads in Nepal and Melamchi Pul is no exception. Shops, simple restaurants and the occasional lodge crowd the road for more than a kilometre. While an eyesore, the road and associated developments are beneficial for every village to the north. Suddenly it is that much cheaper and easier to buy supplies that previously had to be bought from Kathmandu. For villages a road nearby means that cash cropping and many other businesses become possible.

It can be a good idea to call your hotel in Kathmandu to reserve a room. The public telephone is by the bridge to Sarmathang, although there may be more soon. If you are staying here there is little to distinguish the various lodges. A couple aim for the tourist market but really are little different. A friendly face is perhaps the best guide.

Map 25 205

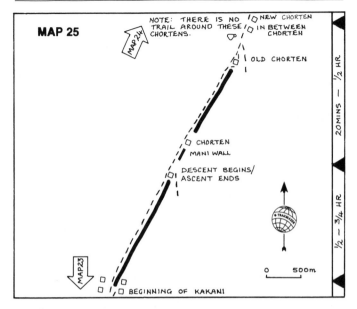

MELAMCHI PUL BAZAAR TO KATHMANDU

There are buses between Melamchi Pul and Banepa approximately every half hour between about 6.30am and 4pm. The service operates year round except when there is torrential rain. The first and last few buses tend to be crowded. There are innumerable buses from Banepa to Kathmandu's Ratna Park bus station. Count on a four to six hour journey.

The road
It is 46 km from Melamchi Pul to Banepa. Initially the road follows the Indrawati River then after an hour or so it climbs the ridge and then drops into another valley. After about two hours the rough dirt road (near Lamidanda) joins the tarmacked Arniko highway that runs between Kathmandu and Lhasa.

Banepa
The dusty noisy main road deserves no more time than that required to catch a bus to Kathmandu, but turn north at the statue of King Mahendra and another world begins. This is the beginning of the old bazaar area. A little further in is a major intersection, the right fork leading to the impressive Chandesvari Mandir (temple). Continuing left is the older part of Banepa. While this is a fascinating place, there are few restaurants to suit the hungry trekker.

❑ **Things that munch in the night**
We should have sensed the danger when we first caught sight of the suspiciously smooth white sheet so carefully pinned over the ceiling in an otherwise rough hotel. However 'This is us', we declared, our thoughts already on dinner.

We blew the candle out in order to go to sleep; instead of silence the walls around us erupted in noise – an alarming crackling, crunching all-consuming assault of mystifying origin. A worried closer inspection of the walls revealed holes the size of a pencil and oversized wood-borers who weren't the least bit shy about their profession.

Wake up? We scarcely slept. The unseen munchers that were systematically eating the building were soon joined by a pack of howling dogs. Not to be outdone the hotel staff began to make unaccountable forays up and down the stairs and gathered laughing on the veranda. Then fleas made an appearance between the joined beds, despite the clean sheets. And all too soon the dawn chorus of birds, dogs and obscene bus horns began, regardless of the fact that we hadn't yet slept. **Vicky Morrison (UK)**

THE SANKHU START FOR HELAMBU   [MAPS 26 & 27]

Instead of the usual Sundarijal start for Helambu and Gosainkund it is possible to begin from Sankhu and join the standard trail at Chisopani. The main reason for doing this is to visit the Vajra Yogini temple. Having said that, route-finding from the temple is difficult. There isn't a main trail so it is a case of following your nose and asking locals. The reward is a splendid Himalayan panorama. The alternative is to trek, or preferably mountain-bike, up a dirt road where route-finding is easier. This trek can also be linked with Nagarkot for a short jaunt, or with the Shivapuri trek to Kakani (not described in this book).

To Sankhu
By bus This leaves from the Ratna Park bus station in the centre of Kathmandu. Bus No 4 is the one you want and they leave roughly every half hour; the fare is less than US$0.20. The 1- 1½ hour journey takes a circuitous route, travelling the southern Ring Road so to save time flag down the bus on the road to Baudha, (and squeeze in a visit to Baudha). Sankhu is the last stop.

By taxi A taxi can take you closer to Vajra Yogini but is hardly worth the extra distance on the rough road; stop in Sankhu instead. The cost is likely to be US$8-16. Generally it is best to bargain with a metered taxi. Since he probably won't have passengers for the return journey bargain for between 1½ and two times the meter fare.

By bike Once past Baudha the road to Sankhu becomes a country lane. Without stops, but at a leisurely pace the ride to Sankhu should take no more than a couple of hours.

Map 26 207

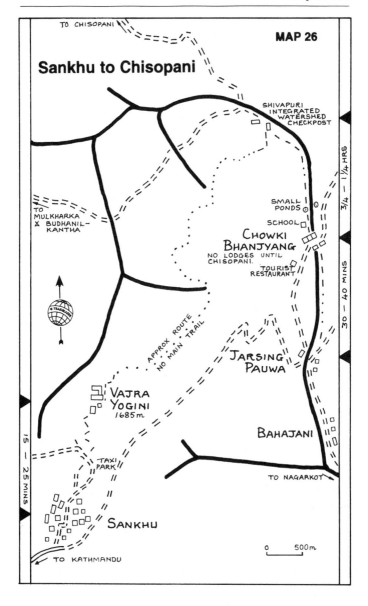

TO CHISOPANI

MAP 26

Sankhu to Chisopani

SHIVAPURI
INTEGRATED
WATERSHED
CHECKPOST

3/4 – 1¼ HRS

SMALL
PONDS

TO
MULKHARKA
X BUDHANIL-
KANTHA

SCHOOL

CHOWKI
BHANJYANG

NO LODGES UNTIL
CHISOPANI.

TOURIST
RESTAURANT

30 – 40 MINS

● TRAMMANDI

APPROX ROUTE
NO MAIN TRAIL

JARSING
PAUWA

VAJRA
YOGINI
1685m

BAHAJANI

15 – 25 MINS

TAXI
PARK

TO NAGARKOT

SANKHU

0   500m

TO KATHMANDU

Sankhu 1400m/4600ft

The historic Newari village of Sankhu is a delightfully simple and time-less town and a great place to wander around, or relax over chiya and watch the world roll by. It has a few basic shops but no real lodges or restaurants. It is also worth noting that there aren't any more shops or tea-houses until Chisopani, a day's walk away.

From the bus park, pass through the colourful arch and follow the road. At the village square turn left (north) and moments later the road suddenly leaves the village by some beautiful stone gods. From this point a red building, part of the Vajra Yogini complex is visible up on the hill-side. The old pilgrim's path leads directly there while a newer road winds a torturous route.

Vajra Yogini 1685m/5528ft

A blood-spattered stone Bhairab protected by a metal grill greets the trekker. A little further up set on stone and surrounded by pines are two pagodas. Countless bells and a policeman guard the main temple. Vajra Yogini is a tantric goddess, a protector of Buddhist beliefs. She has been embraced by Hindus too, as a form of Durga, so non-Hindus are not allowed inside and leather shouldn't be taken near the pagoda.

To Chisopani

For trekking pilgrims the trail to Chisopani begins on the east side of the victorian-style building above the temples. At the collection of prayer flags you have to decide whether to go roughly up the ridge until you reach the dirt road or to continue traversing and climbing along the hill-side to some villages. Judge from the map roughly where you are head-ing and stay on trails. You are bounded by a dirt road above and a trail on the far ridge so you can't overshoot. With luck, you'll arrive at the Shivapuri Integrated Watershed Checkpost: a Rs250 entrance fee has to be paid. The trail continues up the ridge and in a few minutes meets the dirt road from Mulkharka and Budhanilkantha. From here on the route is straightforward, simply follow the dirt road. In a couple of places the road winds around while a trail shortcuts it.

If it's fine the mountain panorama is magic. Beyond the extensive middle hills is a serrated horizon of lofty peaks. The three bulky peaks to the west are the Ganesh Himal and, perhaps hazy in the distance, are the triple peaks of the Manaslu range. The brown (dry season) rocky skyline east of the Ganesh range is the Gosainkund Lekh. Running towards you from this, although far from obvious, is the ridge to Tharepati. Tarkeghyang and Sarmathang sit on the next ridge over; Sarmathang is just visible in a slight saddle. The chorten atop Yangrima peak is just dis-cernible too. Dorje Lhakpa is the central and highest of the three peaks to the north-east. To the east the distinctive snow-fronted twin peaks of

Map 27 209

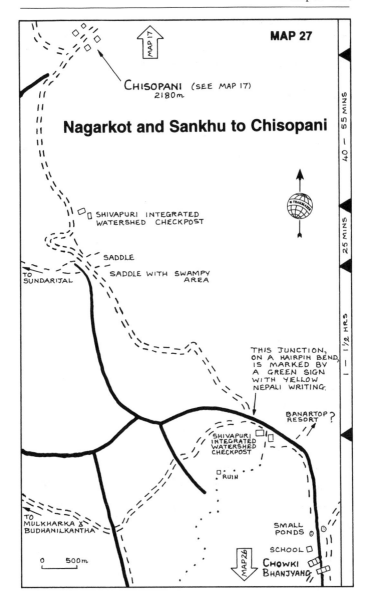

MAP 27

CHISOPANI (SEE MAP 17)
2180m

Nagarkot and Sankhu to Chisopani

☐ SHIVAPURI INTEGRATED
WATERSHED CHECKPOST

SADDLE

SADDLE WITH SWAMPY
AREA

TO
SUNDARIJAL

THIS JUNCTION,
ON A HAIRPIN BEND,
IS MARKED BY
A GREEN SIGN
WITH YELLOW
NEPALI WRITING.

BANARTOP ?
RESORT

SHIVAPURI
INTEGRATED
WATERSHED
CHECKPOST

RUIN

TO
MULKHARKA &
BUDHANILKANTHA

0   500m

SMALL
PONDS

SCHOOL ☐

CHOWKI
BHANJYANG

40 – 55 MINS

25 MINS

1 – 1½ HRS

MAP 17

MAP 26

Gauri Shankar can be seen. Slightly to the right of these are three minor peaks, the most distant of which, is Everest! Its profile is the same as the postcard pictures taken from Kala Pattar. To the right of it is the tip of Lhotse, which disappears as you wander along the road.

Chisopani is covered on p184.

NAGARKOT START FOR HELAMBU

Beginning a Helambu trek from Nagarkot is an appealing idea but there is a difficulty: there is no decent accommodation between Nagarkot and Chisopani and it is too far to walk in a day. For those willing to rough it there are simple local teahouses along the way so it's possible to break the walk into two short days. In contrast to beginning from Sundarijal, the walk to Chisopani follows dirt roads (perfect for mountain-biking, see p180), so it's not a real nature walk. It is scenic, though, if the Himalaya are in full glory.

Chisopani is a solid six to eight hours walking from Nagarkot. So in the opposite direction, fit and flying, this is possible in a long day.

To Nagarkot

Kathmandu hotels and travel agents are fond of selling Nagarkot packages but it is also easy enough to do alone. The tourist bus is booked through travel agents and leaves Kantipath at 1.30pm. Local buses leave the Ratna Park bus park every hour, take the No 7. The bus passes through Bhaktapur so it can also be picked up there. The road is tarmacked all the way, definitely uphill, but a pleasant drive. It would be a nervous ride on a cycle or motorcycle, given the Nepalese style of driving.

After winding up the long hill the bus stops at a road junction where the flash Club Himalaya resort can be seen. Hotel touts jump on the bus here. The main group of resorts is slightly further up the hill.

Nagarkot 1950m/6400ft

This is just a collection of 15 or so hotels offering Himalayan views.

Leaving Nagarkot

Walk along the dirt road to the north and pass more resorts. The first part of the first village consists of the teahouses of Kartiki Bhanjyang, which cater to travellers. The real village tumbles down the hill to the north.

▲ **From the opposite direction** You know you have reached the main part of Nagarkot when you see the sign for Hotel Snowman. Try hitching a ride down or walk below to a junction surrounded by shops and wait for a bus.

Jarsing Pauwa

From Kartiki Bhanjyang the road continues past scattered houses. In a

Map 28 21.

section of forest are a couple of possible shortcuts. The road moves from the top of the ridge to contour slightly north of the main ridge line.

The settlement of Jarsing Pauwa is at a collection of intersections. It has a couple of shops. Leaving, you have a choice of following the ridge or taking the road that contours.

Chowki Bhanjyang

This Tamang village has a row of shops that sell coke, biscuits, noodles and other snacks. Dal bhaat is also available or, for a wider menu, there's a tourist-style restaurant five minutes south along the road. From this point to Chisopani there are no shops or lodges. Only water is available along the way.

Continue up the ridge and past the school. The route is less defined now but keep heading up hill and you can't go wrong. The trail avoids the terraced fields nearby.

The Shivapuri Integrated Watershed checkpost is slightly to the south of the main ridge line. The trail description continues on p208.

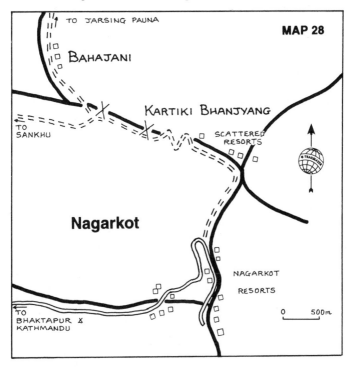

The Kangja La

Sometimes spelt Ganja La, this pass is occasionally used by locals visiting friends in Helambu or vice versa in Langtang. Now it is used more by trekkers. The route description and the timings on the maps are written for crossing from Kyangjin to Tarkeghyang, the direction that most trekkers will choose.

PLANNING AND PREPARATION

The Austrian Alpine Club map East sheet is useful but rely on your eyes more than anything else. Unless conditions are perfect the most difficult decision is whether to attempt the pass or not. Before leaving Kyangjin check with the locals the state of the facilities that you plan to use. Also ask if there is snow near the pass. Snow lower down means trouble on both sides and avalanche danger in some areas. You should always bear in mind that you might have to turn back if conditions get difficult.

The best view of the pass is from the top of Cherko. Binoculars would be handy.

Equipment needed by groups

Groups should carry a full 45 or 50 metre rope, not the short 10 metre section that local trekking agencies often suggest. In addition there should be several ice axes, at least one pair of crampons and, most important, a sirdar who can use this equipment competently. All porters should have sunglasses no matter what the season, something that trekking companies have to be pushed into providing, and even then what they say and the truth is sometimes different. Four hours in bright sun on mixed rock and snow is enough to cause snow blindness (as happened to a group I met). This is a terribly painful and completely unnecessary affliction and a few

> ❏ **WARNING**
> Several people have gone missing around Keldang. At least one person and probably two or three have been killed by bandits. After several extensive searches the body of one American man was found. It seems that he had been lured off the main trail by a series of plastic ribbons to some steep cliffs where he was pushed to his death, all for the sake of a few hundred dollars. In late October 1995 a German, Johann Karstens, (blond and 30 years old) went missing. It is possible he lost his way but the body has yet to be found, suggesting more suspicious circumstances.
>
> Significantly, it seems all the missing trekkers were alone; the moral, join with other people to cross the pass.

bad cases will hold everyone up a day.

Frostbite is another concern. For the sake of your pleasure it isn't worth putting a porter's feet at risk. All porters must have shoes, socks and plastic bags to put between them. Although not particularly comfortable, this combination is enough to prevent frostbite in wet or light snow in fine weather but not in cold powder snow or in difficult conditions. Even if your sirdar wants to push on in fresh cold snow which is more than ankle deep, don't! You might have to make the decision to turn back.

Equipment for independent trekkers

This will vary with the season and your ambitions. If you are quite willing to forgo the crossing unless the pass is entirely snow-free then an extra water bottle, good sleeping bag, emergency plastic sheet, stove, pot, four days' supplies and a ski-pole will do. A tent isn't strictly necessary since there is a lodge before the pass and down the other side, well down, are some stone shelters. Anyway, the weather should suit sleeping under the stars. Perfect enough conditions on the pass are only likely to occur from sometime in October to perhaps mid-December, and even then there is less than a 100% chance. You must be sure-footed and unafraid of heights.

Carrying tents, crampons, ice axes (at least one per group, and more are better), ski poles for everyone and 15m+ section of rope significantly increases your chances of a successful crossing. For spring this is the absolute minimum, and even then success is still very much conditions-dependent. Although you may only end up eating two days' food you should have some (minimal) insurance against an ill-timed dump of snow. At least one trekker has died, caught by snow once over the pass. If you are taking porters ensure they have hats, sunglasses, warm socks, space in a tent, reasonable blankets and a stick or ski pole.

To take a guide or not

A number of trekkers have got into trouble, and some have possibly died, taking the wrong route to the pass summit or getting lost on the other side. I sincerely hope the following detailed route description prevents further deaths. It is still with caution that I say it is possible to cross without a guide. If the trail notes make sense and conditions are good you may wonder what all the fuss is about but in snow and caught by thick fog you might curse me instead. The decision boils down to your confidence.

Local guides are available in Kyangjin and it may be worth taking one up at least to the pass summit, the section where a rope can be needed, and have him point out the route down. He can also carry a useful load. However expect to pay dearly, at least US$20 a day, and definitely more during peak season. Another option is to take a porter-guide from Kathmandu who has crossed the pass before. Be aware that they rarely know how to use ropes or tackle difficult conditions.

Planning the days

From Kyangjin, the Base Camp Lodge is only half a day's walk. However this is where the majority of groups stay and where most independent trekkers should stay. Well acclimatised trekkers with good camping equipment could stay higher at stony Chusangma 4850m/15,912ft, or at a slightly higher camp.

The time taken from Base Camp to the pass is very dependent on conditions. When completely snow-free the fit could make the summit cairns in two hours. More normal is three to four hours, especially for groups. If a rope has to be set up anywhere this can easily add several hours more, making it a demanding six to eight hours to the summit – hence the need for a dawn start.

Once over the pass the critical factor is the availability of water. The lower of the two normal camping spots always has water but between there and Dhukpu, especially during the autumn season, there may be no water at all. During spring there is more chance of finding snow or one of the small lakes still having water but these may not be at convenient spots. Even at Dhukpu finding water sometimes requires a search and then carrying it some distance. Water is also scarce the following day to Tarkeghyang.

Acclimatisation considerations

Whether you're an independent trekker carrying a heavy rucksack or part of a group with porters getting over a 5100m/17,060ft pass will be less of a struggle if you're well acclimatised. Three nights at Kyangjin should give adequate acclimatisation but four nights and some day trips to higher altitudes or sleeping a night somewhere else above Kyangjin will give better preparation. Many trekking companies plan only two nights; this is definitely not enough and will considerably lessen the chances of a successful crossing. If you have already crossed Gosainkund, two nights at Kyangjin may be adequate but three is even better.

Base Camp at 4350m/14,275ft is 450m/1475ft higher than Kyangjin, this is enough of an altitude difference to induce a slight headache in people easily affected. Some trekkers also report minor problems at the top of the pass. On the other side the various camps used range in altitude from 4400-4600m/14,435-15,100ft.

The above assumes that the crossing goes smoothly. Occasionally difficult snow has forced groups to camp further up the pass at 4850m/15,912ft or higher, meaning the majority will experience some AMS that might only be relieved once well down the other side.

▲ Crossing in the opposite direction

The major difficulty is acclimatisation. If you have just been to Tibet, the Everest region or around the Annapurna Circuit this shouldn't be a problem although you should still be watchful for symptoms.

Where you stay above Tarkeghyang is determined solely by the availability of water and thus requires careful planning. The description begins on p221.

LEAVING KYANGJIN

A few minutes out of Kyangjin the trail divides. The larger path returns you to Langtang village while the smaller trail that roughly follows the stream leads to a couple of small bridges which jump the large boulders in the khola. At the kharka and beyond, occasional yellow arrows have been painted on rocks to point the way across hillocks to the forest on small trails. Taking a 45° line relative to the forest line should put you in roughly the right spot. You don't need to pass by any of the scattered small lakes and if you pass beside more than one you have taken the wrong trail. The trail through the forest begins just above a boulder which is bigger than many around it, although this is more obvious once you're above it. It is critical to find the correct path into the forest.

In the warmer months the forest floor is carpeted by bright wild flowers. There is little evidence of large scale cutting but the moss hanging everywhere tells another story. This is a favourite food of the musk deer who will even climb trees and along branches to reach it, often falling out of the tree in the process. So from the abundance of easily accessible moss one must conclude that there are very few deer, if any, left around here.

Leaving the forest the obvious trail climbs to Negang Kharka with its collection of roofless kore. Looking at the route ahead a trail cuts up to a small pass just north of a rocky point. Keen eyes may spot a cairn. This is the trail, not the one on the smoother grassy hills. Just out of Negang the trail briefly bends to put it closer to the hills above, then it roughly contours.

From the minor pass you can see the Base Camp Lodge but reaching it is another matter. A delicate trail, indicative of what is to come, dances across square boulders.

▲ If travelling in the opposite direction, the edge of Negang Kharka is is visible from a little way along from the pass. On the opposite side of the valley you can also see Kyangjin: east (right) of the glacier pushing into the valley is a stream running down the ablation valley. Just east (right) of where this and the stream from the glacier meet is Kyangjin.

Base Camp 4350m/14,275ft
The locals quite happily call this area Base Camp and didn't have another name for it. On the Austrian Alpine Club map, a little south of this area, there is a pool (which I didn't see) called Yeshekupedakta.

The hotel/camping area is a bit of a mess. There are few flat spaces for tents and even a small group can fill the area plus the building (where the staff sleep), something that independent trekkers should note. Also check at Kyangjin that the lodge owner is there. It is normally open for the autumn season but just when you rely on it the lodge owner may have gone shopping. The lodge is usually closed during spring but the building is not normally locked since groups would anyway simply break in. In late 1996 the partially collapsed lodge roof still hadn't been repaired.

To the pass

What time you set off is very much conditions-dependent. If there is no snow a dawn start is best but if some is expected on the pass groups espe-cially should leave as early as possible; as soon as it is just light enough for walking – this can be as early as 4.30am. The rope carrier should stay near the front. To keep strength up it is important to drink plenty of flu-ids and eat snacks. This applies equally if not more so for the crew who cannot be expected to provide for themselves as there is no place (or probably time) to cook a proper meal.

An obvious trail leaves Base Camp and immediately begins climbing. Around the first minor ridge is the first obstacle, a stream. Without snow, crossing the smooth slabs is easy enough but often the smooth rock can be coated with lethal ice. If the stream is covered with snow beware of breaking through it; ropes have sometimes been used here. A large amount of snow brings the possibility of a second danger – avalanches.

Near the top of the next minor ridge is a *maanche-ko dunga*, a man-sized cairn. It is this cairn that is visible from Kyangjin and several other places around the valley. This point is 420m/1380ft up (vertically) from Base Camp so you have already completed well over half the climbing for the day. The ground below has dropped away dramatically and to the north-east the sheer south-west face of Shishapangma 8027m/26,335ft rises above Yala Peak (the one at the southern end of the glacier).

The cairned route follows another ridge then at a point where this steepens, it drops off it. The descent is short and sharp and in snow may require a rope, especially for the crew. It is also possible to continue climbing then descend a little later. A couple of hundred metres further on and just visible from the descent point is an alternative rocky high camp.

At some stage move to the stream and continue climbing on the rough rock. Above, invisible from here, are a couple of lakes that the hardy and adventurous could camp by. Above the lakes is the large, almost flat snowfield seen from Tsergo Peak.

The Kangja La 5120m/16,800ft

Eventually you look up at a daunting bowl. Although cairns mark the top of the pass the exact route is difficult to pick. The best line heads up to beneath a small wall on the right then crosses the funnel left of that to a narrow very exposed path that is barely visible from below. Approaching the pass from the left, or west side face, is not possible. In perfect snow-

Map 29 217

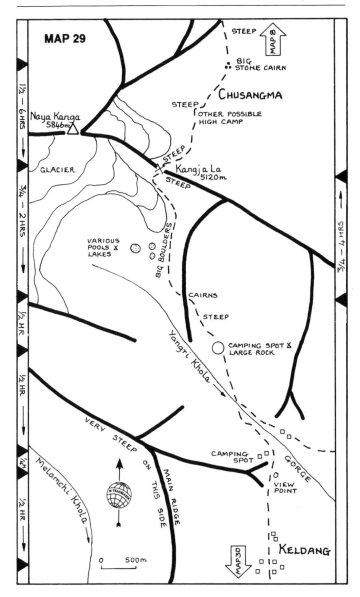

MAP 29

STEEP

MAP 8

BIG
STONE CAIRN

CHUSANGMA

STEEP
OTHER POSSIBLE
HIGH CAMP

Naya Kanga
5846m

STEEP

Kangja La
5120m

STEEP

GLACIER

VARIOUS
POOLS &
LAKES

BIG BOULDERS

CAIRNS

STEEP

Yangri Khola

CAMPING SPOT &
LARGE ROCK

VERY STEEP ON THIS SIDE

MAIN RIDGE

CAMPING
SPOT

GORGE

VIEW
POINT

Melamchi Khola

TRAILBLAZER

0   500m

MAP 30

KELDANG

½ — 6 HRS

¾ — 2 HRS

½ HR

½ HR

¼ H

½ HR

¾ — 4 HRS

free conditions getting to the top of the pass is easier than it at first appears and doesn't require a rope although people frightened by vertical drops and heavily laden porters will appreciate a helping hand. Note that the Austrian Alpine Club map marks permanent snow here though there isn't.

Crossing with snow lying around is dangerous. It is imperative to find the correct ledge that forms the path then thoroughly clear the snow and underlying ice. If the snow is too deep for this, cut solid steps and fix a secure line traversing to the top of the pass. Crampons for at least a few people are essential. Crossing this section could take several hours. Less well prepared groups have turned back at this point.

Although there is little room on the top, the panorama is captivating. This is as grand as it gets anywhere. To the south is an impressive bowl of mountains and glaciers that could tempt a climber and beyond the long southern-pointing ridges the crinkled middle hills extend forever. With a good map you may be able to pick out Shivapuri and behind, unseen, is the Kathmandu Valley. Study the route down.

▲ Climbing to the pass in the opposite direction
The many summit cairns are visible but the route isn't entirely obvious. Head to the brown vertical wall to the west (left) of the pass and pick up the steep rubble trail from there. In snow or ice either fix a rope or spend some time clearing away the snow. At the top the scene is truly alpine. Shishapangma (8027m) rears to the north-east and with a good map you should be able to pick out the majority of the peaks. The top may also bring a shock; there's an almost vertical drop to the basin below. Traverse west (left) on the ledge a metre below the pass summit.

If you found the crossing tough imagine what it was like for the porters for most of whom it will also be their first crossing. You have to admire their stamina; if it was hard ascending the pass with just a daypack just imagine what it would be like with 30kg. They would appreciate you remembering the hardships when it comes to tipping time!

The descent
The descent is steep and, in snow, tricky – it might even require a rope. Beware of rock fall from above and dislodging rocks onto your fellow trekkers below. After the steep section bear left (south-east), avoiding the glacier and the flats at the end of it. Basically follow the rough line of large boulders and some cairns. This area is also exposed to high velocity stone fall from the cliffs above.

A line of cairns (not visible until you're upon them) at around 4800m/15,750ft marks the end of a rough but flattish area. There are a couple of trails that descend fairly steeply to the flat area at 4600m/15,100ft in this small valley. You shouldn't be descending into the main valley just yet.

Map 30 219

This small flat area with a large rock just south of it is the first reasonable camping spot (or the last in the opposite direction) from the pass. Large groups may not easily fit here. Continuing down, the trail skirts to the left (east) of this large rock. A faint track descends to the banks of the Yangri Khola which must be crossed at some stage though there is no bridge. If you crossed the pass quickly you could camp at the kharka, often called Base Camp, on the far side of the khola.

TO KELDANG

The trail leaves the Yangri as it runs into a gorge and briefly ascends past a kore around a ridge. From the cairns there is an extensive view of the route ahead. On no account should you descend to the wide valley floor with the intention of following the Yangri down to civilisation. This is impossible.

The trail turns into a rollercoaster climbing up and down ridges but never approaching the crest of the ridge above or the Yangri Khola below. Soon it passes through Keldang, a series of spread out kore many of which have roofs. For the majority of the year these kore lie empty. Only at the beginning of June do the Tarkeghyang herders move up to occupy them. The milk from naks and dimo (crossbreeds) are used to make cheese and great quantities of butter, mainly to be burnt in butter lamps or mixed in Tibetan tea. Goats and sheep aren't allowed in the national park. By October most kore are empty again, although at least

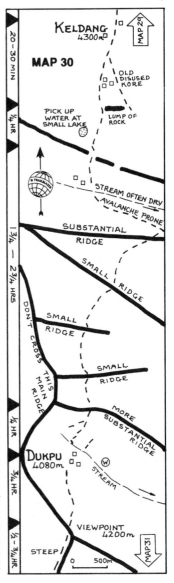

one family now waits out the first part of the main pass-crossing season to sell curd and biscuits to trekkers. No doubt this will gradually meta-morphose into a lodge situation but this is still unlikely to stay open past November and certainly won't be open in the spring. Many minor trails and distracting cairns litter the area.

To Dhukpu

At the end of Keldang is a great lump of rock. There are cairns and good paths around both sides but only the western (right) path actually leads anywhere useful. On the other side is a lake and a stream, both of which may be dry in late autumn. After the notched ridge is a more substantial ridge with a clear path climbing around it. These slopes are avalanche prone and in a bad year snow sticks around here well into May making the traverse difficult.

Zigzag around several more ridges to one that, once at the top, seems more major than the rest. Across the minor valley in front is another ridge with cairns marking a view point and the route past Dhukpu. The kore of Dhukpu are hidden in the bottom of this valley. Ten metres down take the lower trail that leads through juniper scrub.

Dhukpu 4080m/13,385ft

Trekking groups like to stop here because water can always be found, although often with difficulty, and the kore make a good kitchen.

▲ If heading in the opposite direction take the higher trail out of Dhukpu, about 50m up the stream, then begin the climb.

The viewpoint Leaving Dhukpu you can see the cairns that you are heading for, although it's farther than it initially looks. On a clear day you can see the twin-peaks of Gauri Shankar, a mountain above Rolwaling which is holy to all Sherpas and Hindus. Even further away is Numbur, one of the twin holy peaks for the Solu Sherpas. You can also see much of Helambu and Shivapuri, behind which is Kathmandu.

To Tarkeghyang

Between here and Tarkeghyang you lose 1650m/5400ft in altitude, begin-ning immediately with a steep 300m/1000ft descent. The forest cover gradually thickens. Ten to 15 minutes after a kore is a clearing with a trail junction and, just below, a small spring. This may be the only water until Tarkeghyang. Groups occasionally camp here.

Two kore later the trail passes a small moss-covered stupa. From either here or perhaps 15 minutes further down the main ridge is a choice of routes: the short quick way to Tarkeghyang which features a steep and thoroughly nasty narrow bit of trail, or the longer slightly gentler route. I descended in thick cloud taking the shortcut route without even seeing the other trail so the descriptions and map may not be exactly right. A local

Map 31 221

guide would be useful here! In May little wild (edible) strawberries are plentiful.

For the standard route the idea is to skirt around the east Yangrima then meet the main trail from it and descend to an obvious saddle between Tarkeghyang and Lhakhang. From the saddle there's a trail to Sarmathang too.

Tarkeghyang 2550m/8350ft

You've made it to civilisation!

After crossing the Kangja La the Tarkeygyang Hotel could well be called the Tarkeghyang Hilton. This rambling hotel was built in the early 1970s. It even has several rooms with attached bathrooms.

The descriptions of the village and the Helambu routes to Melamchi Pul begin on p191.

▲ If you are about to leave Tarkeghyang for the Kangja La, beware! There are many confusing trails for the first half day. If you wish to take the shortcut take a local guide. For the standard route a guide isn't necessary but with all the cattle trails everywhere the route isn't always obvious; be prepared to backtrack. Either way once past Yangrima and on the main ridge proper route-finding becomes easier. Then the concern is finding a place where you can stay where there is water. Again taking a local guide further would be useful, although not necessary. For an itinerary planner and the altitudes see Appendix A.

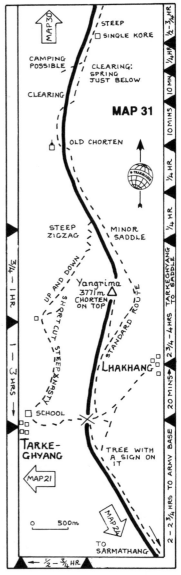

Tilman's Pass

In 1949 Tilman, a few sherpas and a team of porters crossed a glaciated col beneath Dorje Lakpa. It was an ambitious plan, all the more so because Tilman had little idea what was on the other side. He may have seen part of the possible route while surveying the area, but the only way to test whether it was practicable was to try it. He knew that well down the other side along a ridge was Panch Pokhari, a series of five holy lakes that would have a track up to them. It was just a question of reaching them:

'By late afternoon we were more lost than ever: we could not find either our companions or a village or a trail or anything, and it looked as if we would have to spend the night without food or shelter. Then we heard a sound ahead and came upon one of the native tribesmen of the region, who in this part of Nepal are called Limbus. Dawa Namgya and I spoke to him and gave him Rs5 to lead us to his village, and he was just about to do so when Tilman came up and joined us. As I have said, Tilman, when on an expedition, was usually so hairy and shaggy-looking that we called him Balu – the bear. His eyebrows were so big and jutting that when, in the mountains, he got snow on them they looked like the edge of a roof or the cornice on a ridge. Now in the jungle there was no snow, but he looked wild enough without it, with his long hair and beard and more hair sprouting from under his shirt. Like many Asians, the Limbus are almost hairless on face and body. This one had certainly not seen such a sight before, and one look was enough. Before we knew what was happening, he gave a yell and disappeared, Rs5 and all, and we were as lost as ever.' Tensing Norgay (Sherpa), *Man of Everest.*

Tilman and Tensing faced more difficulties than you might – just. Although Tilman took porters over this glaciated pass this is hardly advisable.

❑ **Julie Dawson and Wayne Horsfall** (UK) crossed in December 1996 and reported: 'It's possible to stay at a simple lodge at Jalbari/Jalbiri but from there on, it's camping only, three days to Panch Pokhari. Spend time acclimatising there. We spent two days exploring and searching for the trail. Leaving, head north and drop down more than 100m to a good path. This is around 4000-4200m, not 4500m as marked on maps. There are plenty of streams along the way. After about half a day the path splits: take the lower trail. Another day puts you on the Balephi Glacier. Getting to the top of the pass was tough. We cramponed up the bottom half of the icefall but without icescrews and a second axe we couldn't climb the rest and so were forced to go right over loose scree with stonefall, up and then back onto the icefall. There were crevasses on the 5300m/17,400ft top. The descent on the other side wasn't so simple either... Have fun!'

Naya Kanga 5846m/19,180ft

During my two climbing research treks snow conditions proved to be too dangerous for an ascent of the mountain. Instead Jamie Carr (Equator Expeditions/Exodus UK) provided this information.

PLANNING AND PREPARATION

Many groups attempting Naya Kanga in a quick time frame have failed the mountain or indeed often haven't even made Glacier Camp because of inadequate acclimatisation.

Climbing equipment

On an organised climb the climbing sherpas will fix a rope on the more difficult sections so it is simply a case of following their advice.

Climbing alpine style, a few stakes/deadmen and perhaps three or four ice screws with slings and prussiks should be enough for the standard route. The leader may want two axes.

Maps

The Austrian Alpine Club map, Ost (East) sheet covers the entire climb and in more detail than the Schneider map.

ITINERARY PLANNING

You could acclimatise by crossing Gosainkund first, exploring above Kyangjin or by climbing Yala Peak, which also gives valuable rope practice for the inexperienced. Plan an acclimatisation programme that prepares you for sleeping at 5100m/16,800ft The climbing base camp is, in good conditions, a half day from the base camp hut.

THE STANDARD ROUTE

To Glacier Camp

Close to the Kangja La but before steep walls surround you; leave the rubble-filled valley and climb up onto the glacier to the west. Most groups camp here, on the edge or just before. Note that the glacier is crevassed.

The climb

Traverse the flattish glacier following the occasional cairn (note that it is easy to miss the way when returning). While some groups don't use a rope here, caution is advisable and the prudent would use a rope. Pass well below the inviting but avalanche-prone gully and head for the snowface that ascends to the north ridge of the mountain. Groups often fix a rope on this. Sometimes deep spring snow prevents teams reaching even this point. Gain the ridge and continue up to a rocky outcrop, a convenient resting spot. From this point the summit isn't visible but climb to a high false summit, often the summit attained by groups. The real summit, perhaps 30m higher, can be tricky or dangerous to reach, requiring belays. It is likely to have a large cornice. There are phenomenal views along the Himalayan chain.

Paldor Peak 5928m/19,450ft

This description of the Paldor climb is also a taster for the Ganesh Himal region. Another now rather dated reference is Bill O'Connor's *Trekking Peaks of Nepal*, which covers the same routes. In it he bemoans the fact that a road was being built through the area and wonders what the impact will be. More than a decade later relatively little has changed. The occasional truck belches smoke at the army post below Goat-hen but few vehicles venture further, stopped by winter ice or summer rain. The villages, instead of being destroyed by development, are suffering because little has materialised.

PLANNING AND PREPARATION

Despite the road to Somthang, trekking to Paldor means traversing country with few villages and is almost entirely devoid of shops or lodges. At the minimum this means a few porters to carry the supplies but for most people organising an expedition-style trek through a trekking company is the more practical option. Officially, to attempt to climb Paldor, your group should have a trekking peak permit obtainable from the Nepal Mountaineering Association through a licensed guide, or more usually, through a trekking company. This costs US$150 for up to 10 foreign climbers. Not all groups heading there, however, climb with a permit.

Acclimatisation

Planning a good acclimatisation programme is critical to the success of a Paldor expedition: high camp could be reached from Syabru Bensi in three and a half days' walking, resulting in probable death en route or soon after. Unless you have just been to altitude the best plan is to take a

---

(Opposite) The Buddhist prayer 'Om Mani Padme Hum' is carved onto flat 'mani' stones, piled up into 'walls' throughout the region.

longer route in to partially acclimatise and then, from base camp, take it slowly. Note that the following itinerary is a minimal acclimatisation programme; it's still quite possible to come down with AMS by following it.

Maps
There is only one readily available map of the Ganesh Himal region; Mandala's blue dyeline *Kathmandu to Manaslu Ganesh Himal* 1:125,000. Its uses are for route-planning and then as toilet paper once on the trail. The maps of the Langtang region miss Paldor Peak but do partially cover the walk in/out from Syabru Bensi (although the road isn't marked) and the Singla route.

Climbing equipment
If climbing with a group lead by a climbing sherpa the company should provide most of the equipment. Often groups fix around 400-500m of rope. Then climbers only need a harness, a couple of slings and carabiners or a jumaring device. Climbing alpine style on the standard route, a rope team might want three snow stakes or deadmen, three ice screws, prussiks and enough slings, including a few large rock slings. If attempting another route, bring a bit more gear. All climbers will, of course, need a harness, crampons and an axe. The leader may want two axes.

More information Most trekking companies have at some stage run a Ganesh Himal trek but few have organised the Paldor climb. Aside from getting clear information, it is most important that the sirdar, a sherpa and the cook have been in the region recently. Most will say they have, the truth may be another matter though.

ITINERARY OPTIONS
From Syabru Bensi
The quickest way in and out is from Syabru Bensi but this is almost missing the point. On the way in at the very least the side trip to Jagesworkund (lake) should be undertaken. For more variety, and some extra acclimatisation trekking, the Langtang valley or Gosainkund (and suffering a couple of nights at the 4600m/15,100ft lake) are two easy options. These have the advantage that they can be teahoused; the full trekking crew need only meet you at Syabru Bensi.

Ganesh Himal start
By beginning in the Ganesh Himal, whatever route you choose, you will be trekking through country that sees relatively few trekkers. You will also begin in low, hot but cultural country then cross over or traverse beautiful forested ridges.

(**Opposite**) **Top:** The children of Nepal are one of the special joys of trekking.
Bottom: The May planting season around Langtang village is a busy time for all.

❏ Mountain-biking the Somthang road

Phew! From Syabru Bensi to the top of the first pass is a 750m/2460ft (measured vertically) warm up for the next 1650m, to the top of the main pass. Then down to Somthang is a drop of 350m/1150ft. In between the stiff climbs (or brakepad-searing descents in the other direction) are some gentle stretches with occasional impressive mountain views.

There is little traffic on the road from Trisuli but again there are some killer hills (Betrawati and Kalikastan are 1400m/4600ft vertical apart). Perhaps cycling from Kalikastan, near the top of the first hill, makes more sense. Once past Syabru Bensi there is the odd place where simple food and crude shelter may be available but the prudent would carry a fly sheet, kerosene (for starting a fire), pot and some food. A sleeping bag and enough snacks for a couple of meals are essential. Remember the nights are always cold above 3000m/10,000ft.

Although Department of Immigration rules state that no trekking permit is needed for travelling on a road, this is unlikely to wash with officials at Dhunche. Get a trekking permit to save undoubted trouble. Since you also cross the national park conservation area you'll also need to fork out the Rs650 entrance fee.

Perhaps the best shorter route in is across the Singla and along the Tiru Danda to Pangsang. This could be started from Trisuli, Betrawati or even Dhading. Although the highest point is only 4000m/13,123ft, the time spent at this altitude and the lack of descent still mean useful acclimatisation.

The more standard Ganesh Himal trekking route begins from Gorkha and heads up to the large Gurung village of Barpak and crosses the ridge to Laprak. Across the Buri Gandaki the climbing begins again to Mangeythanti Bhanjyang (approximately 2750m/9000ft). A shorter route to Mangeythanti Bhanjyang begins from Arughat (this is two days from Gorkha) and initially follows the Buri Gandaki up. Drop to Burang on the Ankhu Khola. From here the standard route heads directly to the Singla but this could be varied by heading directly to the Pangsang Bhanjyang first or by crossing a pass even further to the north, which is perhaps the best option. Whichever you choose, putting the climb last also gives the option for non-climbers to join and enjoy the majority of the trip together.

Jagesworkund Although it's not mentioned in the following route description a good alternative to staying three nights at Base Camp is staying at Jagesworkund (lake). This is a short day's walk from Somthang. However it is possible to camp by the lake at an altitude of around 4380m/14,370ft and scramble up the ridge to a little over 5000m/16,400ft during a rest day. From the lake it is a long day to Base Camp; it may only be possible to make the lower base camp in a day.

	Syabru Bensi start	Tiru Danda route	From Arughat
1	Ktm-Syabru Bensi 1450m	Ktm-Trisuli – camp	Arughat
2	Goldzong or near 2200m	Bhalche	Buri Gandaki
3	Goat-hen/Yuri 3000/3500m	Gongur	Dumchet
4	Somthang/above 3270/3600m	Singla	Mangeythanti
5	Mine or above 3900m	Spare day	Laba/Burang
6	Jagesworkund 4380m	Pangsang	Spare day
7	Jagesworkund 4380m	Somthang or above	Serthang
8	Base Camp 4600m	Mine or above	Forest camp
9	Acclimatisation day 4600m	Base Camp/explore	Base Camp
10	High camp 5400m	Acclimatisation day	Acclimatisation day
11	Acclimatisation day 5400m	Acclimatisation day	Acclimatisation day
12	Climb 5400m	High camp	High camp
13	Somthang	Acclimatisation day	Acclimatisation day
14	Gatalang	Climb	Climb
15	Syabru Bensi	Somthang	Somthang
16	Kathmandu	Gatalang	Gatalang
17		Syabru Bensi	Syabru Bensi
18		Kathmandu	Kathmandu

Buses

Bus details and the journey to Dhunche and Syabru Bensi are covered on p123.

There are at least six buses a day between Gorkha and Kathmandu and Dhading and Kathmandu. These start at around 6.30am with the last bus leaving around 4pm. The Dhading road has been rapidly extended, reaching the Ankhu Khola near Salantar by March 1997 and by the time you read this the bus service may even extend to Arughat. Betrawati is served by one bus a day (9.30am) and old Trisuli by at least four, the last one at 2.30pm. And of course buses from Dhunche and Syabru Bensi pass through Betrawati and new Trisuli. All buses leave from or arrive at Kathmandu's new bus station.

SYABRU BENSI TO BASE CAMP   [MAP p229]

Syabru Bensi 1450m/4750ft is covered on p133. Getting there is on p135. Virtually everyone begins walking from Syabru Bensi although it may be possible to hitch a slow ride at least part of the way up the hill.

From Syabru Bensi, the direct and well-used track heads straight up (and I mean up). It meets the road several times and again at the top of the ridge at a minor pass of 2200m/7200ft. Follow the road down: at the split is a choice – take the upper road for the most direct route to Yuri Kharka and the lower one to the village of Goldzong for the lower, old trail to Gatalang. Dal bhaat is usually available at Goldzong and certainly porters will be able to find a place to stay and eat.

About twenty to thirty minutes along the upper road is a collection of buildings beside the road; this is Chauwadar. Groups often camp here and there is a small shop where dal bhaat may be available. Chauwadar is 2³/₄-4 hours from Syabru Bensi.

Gatalang and Shiva Parvati Mandir

The trail continues to follow the road apart from a shortcut through a bend or two. Between 2¹/₄ and 3 hours further up is the Shiva Parvati Mandir and a walled off area, Parvati Kunda (lake). Parvati is Shiva's wife, who waited 10,000 years for him – see the story of Gosainkund lakes on p31. Soon after this you come to the houses of roadside Gatalang, where Nepali food is sometimes available. The true village is perhaps ¹/₄hour below here. It is also possible to eat there and certainly local porters can find a bed and food for the night. If you have taken the lower trail through villages rather than the road it's time to rejoin the road.

The trail continues up, crossing the road a few times. About ¹/₂-³/₄ hour up is a small kharka with a creek beside it which is suitable for a few tents. One to one and a half hour's further up through pleasant forest is Goat-hen, a large kharka close to the road. There are two stone shacks that are popular with porters, plenty of dead wood and lots of room for tents. Water is 20 minutes or more away. One source is the creek further up the main trail, straight through the road zigzags. Around here and slightly further up are a few more possible camping spots.

Yuri Kharka 3520m/11,550ft

This collection of stone shelters and tenting spots is now nestled in a bend of the road. It is a frequent lunch or overnighting point for groups. The panorama includes the major ridge of the Jugal Himal on which Gosainkund rests and the ridge to the north which includes the western flank of Langtang Lirung. If sleeping here or at Goat-hen expect to feel, and perhaps suffer, the altitude.

Leaving, continue in a similar direction, leaving the road behind.

Kurpu Danda Pass 3740m/12,270ft

You are likely to feel the altitude. The pass is marked by a chorten and new vistas. Descend through the zigzags of the road until it flattens out and heads for Somthang.

There may be an alternative direct route to base camp along the ridge; there is certainly a trail to kharkas further up, however porters are generally reluctant to take it.

Somthang 3270m/10,730ft

Despite the grand name and being the important end of the road, this place is only a grazing area that now houses a few staff of the Ganesh

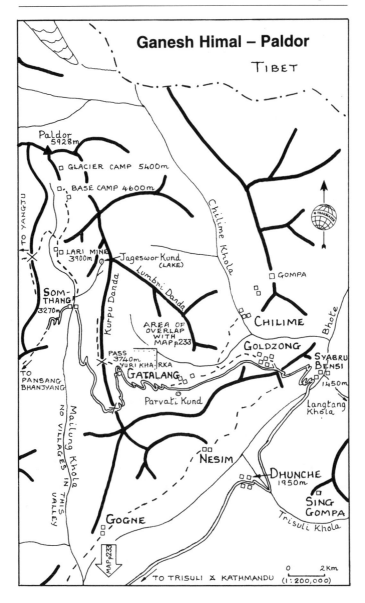

Ganesh Himal – Paldor

TIBET

Paldor 5928m

☐ GLACIER CAMP 5400m

☐ BASE CAMP 4600m

TO YANGJU

☐ LARI MINE 3900m

Jageswor Kund (LAKE)

Chilime Khola

☐ GOMPA

Lumbri Danda

SOM-THANG 3270m

Kupu Danda

AREA OF OVERLAP WITH MAP p.233

CHILIME

GOLDZONG

Bhote

PASS 3740m YURI KHA RKA

GATALANG

Parvati Kund

SYABRU BENSI 1450m

Langtang Khola

TO PANSANG BHANJYANG

Mailung Khola

NO VILLAGES IN THIS VALLEY

NESIM

DHUNCHE 1950m

SING GOMPA

GOGNE

MAP p.233

Trisuli Khola

TO TRISULI & KATHMANDU

0   2Km
(1:200,000)

Himal Lead-Zinc mine on the west bank and a large electricity trans-former and associated buildings on the east bank. There is no village or lodge, only a few stone shelters and camping spots. Supplies are not gen-erally available.

Leave following the power pylons and the obvious trail on the west side of the khola. After another 1-1½ hours, the trail leaves the pleasant forest for river flats and a series of possible camping places at around 3600m/11,800ft.

Lari Mine 3900m/12,800ft

Power pylons lead up the ridge to an uninviting collection of buildings. The ascent takes 1-1½ hours depending on acclimatisation and loads. I visited in winter and not a lot was going on. It looked as if that might be the general situation year-round, although somehow the stream has been polluted. It is possible to camp just below the main collection of build-ings, a place that will appeal to crews since they can often snag an elec-tric heater. A series of more pleasant camping spots begins 10 minutes above the mine, the first of which basks in early morning sun. From near here several trails cross to the west side of the khola for the high pass out (or in) from Yangju.

Jagesworkund is somewhere above on the eastern side of the khola.

Base Camp 4600m/15,100ft

Further above the camping spots the track becomes less obvious and breaks into two. Both routes involve minor scrambling up gullies that challenge heavily laden porters. Break out to the semi-flat high valley and you'll find several possible sights for a base camp but beware, the sun arrives late. The more usual spot is another extensive flat west of the high dividing moraines. Looking up from the lower base camp the location doesn't make sense, but get there and it will. It is a large flat area that can accommodate large groups. Both are fed by glacier waters.

During an acclimatisation day loads could be carried up to high camp. Porters can carry loads higher than base camp but shouldn't be expected to overnight higher. Indeed all but the best equipped shouldn't even be expected to overnight at the cold base camp. Anyone, including kitchen boys, who heads to high camp must have socks and sunglasses.

Between Base Camp and glacier camp are several more rough camp-ing spots. The first is up the ridge immediately out of Base Camp. Further along are a few more tent spots, some of which may be exposed to rock-fall.

High/Glacier camp 5400m/17,700ft

Ascend the moraine ridge to some old glacier-rounded rocks; you then come to a small flat area which is suitable for camping. From near here it is possible to move onto and ascend the glacier but most people go up considerably higher, across the rubble, before stepping onto the glacier. The glacier isn't obviously crevassed to high base camp but a wise team would scout the route with a rope team first. It is possible to camp just around the corner but groups favour a flattish area further up under Paldor's south-east shoulder. Small parties could camp closer to Windy Col or even on it but be warned it often lives up to its name at night.

THE CLIMB

A sunrise or even earlier start is advisable. From high camp to Windy Col the route crosses a potentially crevassed area and there is a bergschrund; consider scouting round the day before. Be sure to carry plenty of snacks, water, Diamox, spare socks and a torch.

The standard north-east ridge route

This is a route that, in perfect conditions, could just be soloed by the keen, especially if there is a track up. Groups will always fix ropes (the day before) across the trickier sections of rock (in spring these are partially covered by snow) and sometimes along sharper sections of the snow ridge and up the final 100m to the summit. The rock is loose but there is no rockfall danger so a hard hat isn't essential. Crevasse rescue equipment isn't needed from Windy Col.

The cheat's route

Rather than climb the ridge from Windy Col head over behind it and onto the glacier. This is definitely crevassed but is otherwise straightforward in hard snow conditions. It leads around a corner (don't ascend too early) then to a minor north ridge of around 45° directly to the summit.

The south-east ridge

Several snow couloirs – all of which are visible from near Windy Col – lead to the ridge. Watch for crevasses and a bergschrund on the way in. Once on the ridge climbing should be straightforward on 30-45° or perhaps 50° slopes. If conditions are good, consider a traverse of the mountain.

The alternative access to the ridge is from the glacier to the west of Paldor. It looks as if climbing a couloir there means a mixed technical route probably requiring a helmet and a modest rock rack, as well as snow toys.

From the summit

Which is the higher point on this flattish (in one dimension) ridge? Who cares, but the views are sufficiently different to justify photographing from both ends. The summit way to the east with a distinctive front ramp of snow is the twin-headed Gauri-Shankar.

EXIT VIA TIRU DANDA AND SINGLA TO BETRAWATI

Looking south from above Base Camp you can see a long ridge extending to the south. We instinctively took it as it looked the most attractive route but wondered where Bill O'Connor's Tiru Danda, *Trekking Peaks of Nepal* was; it wasn't until we got to Kathmandu that we realised we had just walked it.

From Somthang follow the new road (under slow construction January 1997) past a forest nursery and across the stream. Shortly after, the climb begins with a trail that takes shortcuts through the zigzags of the road. The route heads roughly south. Less than two hours out of Somthang are a series of kharkas and small camping spots. Groups will probably plan to stay slightly higher at the extensive Pangsang kharka, where the water and roofed shelters are convenient for kitchen crews and porters. It also affords good views of the ridge to Syabru Bensi and of the Langtang area. This takes three to five hours including breaks (but not lunch) from Somthang. From the kharka to the pass takes $^1/_2$-$^3/_4$ hour. Several trails merge but the main trail is well-defined in the increasingly steep country.

Pangsang Bhanjyang 3856m/12,650ft

The open pass is marked by stone guardians and prayer flags; there is no water. The new views include the Manaslu range and parts of Annapurna. To the north the magnificent Ganesh Himal begins to come into view while to the immediate west complicated creased ridges descend to become the middle hills of the Ganesh range. To the south, ridge after blue ridge of hills extends towards Kathmandu. From just south of the pass most of the route to the Singla is visible. Singla is the highest point of the high ridge that runs east-west at the end of the north-south ridge that you are standing on.

The trail that drops west from the Pangsang Pass leads to Tipling and several other villages, the main users of this area. In winter they light fires to encourage more grass growth and discourage other plants from taking hold. This can also reduce plant disease, but with horrifying pollution consequences. It is possible to walk from Tipling along the Ankhu Khola to the new roadhead of Dhading where buses leave for Kathmandu. To the north are more kharkas and those with time might like to climb one of the rough peaks.

From the Pangsang Bhanjyang to Singla takes $5^1/_2$-$8^1/_2$ hours including breaks. The first half is a stunningly beautiful ridge walk that stays mainly on the western side of the ridge. There are a few steep rocky sections but the trail is easy to follow. There are many kharkas along the way but little or no water, depending on the season. In winter a few frozen streams provide ice for melting.

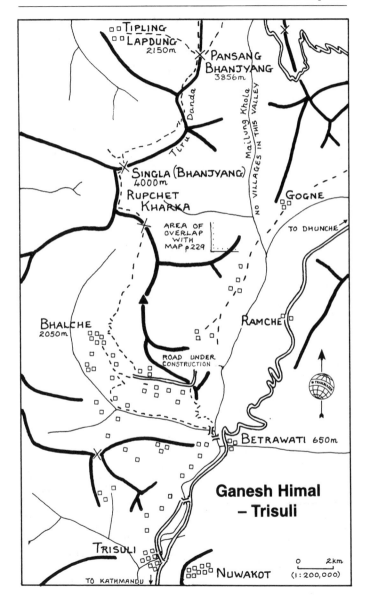

TIPLING
LAPDUNG
2150m

PANSANG
BHANJYANG
3856m

Tiru Danda

Mailung Khola

NO VILLAGES IN THIS VALLEY

SINGLA (BHANJYANG)
4000m

RUPCHET
KHARKA

GOGNE

AREA OF
OVERLAP
WITH
MAP p229

TO DHUNCHE

BHALCHE
2050m

RAMCHE

ROAD UNDER
CONSTRUCTION

TRAILBLAZER

BETRAWATI 650m

Ganesh Himal
– Trisuli

TRISULI

NUWAKOT

0   2km

(1:200,000)

TO KATHMANDU

Singla 4000m/13,123ft

This is often called the Singla Bhanjyang and is given an incorrect height of 4600m on the Mandala map. Rather than a single pass, this is a series of high kharkas and the meeting point of several trails. There is little or no water at the top. During spring there is usually snow lying around, otherwise groups cart water from below.

If at all possible, stay near the top of the ridges for a stunning sunset and sunrise panorama. Views include, from the west: the Annapurnas with Annapurna II's distinctive black rock summit looking the highest in the range although the more distant middle summit is Annapurna I (8091m/26,545ft); Machapuchare's (the Fishtail) double summit blends with Annapurna South. The next range is the Manaslu with Manaslu I to the right. The three large peaks to the north are the Ganesh Himal and more peaks are hidden behind. Paldor is the highest snow point of the ridge that runs off the central peak. The peaks to the north-east are (unfortunately) in Tibet and some form a barrier around the head of the Langtang Valley. Highest on this skyline is the western summit of Langtang Lirung and further right is the snowdome once called Dome Blanc, now Pemthang Karpo Ri, which is distinctive for its tumbling glaciers.

The trail for Betrawati and Trisuli heads south without crossing a clearly defined pass. You are initially aiming for the saddle between you and the next lump of a hill to the south, the Phikuri Danda. Usually arrows on rocks and in the dirt made to guide groups point the way.

The trail soon begins a steep and rocky ascent. Between $^3/_4$ and $1^1/_4$ hours down is Rupchet kharka; it often used by groups. There is no obvious water in winter. Head through this kharka on a trail that looks as if it is leaving the main ridge. In fact this follows the lower ridge to the Gongur Bhanjyang (saddle), a further $1^3/_4$-$2^1/_2$ hours down.

Gongur Bhanjyang 2950m/9680ft

The saddle is often used by groups as a camping or lunch spot. East leads to the kharka previously visible while dropping west leads to many villages and the valley floor. The standard trekking route is the straight, flat option. Five minutes along and slightly off this trail is a water source.

The altimeter stubbornly remains at the same altitude as the pass for a couple of hours; by Nepalese standards the trail is flat but in reality it's a series of minor ups and downs. There are increasing signs of civilisation in the form of a buffalo settlement (milk may be available) and several ugly clear-felled areas that are being turned into kharkas. There are also some interesting rock formations reminiscent of the faces photographed in the *Honey-hunters of Nepal*, a 1988 National Geographic article and book available in Kathmandu. The actual area where Eric Valli photographed the honey hunters was somewhere up the Buri Gandaki valley.

Bhalche/Phalje 2050m/6725ft

Three to four hours from the saddle the trail enters the extensive fields of Bhalche. Stay on the main trail as it descends for $^1/_2$-$^3/_4$ hour to the village. Porters who know the area may take a shortcut that misses the village.

This is a typical traditional Tamang village complete with shit-lined trails, throngs of kids and women who beg for or offer cigarettes. In the village bear right or west (ie away from Trisuli) and ask to find the main stone-stepped trail down. Five minutes down is an old stupa called a gompa by locals. Either take the flat smaller trail heading east or walk through the cluster of houses below and bear east for the main Betrawati trail. This traverses and descends to a new (1997) irrigation canal system. By now terraces extend almost as far as the eye can see with occasional trees and houses breaking the lines, a particularly beautiful region. From here on there are many trail junctions but for the most part the main trail is readily followed. Later is a choice: the old main trail that continues to descend gently through various villages to the valley floor, or a minor trail that shortly leads to a road under construction. This easy-walking route contours to Sattobhatti (1380m/4525ft), a collection of simple lodges in a saddle. Dal Bhaat and simple lodging is available. From here the road curves north around the hillside while the shorter main trail heads southwards and descends steeply. The bridges across the Salangkhu Khola and the Trisuli River and the town of Betrawati are sometimes visible so, although there are many trails, it is hard to go wrong.

To Trisuli

Although the closest road and bus is at Betrawati the slightly longer walk to Trisuli is also rewarding. The easiest but least exciting option is to cross the Salangkhu Khola at the confluence with the Trisuli then simply stay on the west bank and head south to old Trisuli. The more direct route from Bhalche is the Nepalese style: shorter as the crow flies, but crosses another ridge. It is a follow your nose route; simply head due south aiming for a minor pass and ask frequently. Bill O'Connor mentions going via the village of Bumdang before reaching old Trisuli.

APPENDIX A: ITINERARIES & ACCLIMATISATION

The preceding trail guide was deliberately not written on a 'Day 1, Day 2' basis so as to encourage trekkers to travel at their own pace and not stop all in the same places. However, some guidelines are useful for overall planning. Overnight stops are given in the tables below.

ACCLIMATISATION PLANNER

If trekking above 3000m/10,000ft remember to allow time for adequate acclimatisation. Note that it is the sleeping altitude that is important. How high you go during the day is of little importance.

Night 0	below 2000m/6562ft
1	2-3000m/6562-9842ft
2	2-3000m/6562-9842ft
3	3000m/9842ft
4	3300m/10,827ft
5	3600m/11,811ft
6	3900m/12,795ft
7	3900m/12,795ft
8	4200m/13,779ft
9	4500m/14,764ft
10	4800m/15,748ft
11	4800m/15,748ft
12	5100m/16,732ft
13	5400m/17,716ft

On the Langtang trek people often feel the altitude at Langtang village (3480m/ 11,417ft), especially if they have ascended quickly; similarly at Phedi (3600m/11,800ft) on the Gosainkund trek. Mild altitude sickness is commonly suffered on the first night at Kyangjin (3900m/12,800ft) or at Gosainkund (4385m/14,346ft) itself. It is rare for this to get worse but it is possible. All this discomfort can be avoided by planning how you are going to acclimatise, ie where you are going to have a rest day or a couple of easy days.

Note: Syabru B means Syabru Bensi. Syabru means Thulo Syabru. Although main centres only are mentioned, lodges nearby are included. For example Changdam means staying somewhere between the three lodges before Changdam, at Changdam itself or at the two lodges slightly higher. The Helambu Circuit itinerary planner is on p178.

Langtang Valley

Pace	Medium (group)		Altitude-aware	Fast	The quickie
Night	Kathmandu		Kathmandu	Kathmandu	Kathmandu
1	Dhunche	1950m	Dhunche/	Bharkhu/	Bharkhu/
			Bharkhu	Syabru Bensi	Syabru Bensi
2	Syabru	2200m	Langmoche	Changdam	Changdam
3	Changdam	2480m	Ghora Tabela	Langtang	Langtang
4	Langtang	3480m	Langtang	Kyangjin	Langtang
5	Kyangjin	3900m	Kyangjin	Kyangjin	Syabru Bensi
6	Kyangjin	3900m	Kyangjin	Langtang	Kathmandu

7	Kyangjin	3900m	Kyangjin	Syabru Bensi
8	Changdam	2480m	Changdam	Kathmandu
9	Syabru Bensi	1450m	Syabru Bensi	
10	Kathmandu		Kathmandu	

Note: spending two nights at or near Langtang village is the most sensible acclimatisation option.

Gosainkund

Pace	Fast but silly		Fast but sensible	Medium	Medium (group)
Night	Kathmandu	1400m	Kathmandu	Kathmandu	Kathmandu
1	Pati Bhanjyang	1750m	Chisopani	Kakani	Chisopani
2	Kutumsang	2480m	Kutumsang	Sarmathang	Gul Bhanjyang
3	Tharepati	3600m	Tharepati	Tarkeghyang	Magin Goth
4	Phedi	3740m	Tharepati/Gopte	Melamchighyang	Tharepati
5	Laurebina	3925m	Phedi	Tharepati	Gopte
6	Dhunche	1950m	Gosainkund	Gopte	Phedi
7			Gosainkund	Phedi	Gosainkund
8			Syabru	Gosainkund	Sing Gompa
9			Bharkhu/Syabru B	Syabru	Dhunche/Bharkhu
10			Kathmandu	Bharkhu/Dhunche	Kathmandu
12					Kathmandu

Langtang and Gosainkund combined

Pace	Fast	Medium (group)	Relaxed	In reverse
Night	Kathmandu	Kathmandu	Kathmandu	Kathmandu
1	Bharkhu/Syabru Bensi	Dhunche	Bharkhu	Chisopani
2	Changdam	Syabru	Langmoche	Gul Bhanjyang
3	Langtang	Changdam	Ghora Tabela	Magin Goth
4	Kyangjin	Langtang	Langtang	Tharepati
5	Kyangjin	Kyangjin	Kyangjin/Langtang	Gopte
6	Kyangjin	Kyangjin	Kyangjin	Phedi
7	Langtang/Chamdan	Kyangjin	Kyangjin	Gosainkund
8	Syabru/Sing Gompa	Changdam	Changdam	Sing Gompa
9	Laurebina/Gosainkund	Syabru	Syabru Bensi	Syabru
10	Tharepati	Sing Gompa	Sing Gompa	Ghore Tabela
11	Kutumsang/Gul Bhanjyang	Gosainkund	Gosainkund	Kyangjin
12	Pati B/Chisopani	Phedi	Phedi	Kyangjin
13	Kathmandu	Tharepati	Tharepati	Kyangjin
14		Gul B/Kutumsang	Melamchighyang	Changdam
15		Chisopani	Tarkeghyang	Syabru B
16		Kathmandu	Timbu	Kathmandu
17			Two Rivers	
18			Kathmandu	

Kangja La and Langtang Circuit

Night	Kangja La fast	Langtang Circuit fast		Medium (group)
0	Kathmandu	Kathmandu	1400m	Kathmandu
1	Bharkhu	Chisopani	2150m	Chisopani
2	Changdam	Kutumsang	2480m	Gul Bhanjyang
3	Langtang	Tharepati	3600m	Magin Goth
4	Kyangjin	Tharepati/Gopte	3600m	Tharepati
5	Kyangjin	Phedi	3740m	Gopte
6	Kyangjin	Gosainkund	4390m	Phedi
7	Base Camp	Syabru	2200m	Gosainkund
8	Keldang	Gumna/Chhunamna	2780m	Sing Gompa
9	Dhukpu/further	Kyangjin	3900m	Syabru
10	Tarkeghyang	Kyangjin	3900m	Changdam
11	Sarmathang/ Melamchi Pul	Base Camp	4350m	Langtang
12	Melamchi Pul/ Ktm	Over pass to Keldang	4300m	Kyangjin
13	Kathmandu	Dhukpu/further	4080m	Kyangjin
14		Tarkeghyang	2550m	Base Camp
15	Alternative exit	Sarmathang/Melamchi	2590m	Yangri Khola camp
16	Tarkeghyang	Melamchi Pul/Ktm	850m	Dhukpu
17	Kiul Tar			Tarkeghyang
18	Melamchi Pul			Sarmathang
19	Kathmandu			Melamchi Pul
20				Kathmandu

APPENDIX B: HEALTH

STAYING HEALTHY WHILE TREKKING

In developed countries we take for granted clean drinking water, hygienically pack-aged food and comprehensive sewage systems, none of which exist in the villages of Nepal. New arrivals to Asia will be lucky to escape without some form of upset stom-ach, although in many cases this is quite mild and soon clears up of its own accord. It seems to make little difference whether you trek with an expensive group package or independently, and whether you camp or stay in lodges. Most group cooks working for the bigger agencies have completed a basic hygiene course. Their assistants, however, usually have not and the conditions under which food is prepared are far from perfect. Some lodge owners have attended basic hygiene courses, their working conditions are better and they attempt less adventurous dishes.

Diet

The food you will eat in the mountains is nutritious and healthy. The diet is carbohy-drate-weighted – exactly what is needed – with protein coming mainly from eggs, nuts, beans and dal. Walking every day, breathing harder and the cold at higher alti-tudes all mean that you'll burn far more calories than normal. Don't be afraid to eat as much as you like!

Water purification

Nearly all water from taps, streams and rivers in Nepal (even at high altitudes) is contaminated to some degree and should not be considered safe to drink without purification. Only spring water and water made from clean snow are safe without being treated. There are several ways to purify water but first it helps to know who your enemies are. The most difficult to kill of the various pathogens are the cysts that cause giardia and amoebic dysentery; even one or two can cause the disease. These can survive in very cold water and even for several months in freezing conditions. High concentrations of chemicals are required to penetrate their protective shell. They are, however, killed immediately by bringing water close to the boil. Bacteria and viruses are less resilient. Larger numbers are needed before infection occurs and they are destroyed by very low concentrations of chemicals.

Boiling

Water need only be pasteurised (heating it to 75°C/162°F) not sterilised (boiling for 10 minutes) to make it safe to drink. Even at 5800m/19,000ft water boils at around 81°C/177°F so hot drinks like tea, coffee and hot lemon etc, are all safe.

Iodine-based methods

• **Iodine tablets** The active ingredient is tetraglycine hydroperiodide. If the water is very cold allow 30 minutes rather than the usual 10; if it is cloudy double the dose (ie two tablets per litre). The normal dose is enough to kill giardia despite the label's suggestion to double the dose. These tablets are convenient and easy to use but are hard to find in Kathmandu. The two brand names are Potable Aqua and Coghlan's Drinking Water Tablets.

• **Polar Pure** This method relies on dissolving a small amount of iodine directly in water. It is effective and cheap. The iodine crystals come in a glass bottle with a filter to prevent the crystals falling out of the bottle. There's a temperature sensitive strip on the side to determine the dose needed.

• **Betadine/Povidone** This method uses a non-iodine based molecule to bind free iodine. For a 10% solution use eight drops per litre of water. If the water is 20°C wait 15 minutes before drinking; if very cold, one hour.

• **Lugol's Iodine Solution** Unless purchased in the West, the solutions come in different concentrations that are often not indicated on the bottle. The solution could be 2%, 4% or 8%. In addition, the free iodine (the active ingredient) is dissolved in potassium iodide so the total amount of iodine consumed is much higher than necessary. However, if you have no choice, it's definitely better than nothing. For 2% solution use five drops per litre of water and leave it for 15 minutes before drinking. If the water is very cold, or cloudy, then it should be left for 30 minutes or 10 drops should be used. Note that iodine solutions are messy so put the bottle in several plastic bags and the iodine (except Betadine) should be kept only in a glass bottle.

Chlorine based methods

• **Chlorine based tablets** (Steritabs, Puritabs) These are similar to the silver-based Micropur tablets but they aren't effective against giardia. However, if used with a fine filter (to remove the giardia), half a tablet is adequate.

Several purifiers use super-chlorination, a high dose of chlorine that is later neutralised by adding hydrogen peroxide. It's very effective.

Water filters

There is quite a variety on the market and some include an iodine resin. Follow the manufacturer's instructions carefully, especially with regard to cleaning and maintenance. The drawbacks with filters are their size, weight and cost.

Using bottled water

This can be obtained along the trail but because it is carried in, its price rises dramatically. The leftover bottles are also unsightly and difficult to dispose of. Using purifying methods is a far better solution. Boiled water is often available in the lodges but it requires valuable firewood to prepare.

AMS – ACUTE MOUNTAIN SICKNESS

Commonly called altitude sickness, AMS can affect all trekkers going above 3000m/10,000ft. It's caused by going up too high too fast and can be fatal if the warning signals are ignored. Your body needs time to adjust to the smaller quantity of oxygen that is present in the air at altitude. At 5500m/18,044ft, the air pressure is approximately half that at sea level so there is half the amount of oxygen (and nitrogen).

Altitude sickness is preventable. Go up slowly, giving your body enough time to adjust. The 'safe' rates of ascent for the majority of trekkers involve spending two to three nights between 2000m/6500ft and 3000m/10,000ft before going higher. From 3000m you should sleep at an average of 300m/1000ft higher each night with a rest day every 900-1000m/3000ft. These rates are marked on the sample itineraries on p237. Be aware of the symptoms and ascend only if you are symptom-free.

Mild AMS symptoms

You need have only one of the following symptoms to be getting altitude sickness, not necessarily all of them.
• **Headache** This begins as a pressure headache then develops into a frontal or all over headache
• **Nausea**
• **Dizziness or light-headedness (mild)**
• **Appetite-loss, or generally feeling bad**
• **Dry raspy cough**

What to do about mild AMS symptoms If you find mild symptoms developing while walking, stop and relax (with your head out of the sun) and drink some fluids. If the symptoms do not go away completely then stay at the same altitude. If the symptoms get worse, go down. Even a small loss of elevation (100-300m/328-984ft) can make a big difference to how you feel and how you sleep. If symptoms develop at night then, unless they rapidly get worse, wait them out and see how you feel in the morning. If the symptoms have not gone after breakfast then have a rest day or descend. If they have gone, you should still consider having a rest day or only an easy day's walking.

Note that there is a time lag between arriving at altitude and the onset of symptoms. In fact, statistically it is more common to suffer mild symptoms on the second night at a set altitude than on the first night.

Mild symptoms often clear up after taking Diamox, a solution that should be considered especially when trekking with an organised group on a fixed itinerary. It can

---

❏ **AMS can kill in Langtang**
We passed a guy who looked a little puffed. He said the altitude had got to him a bit and he was heading down from Kyangjin. He looked tired but not in any serious difficulty, simply short of breath. Later he reached Langtang village and rested. He felt better but during the night he went into a coma and died. Moral: trek with a friend or if alone ask for people to help you. **Mark Cohen** (UK)

also be useful for climbers who have ascended too fast. Altitude sickness must be reacted to when symptoms are mild: going higher will definitely make it worse. You trek to enjoy, not to feel sick.

Serious AMS symptoms
• **Persistent, severe headache**
• **Persistent vomiting**
• **Ataxia** – loss of co-ordination, an inability to walk in a straight line, making the sufferer look drunk
• **Losing consciousness** – inability to stay awake or understand instructions
• **Liquid sounds in the lungs**
• **Persistent, sometimes watery, cough**
• **Difficulty breathing**
• **Rapid breathing or feeling breathless at rest**
• **Coughing blood, pink phlegm or lots of clear fluid**
• **Severe lethargy**
• **Marked blueness of face and lips**
• **High resting heartbeat – over 120 beats per minute**
• **Mild symptoms rapidly getting worse**

Ataxia is the single most important sign for recognising the progression of AMS from mild to serious. This is easily tested by trying to walk in a straight line, heel to toe and should be compared with somebody who has no symptoms. Twenty-four hours after the onset of ataxia a coma is possible, followed by death, unless you descend.

The patient, supported by several people, must be taken as far down as possible, even if it is the middle of the night. People with serious symptoms may not be able to think for themselves and may say they feel OK – they are not.

Medical conditions at altitude
• **High Altitude Cerebral Edema (HACE)** This is a build up of fluid around the brain. It causes the first four symptoms on the two lists above. HACE can occur in 12 hours but normally takes one to three days. At the first sign of ataxia begin to descend. If the condition has developed doctors usually give 4mg of dexamethadrone six hourly, Diamox* (see p242) (250mg) 12 hourly and 2-4 litres per minute (l/m) oxygen** (see p242). A Gamow Bag*** (see p242) should be used if available.

• **High Altitude Pulmonary Edema (HAPE)** This is an accumulation of fluid in the lungs and can be serious. It is responsible for all the other mild and serious symptoms. Immediate descent is vital and Diamox (250mg) may be given 12 hourly, Nifed orally (10mg, eight hourly) and 2-4l/m oxygen. A Gamow Bag should be used if available.

• **Periodic breathing** Less oxygen than usual in the blood affects the body's breathing mechanism. While at rest or sleeping your body seems to feel the need to breathe less and less, to the point where suddenly you require some deep breaths to recover. This cycle can be a few breaths long, in which after a couple of breaths you miss a breath completely. Alternatively it may be a gradual cycle over a few minutes, appearing as if your breathing rate simply goes up and down regularly. It is experienced by most trekkers at Kyangjin, although many people are unaware of it while asleep. Studies have so far found no direct link to AMS.

• **Swelling of the hands, feet, face and lower abdomen** A few trekkers experience some swelling, usually minor; women are more susceptible. It is not a cause for concern unless the swelling is severe, so continued ascent is OK. Remove rings.

- **High Altitude Flatulence Emission (HAFE)** This is commonly known as HAF (High Altitude Farts). The cure – let it rip! You're not a balloon that needs blowing up.

- **Blood noses or bloody snot** This is caused by rapid ascent but should go away after a few days. It is common when crossing Gosainkund and at Kyangjin.

- **Sleeping** Many people have trouble sleeping in a new environment, especially if it changes every day. Altitude adds to the problems. Apart from the condition known as periodic breathing (see above), the decrease of oxygen means that some trekkers experience wild dreams. This often happens at Kyangjin or Langtang.

- **Appetite** Altitude causes some people to lose an interest in food but you should try to eat as much as you can.

Treatment for AMS

* **Diamox (Acetazolamide)** This is a mild diuretic (it leads to increased urination) that acidifies the blood to stimulate breathing. Using it as a prophylactic (ie to prevent AMS before you have symptoms) is not yet recommended, unless you ascend unavoidably rapidly (eg flying to a high altitude, such as Lhasa, or on a rescue mission), or unless you have experienced undue altitude problems previously. It is a sulfa drug derivative and people allergic to this class of drugs should not take Diamox. People with impaired renal (kidney) function shouldn't take it either. The side effects are increased urination and sometimes tingling sensations in the lips, fingers or toes but these symptoms are not an indication to stop the drug. Diamox can also ruin the taste of beer and soft drinks and increase your skin's sensitivity to sunlight.

Taking Diamox with you on the trek is recommended; you should consider using it if you experience mild but annoying symptoms, especially if periodic breathing if it continually wakes you up. The dosage is 125mg (half a tablet) every 12 hours for one to two days. Diamox actually goes to the root of the problem: so if you feel better, you are better. It does not simply hide the problem. However this does not mean that you can ascend at a faster rate than normal, or ignore altitude sickness symptoms since it is quite possible to still develop AMS while taking Diamox.

** **Supplementary Oxygen** (O_2) does not immediately reverse all the symptoms but it does help significantly. Descent in conjunction with O_2 is more effective.

*** **Gamow Bag** This is the latest device to assist with severe AMS. Basically, it's a plastic tube into which the patient is zipped. A foot pump is used to raise the pressure inside the bag simulating a lower altitude.

Rates of acclimatisation

Individual rates of acclimatisation are dependent on how fast your body reacts to compensate for the altered pH level of the blood. For slow starters Diamox can provide a kick-start but for people already adapting well its effect is minimal.

DIARRHOEA

This is a common problem in developing countries, especially Nepal, and few trekkers escape without some (usually mild) form of diarrhoea. Ideally, you should visit a doctor for a stool test if it doesn't clear up in a few days. While trekking, however, this is usually impossible so self-diagnosis may be necessary.

Many people over-react and start taking medication at the first loose stool. Diarrhoea will not normally kill you so urgent treatment is neither necessary nor always recommended. It's better to wait a few days and see if it goes away on its own. Unless the diarrhoea is particularly severe (eg as with food poisoning) there is no need to stop trekking. Just drink lots of water and listen to your body: if you feel hungry, eat, and if you don't then take soup and light foods. If the diarrhoea is still trouble-some after a few days and you are fairly sure what type it is you may want to treat it. Avoid taking Immodium or Lomotil. These drugs act as a simple cork without curing the real cause of the diarrhoea. Their only use is stopping you up for long bus jour-neys. Be aware too that the effects of several tablets can last from a couple of days to a week! Doctors at home routinely prescribe either of these medicines as part of your medical kit.

Travellers'/bacterial diarrhoea
Hitting many new arrivals to Asia, this kind of diarrhoea is caused by eating food which contains strains of a common bacteria that your body isn't used to. The onset is often accompanied by or even preceded by a fever and/or chills and nausea, followed by fairly sudden, frequent, watery diarrhoea and often cramps.
• **Treatment** If you dislike popping pills it's worth waiting to see if your body can fight it off on its own. Tough Nepalese bacteria, however, often need stronger mea-sures. The most effective is to begin a short course of Norfloxacin or Ciprofloxacin; for Norfloxacin the dose is 400mg every 12 hours for three days. For Cipro, 500mg every 12 hours for five to seven days. Note that Cipro and Norfloxacin can increase your sensitivity to sunlight.
An occasionally recommended drug is Bactrim/Bactrim DS or Septra but as there are now resistant strains these are not nearly as effective.

Food poisoning
This comes on suddenly and severely at both ends, about one to eight hours after eat-ing contaminated food. Luckily, it usually lasts less than 24 hours and recovery is quick, although you feel weakened.
• **Treatment** There are no drugs that can help – the body just has to eject all the con-taminated food and rid itself of the poison. Rest and drink plenty of fluids. Oral rehy-dration solutions are helpful.

Giardia
Common in Nepal, giardia is caught from infected water, especially in Kathmandu and from high mountain streams near areas where yaks graze. It generally takes seven to 14 days to develop and doesn't come on suddenly. The classic symptoms are sul-phurous (rotten egg) smelling farts and burps but these don't have to be present; they can also be the result of eggs for breakfast or a minor viral infection. More reliable symptoms that make it easier to distinguish from other types of diarrhoea include a rumbling upset stomach, bloating and cramps. Stools alternate over several days from loose but not watery to normal and even some minor constipation. Usually there is no fever, chills or nausea. Giardia can also be virtually symptomless: just a slightly rum-bling, sometimes crampy, stomach with occasional soft stools in an approximately regular cycle perhaps of seven to 10 days. Some forms may go away on their own after several weeks but treatment is usually required.
• **Treatment** There's a choice of two drugs. Tiniba (Tinidazole) can be bought at all Nepalese pharmacies without a prescription. The dose is 2g, ie four x 500mg, taken all at once. It's better taken in the evening because the usual side effects (a strong metal-lic taste in the mouth and occasionally mild nausea) may be slept off. **Do not mix with alcohol**. This dose is about 90% effective but, if you feel positive that you have giar-dia, the same dose should be repeated 24 hours later. Alternatively Flagyl/Metronidazole may be used. The dose is 250mg, three times a day for five to seven days. This should also not be mixed with alcohol.

Amoebic dysentery

Only 1% or less of all diarrhoea cases are caused by amoebic dysentery. The onset of amoebic dysentery may be sudden and severely weakening – sometimes to the point where the sufferer is barely able to leave the toilet. However, it usually starts slowly, a mild diarrhoea that comes and goes, something that can almost but not quite, be ignored. This is the most dangerous time because although the symptoms may eventually clear up, your system is still infected and is being slowly damaged. It can also be confused with giardia. If you suspect you might have amoebic dysentery, have a stool test when you return to Kathmandu.

Other diarrhoea

The above are the most common varieties that travellers and trekkers pick up. However there are more: viral diarrhoea, typhoid, cholera etc. If it doesn't clear up trek out and see a good doctor. Stomach ulcers and related problems can also cause diarrhoea.

OTHER HEALTH PROBLEMS

Dehydration

Trekkers lose large quantities of water, not just through sweating but by breathing harder at altitude. Water vapour is exhaled with each breath and the thinner air means more breaths are required. If the fluids lost are not replaced, you'll become dehydrated; this will make you feel lethargic and sometimes give you a headache. The symptoms are similar to AMS so the easiest way to avoid confusion is to always keep hydrated.

A happy mountaineer always pees clear! If your urine is a thick yellow or orange colour you are not drinking enough. Even if you are not feeling thirsty you should still try to drink more. This can include any liquids (soups and tea but not alcohol) and as much water as possible. Many people find that with supper they often drink more than a litre of water, catching up on what they should have drunk during the day.

The trekker's cough

A runny nose and an irritating, usually dry cough is common among trekkers. Smoky lodges and excessive breathing of the thin cold dry air often causes runny nose and an irritating, usually dry cough; avoid smoky rooms and pop throat lozenges at the first sign of a sore throat. Although it's an inflammation of the bronchi, since it isn't caused by a bug there shouldn't be any fever and there is no magic cure.

Chest infections

When travelling you encounter new strains of the common cold and flu viruses. There is, of course, no cure for a cold (ie viral infection). However, especially at altitude, an opportunistic bacterial infection – bronchitis – can develop too. It can be difficult to distinguish between viral and bacterial infections but lots of thick coloured sputum, especially in the morning, and a painful cough is more indicative of a bacterial infection. Steam inhalations are useful and easy to arrange. Drink plenty of fluids. Unless it is particularly troubling wait until you get to Kathmandu to see a doctor and anyway in a warmer climate and lower altitude often your body can overcome the infection. People with a history of chest infections could begin the medication previously used. If you still have a long trek to go consider taking 500mg Amoxicillin three times a day for a week (or Ampicillin, same dosage). These drugs should not be taken by people allergic to penicillin. An alternative is 250mg Erythromycin four times a day but this drug arrests infection rather than completely cures it.

Snow blindness
Burnt skin/burnt eyes Sunburn of the cornea is a painful affliction that feels like hot sand in your eyes. It is entirely preventable by wearing sunglasses that block UV light. Porters trekking in snow must be provided for and it is often up to you since trekking companies usually don't care.

Frostbite
When flesh freezes the results are very serious; amputation may be necessary. Frostbite occurs usually in fingers or toes and takes time to develop unless bare flesh is exposed to winds at low temperatures.
• **Treatment** In the early stages fingers or toes feel numb, clumsy and lose strength. If it's still possible to move them a little they should be warmed up immediately as they are on the verge of freezing. Warm them slowly and evenly (in your armpit or groin) – sometimes this is painful. Blood temperature is the optimum warming temperature and once defrosted you must promote blood circulation (swing your arms around). When deep freezing has occurred the flesh turns white or even blue and fingers or toes become wooden, incapable of movement. At this stage don't begin rewarming them until you're in a position where refreezing cannot occur since this is even more damaging. Rewarming is painful and blisters will probably form. See a doctor as soon as possible.

Boils
These are more common in the monsoon season and are usually the result of a staphylococcal skin infection. Boils are not urgent but you must see a doctor when you can.

Unwelcome bed companions
If you're using your own sleeping bag it's unlikely you'll have problems. Rented sleeping bags always carry a very small risk of scabies but not fleas or bedbugs, and this can be further reduced by airing the bag for a day or two in the sun. If you ever use local blankets the risks increase considerably.
• **Bedbug Bites** are normally small, itchy and in neat lines. Bedbugs do not normally live in sleeping bags because when they are aired there is nowhere to hide.
• **Fleas** All local dogs are carriers and fleas also hide in quilts, blankets and old carpets; occasionally trekkers pick them up. The small, red, itchy bites are usually congregated around areas such as the tops of your socks, waist, armpits or sleeves. Try not to scratch them. Wash yourself and your clothes thoroughly. If you can find some flea powder, use this as well.
• **Scabies** Caused by a microscopic parasite this is luckily rare amongst trekkers. It can be caught from sheets or rented sleeping bags (but only if they have not been aired properly) or contact with an infected person, sometimes another trekker. To avoid scabies use a sleeping sheet in your sleeping bag. The itchy red spots look like pimples without the pus and may, at first, be confused with flea bites. As the parasites multiply, the marks spread widely. Visit a health post or preferably a doctor.
• **Treatment** is an ointment or a head-to-toe dousing with Scabex. All clothing should be washed and thoroughly aired and your sleeping bag should be left in the sun for several days. It takes a few days for the symptoms to disappear and a second treatment may be necessary.

Leeches
These monsoon terrorisers are able to put a sizeable hole in you completely painlessly. Found in profusion in damp forest, leeches are adept at penetrating socks and even boot eyelets. They can also drop from trees. Do not try to pull a biting leech off instead

apply salt, iodine or a lighted match and it'll quickly drop off. Leeches don't transmit disease but wounds can become infected.

Blisters

Since you spend most of the time on your feet, looking after them properly to avoid blisters is of paramount importance. Start with boots that have been worn in. This means not just for a short walk on level ground but with a pack in hilly country.

If a blister starts to develop while you're trekking you can usually feel it. There'll be some rubbing, localised pain or a hot spot. Stop and investigate, even if it occurs during the first five minutes of walking or just in sight of the top of the hill. The trick is to detect the symptoms before the blister develops. Apply moleskin or Second Skin, or a strong adhesive tape such as Leukoplast, which is available in Nepal. Check that the hot spot is not being caused by the seam of a sock or a seam in your boot. Once you've applied a dressing, recheck it periodically to ensure that the problem is not getting worse.

• **Treatment** If you develop a blister there are several approaches. If it's not painful then surround it (don't cover it) with some light padding, eg moleskin, and see how it feels. Otherwise you may want to drain it. Clean the skin, sterilise a needle by holding it slightly above a flame for a few seconds and pierce the blister. Don't cut away the blister skin until it has dried out and is no longer useful for protecting the delicate skin underneath. Put protective tape over it with some cotton wool as padding. Some people, however, put the tape straight over the blister, with no dressing.

Tendonitis

Pain in the achilles tendon is usually caused by overuse or by ill-fitting boots.
• **Treatment** is rest and an anti-inflammatory drug such as Ibuprofen, aspirin or paracetamol.

Vaginal infections

If you have experienced these before it is worth bringing a course of the medication you were last prescribed.

FIRST AID KIT

This is a very basic list to cover the more common ailments that afflict trekkers. Climbing groups will need a more comprehensive kit. Quantities stated are for one to two people.

Easily purchased in Kathmandu without prescription:

• **Diamox** This comes in two forms, 250mg tablets and 500mg time-release capsules. One strip of 10 tablets is plenty.
• **Norfloxacin** 10 tablets or **Ciprofloxacin** 20 tablets. These are powerful drugs that can also be used to treat many other infections.
• **Tinidazole/Tiniba** 8 to 10 tablets.
• **Jeevan Jal (oral rehydration salts)** One to three packets for the replacement of salts and fluids lost by vomiting and diarrhoea. Fanta, Coke or Pepsi (with the fizz taken out) and soup are also helpful but not in excessive quantities.
• **Erythromycin** You may also consider taking this for skin infections or bronchitis. The dose is 250mg, four times a day.

Items which are better purchased in the West:

• **Moleskin/Second Skin/zinc oxide based tape** (Leukoplast) – for blisters. Cheap low quality tape is available in Nepal.

• **Painkillers** Aspirin (Disprin), paracetamol or acetamenophen (Tylenol) or Ibuprofen (Advil). These are useful as mild painkillers for headaches and to reduce fever and tenderness or swelling in joints (Ibuprofen and aspirin are particularly effective for this). Some brands are also available in Nepal.

• **Plasters/Band-Aids** Assorted plasters and perhaps a stretch bandage would be useful. If you have had knee or ankle trouble previously a good support bandage is well worth bringing.

• **Betadine/Savlon** Antiseptic for cuts.

• **Throat lozenges** Bring several packets. They are also available in Kathmandu.

RESCUE PROCEDURES

Assessing the situation

On a standard trek there are few situations where the only solution is a helicopter rescue. For severe AMS immediate descent is vital rather than even an hour or two's wait. If somebody has had a serious accident, don't panic. Ensure they can breathe. If they are bleeding, apply pressure over the wound, keep them warm and take stock of the situation. Look at all your options logically and carefully. Helicopter rescue is standard for a broken leg/hip/pelvis, head/back injuries, abdominal injuries and multiple injuries.

Summoning a helicopter

The process of summoning a rescue helicopter can take several days, even once the message reaches Kathmandu, because there must be a guarantee of payment by a trekking company or your embassy. How quickly the helicopter comes also depends on the weather.

There are radio posts at the National Park HQ and at several of the army posts. There are telephones at Dhunche, Tarkeghyang, Melamchighyang, Kutumsang and Melamchi Pul.

When sending a message include as much clear detail as possible: your names and nationalities, the exact location, the reason for the rescue request (this will assist the doctor sent) and an assessment of the seriousness. Helicopters require a flat area to land on, below approximately 5500m/18,000ft.

APPENDIX C: FLORA AND FAUNA

Accompanying the huge range in altitude is a diverse range of flora and fauna.

FAUNA

Animals in the National Park

Many animals are nocturnal or shy or a combination so, apart from seeing monkeys and perhaps pikas, you have to be lucky or vigilant to see more. Some of the shyness comes from hunting – they have learned to fear people.

• **Himalayan black bear** (*balu*) occasionally treat themselves to millet and maize but gone are the days when fields near harvest-time required constant guarding. They also have a taste for goats and calves which is perhaps where the blood-drinking yeti legends originate.

• **Barking deer** (*mirka*) Small and similar to the musk deer, it can be distinguished by the male having (small) horns, is sometimes a reddish colour and is found at lower altitudes. They are hunted (illegally) for their meat, so it's not surprising that they are often seen sheltering, for safety, near the National Park headquarters.

• **Musk deer** (*kasturi*) Delicate and well under a metre high they are illegally hunted for their musk, produced by a gland in the male, which is used to make perfume. The male has two large distinctive fang-like teeth. It's possible that the musk deer has been hunted out of the Langtang Valley.

• *Serow* are bigger than the barking or musk deer. Species-wise this comes between the goat and deer family and, with its ungainly gait, fully looks as if it does.

• **Leopard** (*Chetuwa*) Nepal has three types; spotted, clouded and snow. Before environmentalism became popular anyone who killed a leopard (or tiger) would get a medal from the King. Locals call anything dangerous in the forest *bagh* or tiger but in the Langtang this is always the leopard. The clouded leopard is slightly smaller and paler in colour than the spotted variety. Snow leopards rarely grace the main Langtang Valley but a few may hide in the uninhabited region south of Dorje Lhakpa and other isolated valleys. They cover enormous areas hunting for prey – often blue sheep. A snow leopard can be distinguished by its stocky legs, pale fur and long thick tail.

• **Wild pigs** (*banyal or bungur*) root around forest floors and nearby open areas, often eating villagers' crops. The more aggressive pygmy boar isn't found in Langtang.

• **Langur monkey** (*lamu puchhre*) The name literally means long tail monkey. They are shy but beautiful – grey with a black face edged in white – and are usually seen in the forests of the Langtang Valley

• **Brown monkey** (*bhandar*) Often seen at Swayambhunath, these chimpanzee-like monkeys are also common in the Langtang Valley

• **Wild dog** (*shyaal*) A relative of the domestic dog, this sandy-coloured shy dog often howls dolefully at night and eats chicken and kids (the baby goat kind).

• **Wolf** Usually brown or tan. They have been seen around Laurebina Yak but they move around a lot and are sometimes found above the tree line.

• **Wild cat** Slightly larger than a domestic cat, their delicate footprints are often seen in snow at surprisingly high altitudes where they probably hunt the mouse-hare. The time to spot them is very early in the morning.

• **Himalayan Thar** (*jharal*) Featured on the Rs50 note, thar are the most elegant of the goat family. There are some large herds high in the Langtang valley but they scare easily.

• **Mouse-hare** (*moosa*) or **Pika** A ball of fur with ears, a nose and a stubby tail that lives in the alpine areas. They are often seen sunning themselves around rocks or darting into holes that look far too small for them.

• **Blue sheep** (*Bharal/nar*) Males have thick heavy horns that point out rather than up. Their fur (wool isn't the right word) is thick and straight. For the warmer part of the year it is fawn-brown while in winter it turns to a slate grey and white. They prefer sunny high slopes (about 4000-6000m/13,000-20,000ft).

• **Stone weasel** A graceful lean tan blur which is seen in the alpine areas. They can often be found around lodges and high kharkas.

• **Red panda** A much smaller cousin of the famous giant panda and similarly elusive. Feeds mainly on bamboo so it's virtually never seen. Apparently, there are populations in the Red Panda Reserve below Chalang Pati on the shady side of the ridge.

Domestic animals

A variety of animals are kept in the warmer lower hills. Chickens are kept mainly as egg producers. Goats are numerous and they are also destructive, stripping the ground and shrubs bare of leaves; they are responsible for much of the deforestation close to villages. They are sacrificed and eaten during important Hindu festivals and ceremonies. Cows and buffalo provide milk and pull ploughs. Buffalo are eaten while cows aren't supposed to be, although the Langtang Tamangs and the Yolmo are notorious for doing so. At high altitudes these are replaced by yaks, naks and crossbreeds.

Birds

Nepal is on some major migration routes and is famed for its varied bird life. Birdwatchers should consult *Birds of Nepal* by RL Fleming or *Birds of the Central Himalaya* by Dorothy Mierow, both are usually available in Kathmandu bookshops.

• **Lammergeier/bearded vulture** This large and beautiful soaring bird is a scavenger which is often seen gliding along the mountain sides at Gosainkund and above Langtang, searching for carcasses. Differentiating it from the griffon is easiest by the tail: it is roughly diamond-shaped.

• **Himalayan griffon** Similar to the lammergeier but slightly heavier with an axe head-shaped tail.

• **Golden eagle** This raptor hunts pheasants, snow cocks and smaller mammals rather than being a scavenger. It is smaller and more agile than the other soaring birds.

• **Blood pheasant** (*kalij*) So called because the male has a red throat, red eye rings, a red and white tail and bright red legs. Tamangs believe the bird's sweet meat is medicinal so in this region it is rare to see them.

• **Impeyan pheasant/Monal** (*danphe*) The national bird of Nepal; it is often seen in pairs. The male sports nine iridescent colours and is plump, almost heavy. The female is a plainer brown and white; both have a small head crest. They are frequently seen in high forest or just above the tree line. They are also often illegally eaten by locals.

• **Tibetan snow cock** Both male and female are striped: black, white, grey and brown with orange legs. Easy to approach, they congregate in noisy groups in alpine regions. When scared they glide off squealing to the world about where they are heading.

• **Grouse** can easily be confused with the snowcock but they are smaller and less noisy.

• **Snow pigeon** They fly in compact flocks and as they wheel around in the sky their colour alternates between light and dark.

• **Yellow-billed** and **red-billed chough** Black with red legs, choughs are curious and playful but have the annoying habit of attacking tents, ripping the material with their beaks.

• **Jungle crow** Black and slightly scrawny, crows are great camp scavengers. Younger crows are partly grey.

• **Tibetan raven** ('Caw caw') Completely black, these ravens attain nightmarish proportions.

FLORA

From October to the spring the Langtang is dry and brown. In contrast, during late spring and the monsoon the greenery is surprisingly intense and wild flowers cover the hillsides. The wide range of flowers include the rhododendron (*laligurans*, the national flower of Nepal), gentian, primrose, edelweiss and the beautiful mountain poppy. Above the tree line you can see dwarf rhododendron and juniper scrub. The highest plant of all is the tiny snow rhododendron.

Trees

• **Himalayan Oak** leaves are reminiscent of holly and are used for cattle fodder. There are 17 different types.

• **Juniper** *(doopee)* There are five or six species from the large dark multi-trunked tree with the bark growing in long strips to the alpine scrub form. In Helambu the wood from the large trees was traditionally used to make fragrant cupboards and furniture. Tibetan people everywhere burn juniper as incense; its fragrant and instantly recognisable scent soon becomes very familiar.

• **Chir pine** *(pinus Roxburghii)* A distinctive feature of West Nepal, pockets are found in Langtang National Park. They grow only on dry rocky slopes at an altitude between 750m/2500ft and 2000m/6500ft. The ramrod-straight fire-resistant trunks are covered by a tough scaly bark which is often light in colour. The branches begin high and have only sparse needle clumps. You can find them on the walk out of Bharkhu and between Sarmathang and Melamchi Pul.

The Blue Pine is found between 1850-3400m/6000-11000ft and has five needles that are shorter than the Chir Pine's and big untidy drooping cones.

Rhododendron Native to the Himalaya, 30 varieties are found in Nepal. Between Langtang village and Kyangjin, and around Tharepati and Melamchi, are some beautiful rhododendron forests; they are particularly stunning in March/April.

APPENDIX D: GLOSSARY

AMS	Acute Mountain Sickness – altitude sickness
bergschrund	a dangerous crack (where a glacier meets a rock wall)
bhanjyang	pass
bivvy (bivouac)	small shelter for camping
Brahman/Bahun	Hindu high priest caste
cairn	pile of stones marking a route ('stone men')
chang	home-brew made from barley or rice
chu	river
chombo/chenpo	big
chorten	Tibetan stupa (see below)
chotar	prayer flag pole beside a house
crampons	spikes that strap on boots to aid walking on ice
crevasse	dangerous cracks in a glacier
dal bhaat	staple meal of lentils and boiled rice
deorali	pass
dhai	curds
doko	woven, load-carrying basket
gang, usually *kang*	mountain
gaon	village
gompa	Buddhist temple (literally: 'meditation')
goth	see kore
himal	snowy mountains
kang	mountain
kani	entrance arch
kharka yak	house or grazing ground
khola	stream
kore	shelter or temporary house
kosi	river

kund	lake
la	pass
mani wall	wall of stones carved with Buddhist mantras
mantra	prayer formula
mahi	butter milk, sour and like watery curd
nimki	salt butter tea
pokhari	lake
raksi	local distilled spirit
Sherpa	of the Sherpa people
sherpa	trekking group assistant
sirdar (sardar)	the head Nepali organiser, often leader as well, of a trekking group
solja/suchiya	salt-butter tea
stupa	Buddhist religious monument
suntala	mandarin orange
tal	lake
tarn	small lake without entry or exit stream
trisul	trident carried by worshippers of Shiva
tsampa	roasted barley flour
tsang	crevasse but is called a glacier on the best maps
tse	peak
tsho/cho	lake

APPENDIX E: BIBLIOGRAPHY

Travel guides

Armington, Stan *Trekking in the Nepal Himalaya*, 6th edition, Lonely Planet, Australia 1994

Bezruchka, Stephen *Trekking in Nepal – A Traveller's Guide*, 6th edition, Cordee, UK/The Mountaineers, USA

Chan, Victor *Tibet Handbook* Moon Publications, California 1994

Knowles, Peter and Allardice, Dave *White Water Nepal, A rivers guidebook for rafting and kayaking* Rivers Publishing UK and Menasha Press USA 1992

Moran, Kerry *Nepal Handbook* Moon Publications, California 1991

O'Connor Bill *The Trekking Peaks of Nepal* The Crowood Press, Wiltshire 1992

Reed, David *Nepal* The Rough Guide, London 1996

Maps

Alpenvereinskarte Lhangtang Himal Ost and *West*, Alpenvereinskartographie (Austrian Alpine Club) 1990

Helambu-Langtang, Nelles Verlag, München 1987

Kathmandu Valley, Nelles Verlag, München 1989

Map of Nepal, Mandala, Kathmandu

Map of Nepal, Himalayan Booksellers, Kathmandu

Planimetric Map of Satellite Images, for National Remote Sensing Centre (Nepal) by Institute for Applied Geosciences, Germany 1986

Sheet Nos 2785 06A (Kathmandau), 2785 02C, 2785 02D and 2785 06B, HMG Survey Department 1992-5

Travelogues/History
Tilman, HW *The Seven Mountain-Travel Books* Diadem, London and The Mountaineers, Seattle 1983
Ullman, James Ramsey (as told to) *Man of Everest – The autobiography of Tenzing* George Harrap and Co, London 1955

Research
Desjarlais, Robert R *Body and Emotion – The aesthetics of illness and healing in the Nepal Himalaya* University of Pennsylvania Press, 1992 and Motilal Banarsidass, Delhi 1994
Selters, Andy *Glacier Travel and Crevasse Rescue* Diadem, London 1990
Dr Rajesh Gautam and Asoke K Thapa-Magar, *Tribal Ethnography of Nepal*, Bookfaith India, Delhi 1994

Medicine
Duff, Jim and Gormly, Peter *The Himalayan First Aid Manual* 1994
Houston, Charles S *Mountain Sickness*, Scientific American, October 1992, Vol 267 No 4
Houston, Charles S; Sutton, John R; Cymerman, Allen; Reeves, John T *Operation Everest II: Man at extreme altitude* Journal of Applied Physiology No. 63 1987
Shlim, Dr David R *CIWEC Clinic Travel Medicine Center* http://www.bena.com/nepaltrek/ciwec/immune.html
Wilkerson, James A *Medicine for Mountaineering* The Mountaineers, Seattle, Washington

---

APPENDIX F: NEPALI WORDS AND PHRASES

Namasté
Probably the first word learnt by the newly-arrived foreigner in Nepal is this greeting, which is spoken with the hands together as if praying. Its meaning encompasses 'hello' and 'goodbye' as well as 'good morning', 'good afternoon' or 'good evening'. *Namaskar* is the more polite form.

General words

How are you?	*Bhaat khanu-bayo?* (Have you eaten your dal bhat?)
Fine thanks	*Khai-é* (I have eaten)
Please give me	*di-nus*
Do you speak English?	*Angreyzi boinoo-hoon-chha?*
yes/no (see below)	
thank you	*dhan-yabad* (not often used)
excuse me (sorry)	*naf-garnus*
good/bad	*ramro/naramro*
cheap/expensive	*susto/mahango*
Just a minute/Wait!	*Ek-chin!*
Brother/sister	*dai/didi* (used to address anyone of your own age)
Good night	*sooba-ratry*
Sweet dreams	*meeto supona*

Questions and answers

To ask a question, end the phrase with a rising tone, An affirmative answer is given by restating the question without the rising tone. 'No' is translated as *chaino* (there isn't/aren't any) or *hoi-na* (it isn't/they aren't).

What's your name?	*Tapaiko* (to adult)/*timro* (child) *nam ke ho?*
My name is	*Mero nam.... (ho).*
Where are you from?	*Tapaiko/timro dess kay ho?*
Britain/USA	*Belaiyot/Amerika*
Australia/New Zealand	*Australia/New Zealand*
Where are you going? *Kata janné?*	I'm going to *.......jahné*
Are you married?	*Tapaiko bihar bhayo?*
Have you any children? *chora chori chhan?*	
boy/girl	*chora/chori*
How old are you?	*Kati barsha bhayo?*
What is this?	*Yo ke ho?*

Directions

Ask directions frequently and avoid questions that require only 'yes' or 'no' as a reply.

Which path goes to	*janné baato kun ho?*		
Whereis...?	*kaha chha*	lodge/hotel	*bhatti*
shop	*pasal*	latrine	*charpi*
What is this village called? *Yo gaon ko nam ke ho?*			
left/right	*baiya/daiya*	straight ahead	*seeda jannus*
steep uphill/downhill	*ukaalu/uraalo*	far away	*tadah*
near	*nadjik*		

Numerals/time

1 *ek*; 2 *dui*; 3 *tin*; 4 *chaar*; 5 *panch*; 6 *chho*; 7 *saat*; 8 *aat*; 9 *nau*; 10 *dos*; 11 *eghaara*; 12 *baahra*; 13 *terha*; 14 *chaudha*; 15 *pondhra*; 16*sora*; 17*sotra*; 18 *ataara*; 19 *unnice*; 20 *beece*; 25 *pachis* 30 *teece*; 40 *chaalis*; 50 *pachaas*; 60 *saati*; 70 *satari*; 80 *ossi*; 90 *naubé*; 100 *say/ek-say*; 200 *dui say*; 300 *tin-say*; 400 *charr say*; 500 *panch say* ; 600 *chho say*; 700 *saat say*; 800 *aat say*; 900 *nau say*; 1000 *hajaar*

How much/many?	*kati?*	What time is it?	*kati bajyo?*
It's three o'clock	*tin bajyo*	hours/minutes	*ghunta/minoot*
today	*ajaa*	yesterday	*hidjo*
tomorrow	*bholi*	day after tomorrow	*parsi*

Food and drink

Restaurant/inn	*bhatti*	cheese	*cheese*
Please give me	*di-nus*	boiled egg	*phul/andar*
mineral water	*khanni-paani*	omelette	*unda*
tea	*chiya*	salt	*nun*
coffee	*coffee*	spicy hot	*piro*
milk	*dood*	no chillis	*korsani china*
boiled milk	*oomaleko-dood*	sugar	*chinni*
beer	*beer*	honey	*maha*
rice spirit	*rakshi*		
Cheers!	*khannus!*	It tastes good	*Ekdum meeto*
chicken	*kookhura-ko maasu*	buffalo	*rango-ko*
pork	*sungur-ko*	rice	*bhaat*
lentils	*daal*	vegetables (cooked)	*takaari*
potatoes	*aloo*	bread	*roti*

INDEX